Happy Again!

THE ART OF <u>POSITIVE</u> SEPARATION

Endorsements

"The most practical plan I've seen for creating a positive reality in divorce or separation. This isn't a vague set of ideals or a theoretical exploration: it's a simple, daily, 'boots on the ground' approach that will get you back on your feet and striding confidently into your future. A must-read!" – **Jack Canfield, author of** *The Success Principles***, co-creator of the** *Chicken Soup for the Soul*® **series**

"Eveline Jurry is a strong new voice in the field of divorce and separation. With her easy-to-follow method and no-nonsense approach, she will help you step out of your old life and into your new one with confidence and clarity." – **John Gray,** *New York Times* **#1 best-selling author of** *Men Are from Mars, Women Are from Venus*

"Far from a typical divorce manual, *Happy Again! The Art of Positive Separation* is a guide to reclaiming a joyful, fulfilling life after a relationship has dissolved. Her Method is practical and grounded, but Eveline's *joie de vivre* shines through in every word. This book is one in a million." – **Marci Shimoff,** *New York Times* **#1 best-selling author of** *Happy for No Reason, Love for No Reason,* **and** *Chicken Soup for the Woman's Soul;* **co-founder of Your Year of Miracles**

"A perfect guide for anyone who wants to get out of their head and on with their life after a breakup." – **Janet Bray Attwood,** *New York Times* **best-selling coauthor of** *The Passion Test* **and** *Your Hidden Riches*

"Even if your breakup feels like the end of your world right now, a new door is opening into your future—and this book can be your insightful, loving (but eminently sensible) step-by-step manual to get back on track and steer clear of the slippery slopes of blame, drama, and negative thinking. I highly recommend it." – **Chris Attwood,** *New York Times* **best-selling coauthor of** *The Passion Test* **and** *Your Hidden Riches*

"With the perfect balance of practicality and heart, Eveline Jurry outlines a clear path out of the chaos of separation and into a future full of new and better dreams. I loved this book!" – **Marcia Wieder, best-selling author; CEO, Dream University**

"With Eveline's Positive Separation Method, you'll learn to approach your breakup from a position of strength, integrity, and positivity. The wisdom and daily practices in this book will serve you not only through your separation process, but for the rest of your life." – **Debra Poneman, best-selling author, founder of Yes to Success Seminars and co-founder of Your Year of Miracles**

Happy Again!

THE ART OF POSITIVE SEPARATION

Eveline Jurry

WITH BRYNA HAYNES

NEW YORK

LONDON • NASHVILLE • MELBOURNE • VANCOUVER

Happy Again! THE ART OF POSITIVE SEPARATION

Published in New York, New York, by Morgan James Publishing. Morgan James is a trademark of Morgan James, LLC. www.MorganJamesPublishing.com

The Morgan James Speakers Group can bring authors to your live event. For more information or to book an event visit The Morgan James Speakers Group at www.TheMorganJamesSpeakersGroup.com.

ISBN 9781683509172 paperback
ISBN 9781683509189 eBook
Library of Congress Control Number: 2017919476

Cover Design:
Ingeborg Berghuijs
www.IngeborgBerghuijs.com

Edited:
Bryna Haynes
www.TheHeartofWriting.com

Interior Design:
Chris Treccani, www.3dogcreative.net
Bryna Haynes, www.TheHeartofWriting.com

Illustrations:
Janneke Paalman, www.JansOntwerpFabriek.nl
Chris Mulder, www.Pinta.nl

DISCLAIMER

In an effort to support local communities, raise awareness and funds, Morgan James Publishing donates a percentage of all book sales for the life of each book to Habitat for Humanity Peninsula and Greater Williamsburg. Get involved today! Visit www.MorganJamesBuilds.com

Dedication

This book is dedicated to Boudy, Fréderique, and Charlotte. You are all an incredible source of love, inspiration, joy, honesty, and fun for me as your mother. I am proud of each of you in your uniqueness, and profoundly grateful that we are together on this life adventure.

Also, with great respect and love, to my grandparents, Jacobus Jurry, Christina Plaisier, Flora van Beuningen, and Lucas Peterich, who collectively inspired me to create the Positive Separation Method and share it with the world.

Table of Contents

Foreword

Happy Again! The Art of Positive Separation is the most practical recipe I've encountered to date for how to make gourmet lemonade out of the lemons Life may have handed you. We don't often hear the words "positive" and "separation" in the same sentence, let alone making an art of it. Yet, art it is. Chapter by chapter, the dark uncertainty you may now be walking through will soon begin to occur as an unexpected and even welcome adventure, as you not only pick up the pieces of your life, but discover ways to weave them together again in surprisingly bright and beautiful ways. Let's just say that this book is the literary equivalent of Gloria Gaynor's "I Will Survive," Diane Ladd's *Under the Tuscan Sun,* and a recovery weekend at the spa with your best friend all rolled into one.

What makes this book so profoundly useful is Eveline's ability to meet you where you are, and provide you with concrete, sensible steps to navigate your way through the thicket and into the sunshine of your wholehearted and bountiful new life. She understands that, at the moment, you're likely overwhelmed, hurting, lost, and confused. She knows you may be wrestling with festering resentment, and regret so deep and gnarly that it wakes you with a start in the middle of the night.

Yet, she also knows that a broken heart is an open heart, and that a life torn asunder is also a life newly unencumbered—a life wide open for self-reflection, meaningful revisions, and a glorious Phoenix-rising-from-the-ashes recreation.

Back in the mid-1980s, social psychologists Dr. Hazel Markus and Dr. Paula Nurius did an experiment around the importance of having "a possible self" of the future when moving through a shattering breakup. In their study, they discovered that most people going through a breakup describe their current self in similar ways—as a failure, as all alone in life, as sadly unwanted and rejected. However, those who could imagine a more hopeful future self—who could say, "One day I will be loved, happy, healed, and whole again"—inevitably were more likely to find their way to that future.

Eveline is the wise and loving guide who will lead you to this positive "possible self" of your future. Even if you're having a hard time believing you'll get there, her unstoppable and enthusiastic conviction will carry you through to the other side. In making the choice to follow her lead, one day, not long from now, you will look back on this terrible time and bless it for the bountiful opportunities it gave you to wake up and claim your value, your voice, and your power, perhaps for the very first time. You will see grace in the dramatic ways that falsehoods fled from your life, and beauty in the ever-evolving ways that life inescapably, and ever so graciously, recreated itself.

May you find your way to that future, and may your journey be blessed.

Katherine Woodward Thomas, MA, MFT
New York Times best-selling author of *Conscious Uncoupling: 5 Steps to Living Happily Even After*

Introduction

It was the first week of January. My husband was on a ski trip with my two oldest kids, and I was coming home to a quiet house—a rare blessing. As I climbed my front steps, I slid and sprained my ankle. It didn't hurt that much, and I wasn't really upset about it; it was something I couldn't change. But my best girlfriend, who I'd known since I was eight, was coming in from Spain the next day to visit for her holidays, and there was a lot that I wanted to do to prepare for her arrival. Now, I was forced to stop my preparations and rest my injured leg.

When my friend arrived, she immediately rolled up her sleeves and set to work taking care of me and my youngest daughter (who was only four at the time). She was terribly loving and sweet, and had enough energy for ten people. "Don't worry, Lien," she said. (Lien is my nickname.) "I'll run your life for a while until you are ready to be up and about again. Sit here by the fireplace and relax. Read some magazines. I'll make you a cup of coffee."

After giving birth to three children, throwing parties like confetti, running my creative career, helping my husband with his own big career, and living through years of sleepless nights and endless to-do lists, I was ready for a break. I felt like I was in Wonderland in my own home, and it was incredibly soothing. But this enforced quiet time, combined with plenty of long talks with my friend, also gave me the space to find some serious insight into my own heart. What I saw was not a pretty picture.

I realized that I was no longer connected to myself—to the things I used to love about myself. On the outside, my life was perfect. On the inside, my heartbeat hardly had a sound. And I had no idea *why*.

On one level, I had known it for years. The twinkle in my eye was gone. I missed my vibrancy, my inner joy, the excitement I used to feel about my life. But we were so *busy* all the time that I was able to ignore the fact that I was on a road to a dark place.

For years, I'd tried to communicate on a deeper level with my husband, but I did not have the right tools. I am highly sensitive, and my experience of daily life is, at times, much deeper and more colorful than what might be considered "normal." My husband, on the other hand, was very logical and straightforward, and I loved that about him. However, because of his own personality, he didn't always understand how I felt about things, and I couldn't show him in a way he could interpret—and somewhere along the line, as we both poured our energies into our family and our respective careers, we stopped trying. We both wanted to be happy, but slowly, without recognizing it, we grew away from one another.

I realized all of this for the first time while I rested my injured ankle. But admitting my unhappiness in my marriage and actually ending my marriage were two different things. As "a glass-half-full" kind of person, I had thoughts like, "It's not that bad. We have a good life. I can be okay here." But the truth was, I missed the deep connection I knew was possible—the inner glow and radiance that strength in partnership can boost. I wanted to feel like I could conquer the world with my partner at my side.

What I didn't know at the time—and what took me years to learn—was that I had to love and connect to myself with exactly that kind of grace and bravery before I could receive that love from someone else.

I looked for help to sort out my feelings, and started working with a therapist not long after my friend returned to Spain. I tried to improve my ability to communicate with my husband, and our ability to communicate together, but after several months I realized that a milestone had been passed—probably years before—and we were too far gone to repair the unhappiness and bridge the distance that had grown between us.

Around this time, I remembered the positive model of separation I'd witnessed as a child. My parents and my grandparents were divorced, and all of them had been able to go through this process with grace while minimizing the effect of the separation on me and my siblings. At this point, all three of my kids were under the age of ten, and I was managing my creative career as well as my household, but I trusted it would all work out. After all, my whole family had mastered what I termed "The Art of Positive Separation," and had thrived—why not me?

I was not prepared for the actual experience and work of a divorce. I knew how I wanted my separation to look, but I didn't have the tools to make it happen in the way I envisioned. Turns out, witnessing family members in the process of positive separation and going through it myself in real time were two very different things! Focus and determination were my keywords, but the actual process was chaotic, nerve-wracking, and traumatic. Just a few days after the official decision was made, my entire life was different. The fact that it had been my choice didn't make it easier. There was a huge stone of guilt in my stomach. I felt like I had failed as a wife and as a member of the great family we had created. More, I felt like the worst mom ever. I could hardly look my children in the eyes without wishing I could evaporate this whole situation. I also missed "our" friends, who were suddenly divided into "mine" and "his," and I felt terrible that my actions had upset so many who had been loving and caring toward us as a family.

But in the midst of the emotional and logistical nightmare of separating our family, possessions, and time, the biggest question I had was:

"Will I ever be happy again?"

FINDING MY WAY BACK

Divorce. Breakup. These are plastic words; they mean nothing until they happen to you. Suddenly, the days are ticking away, and they feel endless. Life feels raw and uncertain. It hurts deep in your bones. You feel blocked, and scared, and reactionary. You feel lonely and weak.

I lost weight—too much weight—and as the pounds dropped off so did my strength and resilience. I couldn't sleep. I couldn't relax. My mind told me I'd made the right choice, but in my wounded heart I wondered if I'd ever find the kind of connection and *joie de vivre* that I'd envisioned while sitting in front of my cozy fire with my ankle propped on a pillow. I wasn't whole. I hadn't suddenly found *me* again. I wasn't even certain I would survive this.

One day, a few weeks into the divorce process, I took a detour instead of biking straight home from our mediation meeting, I stopped at a cute little café in the center of Amsterdam, on the Prinsengracht Canal. I didn't see the pretty blossoms on the trees outside. I didn't see the glint of sunlight on the canal, or the boats cruising on the calm water. I felt like a big ball of aching emotion spinning in a void, all alone. I'd been avoiding people for months, processing the whole transition on my own, but now I just wanted someone to hold my hand and guide me through the mess my choice had made of my life—of all our lives. When I'd decided I wanted more from my life—when I decided that I wanted to be the happy, vibrant person I knew myself to be, and not a gray shadow of myself—this sucking, negative spiral was *not* what I had envisioned!

I wanted a different option. More, I wanted an instruction manual.

Sitting there, sipping my coffee, I had a vision. I saw myself on a big, fluffy bed, surrounded by pillows and cushions and fresh spring flowers. Like in one of those old children's movies, that bed took flight, and I knew that it was flying me and my children into a happier, more comfortable future.

For the first time in a long while, I felt a little spark of hope, and it kept me going. I created a vision of what I wanted my life and my children's lives to look like, and I held onto it as tightly as I could. Step by baby step, I cut down on the chaos and started moving forward. I did what I could, every day, and let go what I couldn't control. Soon, the terrible inner ache started to subside. I started to smile again.

That day in the café, I'd wished for an instruction manual—a guide to navigating my breakup in a way that wouldn't shatter me and my family. I wanted an Ikea-style how-to on the art of positive separation, complete with pictures, diagrams, and detailed step-by-step directions I could follow out of the darkness and into my new life. I wanted to master the process of separating in a positive, healthy way.

At the time, such a manual didn't exist. But it does now—and you're holding it in your hands.

This book is your step-by-step guide to a positive, empowering separation. It's based not only on what I learned in my own divorce, but on the Method I created to help people like me—and you—climb out of the chaos and navigate their separations with greater confidence, hope, and love. In this book, I'll share exactly what you need to know about your separation: how it works, what the potential pitfalls are, who you can call for help when you need it. I'll also show you exactly how to find, and maintain, the positive attitude and self-care you need to rediscover your love for your life, spark that light in your eyes, and be happy again.

What "Positive Separation" Really Means

In order to create a positive separation (rather than a traumatic or harrowing one) you need to have the right perspective. You need to get up, roll up your sleeves, and face your new reality head-on. Then, you need to do what you can to nourish your body, manage your tumultuous emotions, complete your daily tasks, care for your family, and let the rest go.

In the Netherlands, we call this the "Rotterdam attitude." The center of that city was bombed into rubble during World War II, its entire heart taken out. In the aftermath, there was only one solution if residents wanted the city to flourish again: rebuild, whatever it took. Today, Rotterdam has one of the largest and most bustling harbors in the world, and is the only truly modern city in the Netherlands, with lots of glass and skyscrapers—but its people still retain the dogged practicality and will to move forward that saved their city from abandonment and ruin.

My family is from Rotterdam. Perhaps that's where I learned this attitude.

The truth is, separation is *hard*. (If all of this was easy, everyone would experience a positive separation!) When our partner is no longer there to blame, we have to look at ourselves. We have to put ourselves back together, step by step, just like the citizens of Rotterdam rebuilt their city from the ground up.

Trying to do this without help can feel a lot like trying to climb Mount Everest with no preparation, no base camp, no support team, and no Sherpa to guide you. If you don't get what you need from the beginning, you're likely to end up scarred, scared, and stranded.

When you separate from your partner—whether you initiated that separation or not—you have a big job to do. You need to keep your life going every day, and move it in a new and positive direction. You need to untangle your finances, your possessions, your friends, and your social life. You need to unravel your emotional ties, your family ties, your entangled hopes and dreams. You need to heal your broken heart, and find wholeness within yourself so you can rebuild your life and create a happy future.

This process shakes you to your very foundation—and while you're falling into that deep hole, and boulders are raining down on your head, you still have to try to navigate the world like a grown-up and fulfill your responsibilities.

The day I had my vision in the café, I was at my lowest point, and I had to make a choice. I could either keep spinning down into the darkness, or I could put on my big-girl pants, identify what I *really* wanted from my new life, and create a future that was as bright and shiny as the one in my vision. I was just forty years old, still full of youth and beauty, and I had a full life ahead of me. I was *not* going to waste it on the drama of my separation. I was not going to be a victim of my life. And although I knew my choice to leave had hurt my children, I wasn't going to let that choice trap all of us in an endless web of negativity.

But how would I shift myself from negativity to positivity? The only way I knew how to do it was to take little steps toward my vision every day.

I promised myself that from that day on, I would spend quality time with myself, my tea, and my notebook every week. I would list out the actions I could take in the week to come, and decide how I wanted to think, feel, and behave every single day. I would schedule positive actions in my calendar. I decided to call this time my "Power Hour."

Setting up my Power Hour was my first big step toward taking back 100 percent responsibility for my life. From that moment on, I was committed. I knew I was resilient, and could conquer any storms that came my way—but only if I worked diligently on myself and my separation. If I wanted to shine for myself and my children, I needed to do this work, and do it to the best of my abilities.

No one was going to climb Mount Everest for me. No one was going to take my hand and lead me to the top. I could gather my tools, my support, and my courage—but in the end, it was my feet that had to climb.

The same is true for you. This book is your instruction manual—but *only you* can implement the instructions I'll give you. *Only you* can decide to move forward with hope instead of fear. And *only you* can take action to reclaim your life, your future, and your happiness.

THE PATH FORWARD

I'd love to tell you that I did everything right from the day I committed myself to positive and constructive action … but I can assure you, I didn't.

There were whole days—and even weeks—when I found it difficult to channel my powerful emotions, and when my negative thoughts were set to replay on a 100-decibel loop. During those times, I engaged in stupid and emotionally-driven behavior I'm not proud of at all.

But there were also whole days when I felt connected with myself in a way I hadn't been in years—days when I clearly saw my vision for a happy future beginning to take shape.

Having a plan comforted me more than I can say. No matter what kind of day I was having, my support team provided their support and love, and helped me stick to my commitment to take care of myself and my body. I learned, bit by bit, how to disconnect from my old life and plug into my new one. I learned to sense what triggered my emotional storms, and to navigate those situations differently. I cleaned out my house, got rid of all of my unnecessary belongings, and started fresh. I did things that were fun, simply because they were fun. I learned to laugh again, and to cry without feeling like it was the end of the world.

My old life was gone. My old love was gone. My old dreams for my family were gone. But I was gaining a new life, and a new love: myself.

How to Use This Book

About a year after my divorce was finalized, I began to wonder how I could teach others to apply the tools I'd used in my separation to their own situations. I developed my Positive Separation Method™ to help anyone going through their own separation to get their life back on track, feel happy again, and move forward into a brighter future. A few years after that, a big Dutch publisher bought the rights to my book, *Je Wordt Weer Gelukkig* (You Will Be Happy Again). Now, I've refined and restructured the Method that has helped so many people in the Netherlands so that you can create your own Positive Separation, starting right now.

The tools in this book are universal. Whether you're going through a formal divorce or separating from a boyfriend or girlfriend; whether you initiated the separation, or it took you by surprise; whether you have children, or you don't; whether you are young, or old, or somewhere in the middle; this book can help you disentangle yourself from your old life, get clear on what your new life will look like, and take action to get your life back on track and moving forward.

The Five Steps of My Positive Separation Method™

Step 1: Disconnect from Your Old Life and Connect to Your New Life

Step 2: Focus on What You Can Control (and Let Go of What You Can't)

Step 3: Empower Yourself and Reconnect to Your Core

Step 4: Take Loving Action to Care for Yourself

Step 5: Move Forward with Confidence!

As you see—and as you'll continue to discover as you read through this book—my Positive Separation Method is all about *you*. It's about your focus, your energy, your actions. It's about taking care of yourself, and loving yourself, so that you can be the person you want to be in your new life, reclaim the essence of who you are, and *be happy again*.

Steps 1 through 4 of the Method are about getting through the initial phases of your separation and reconnecting to yourself on multiple levels so you can move through your separation in the most empowered, positive, and productive way. You may need to work with these initial steps for three months, six months, or even a year or more before you are truly ready to move forward into your new life with Step 5. My advice is: don't rush it. You will know when you are fully ready to leave your old life behind and step into your new, happy future.

There are many ways to use this book, but my suggestion is that you read the entire book in a weekend, or over the course of several days. Once you understand the Positive Separation Method and get a sense of where you're headed, go back and work through Steps 1 through 4, one by one. Dedicate a journal or notebook to your separation process, do the exercises, and use the tools and Empowered

Actions in each chapter. If you follow the instructions in this manual and don't let yourself get sidetracked, you should be on a more positive path within three to four weeks.

After you do this preparation and set up your new positive behaviors, you will need to *keep* doing them for as long as it takes to get through your separation. Then, when you're ready, you can use the tools in Step 5 to modify these new positive habits and carry them forward into your new life. Fourteen years later, I still use my Power Hour every week to set up my schedule and lay out my intentions for the week. It's a powerful practice that's kept me on track through all of life's ups and downs.

At its heart, this book is the practical, action-oriented manual I was looking for when I was in the throes of my own separation. Although you will find plenty of helpful tips in Steps 3 and 4 of my Method for coping with emotions and keeping a positive mindset on a daily basis, you would also be well-served to consider using this book alongside other methods which focus more deeply on emotional and spiritual health. Katherine Woodward Thomas, author of *Conscious Uncoupling: 5 Steps to Living Happily Even After*, who wrote the Foreword for this book, is one of the best resources I know for this kind of work, and her Conscious Uncoupling method is a perfect complement to my work and message.

A Happy and Radiant Future

Two years after my divorce, I met John. Like me, he had recently gone through a separation, and all of the grief and struggle that went with it. At first, I was afraid to dive into a new relationship. I had just found myself again, and I was scared to lose that new connection. But I was sturdier than I thought. I had grown into a fully-realized, happy woman, and could talk about my feelings in a way I hadn't been able to do before. John took me gracefully by the hand and became a loving, dynamic life partner who helped me flourish even more.

We made our union official in 2008, with rings and a ceremony in the rainforest of the Suriname with the villagers of Apetina as witnesses. Our newly blended family—seven children in total—were all in attendance. When we returned to Amsterdam, we celebrated with a big dinner for family and friends in an old mansion. It was a night full of flowers, music, speeches, and happiness. When I was first going through my separation, I never imagined that my life could be so full, so rich, or so surprising!

I'm also happy to say that my children have a wonderful relationship with their father, who is remarried and lives around the corner from us in Amsterdam. Since the day we separated, my ex-husband and I have both been present for all the highlights of our children's lives along with our bonus kids on both sides. We are truly a happily blended family. It took work, but everyone has been so positive through the entire process, and I'm extremely grateful for the way things have turned out.

In life, change is constant. We learn and we grow. We turn this way or that way. We try new things. We stop doing other things. We evolve, and we leave behind what we no longer need. We come together, and we separate. I know where you are right now, and how you feel. I also know where you can go from here—and I promise, if you keep your heart open, remember the lovely days of your past, and envision the lovelier days in your future, that radiance will become part of you. You will smile again, and your smile will be even bigger than before. You will dance in the sun and celebrate your life to its fullest.

Just hang in there, trust yourself, and follow this guide to the Art of Positive Separation, and I know you *will* be happy again!

POSITIVE SEPARATION STEP 1

Disconnect from Your Old Life and Connect to Your New Life

Disconnect from Your Old Life and Connect to Your New Life

Before you can take any steps to get your life back on track and start finding your happiness again, you need to untangle yourself from your old life. To do this in an empowered way (as opposed to a chaotic, stressful, and disempowering way) you need to understand *all* of the details of your separation—the good and the bad, the inner and the outer, the physical and the energetic. Then, you need to create a structure for yourself that will allow you to cope with the physical and emotional tasks of creating your new life.

Separation, even if the decision is mutual, is never easy. It turns your life upside-down, and you lose control of things that you once felt secure with. There will be days when you feel ungrounded, adrift, and stressed out. You will cry, a lot. You will also laugh, and rage, and wallow in regret. Your relationships with friends and family will change. You will have new worries and new challenges.

The only way to navigate this in a positive way is to draw a hard line between your old life and your new one. You need to make choices based on where you are right now, not where you were, or where you wish you were. And to do this, you need to take an honest look at your current situation.

In Step 1 of the Positive Separation Method, we will look at all the hard facts of your separation one by one. By choosing to look at things for what they are, you will feel less like a victim and more like a person who's committed to moving toward a better, happier life. You'll be better able to break down your tasks into manageable chunks that don't feel overwhelming, and manage your store of personal energy so you don't burn yourself out.

Once you have gotten crystal clear on where you are and what's happening in your life, you will close the window on your old life and open the door to your new one. In other words, you will disconnect from your old life and connect to your new one.

If you are a parent, this work of disconnection and re-visioning your life is especially important for you. Many people in separation want to prioritize their children above all else, and so have trouble disconnecting from their ex-partners in a complete way which enables them to move on with their new lives. Instead of basing your actions and feelings on what seems best for your children, I encourage you to make *yourself* the top priority. When you lift yourself into a better and more empowered place, you set the tone for your children, and they will follow your example. More, you will be in a better position to begin your new parenting role.

Approaching your separation in this way—by deliberately disconnecting from your old life and connecting to your new one—requires courage and conviction. You need to take an active role in empowering yourself. No one else can do this for you. Just as I made a choice that day in the café, you need to make a choice in this moment. Will you be a victim, and allow yourself to spiral downward into blame, shame, and negative emotion? Or will you take stock of the situation, make a plan, and move forward knowing that you're doing all you can to honor yourself and your vision for a better life?

Once you actually start implementing the suggestions and doing the exercises in this Step, you'll notice that you are better able to function on a daily basis. You'll make better decisions regarding your home, your children (if you have them), your work, and all areas of your life. Those around you will also benefit from your empowered mindset.

Above all, remember that your old life is over. If you hang on to what could have been, or continue to make decisions based on what your ex-partner thinks, feels, or does, it will only hurt you in the long run. You can't go back to the past. You can't change what has happened. But you *can* choose a happy future for yourself.

Again, I want to be clear: Separation is hard work. There are a lot of things that will need to be done to bring the process to a positive conclusion. A large part of mastering the art of separation lies in accepting what is happening and working with what's in front of you.

It takes courage to make a new start and give your happy future a chance—but the sooner you begin to chart a path through the chaos, the sooner you will start to feel like you have solid ground under your feet again. So, let's get started!

CHAPTER ONE

Start from Where You Are

Sometimes, separation is a long time in the making: a slow drifting apart, a gradual distance that eventually becomes irreparable. And sometimes, it hits you like a sledgehammer out of nowhere. But regardless of the story of your separation and the drama that accompanies it, it's vital to start from where you are and make a clean break from your old life.

ISABELLE'S STORY

Isabelle, a successful museum conservator in her late twenties, learned this firsthand when she discovered that her partner was hiding some big secrets.

"I had been with my boyfriend for several years. We lived together in a beautiful condo in the city, a modern space filled with light and high-tech amenities, and just as often filled with our friends and family. I had a job I loved that took me around the world, and he had a creative career with an ad _gency. Our life felt like a comfortable blanket wrapped around us—except for one thing.

"My man had a secret. Well, it's actually more accurate to say that *I* had a secret—one I was keeping from my friends and family on his behalf. He was using drugs. Not just smoking a joint here and there, but hardcore drugs—cocaine, painkillers, and other stuff, too. It wasn't all the time, but I didn't agree with it at all. We fought about it regularly, but I kept thinking, 'We are still so young. It's just temporary. He's living it up while he still can. One day, this will just stop.'

"But it didn't stop.

"Just before I was due to leave on a work trip out of state, we had a huge blowout. He had gone out with some of his agency friends the night before, and hadn't come home. I knew they had been partying. He cried, and said he was sorry, and promised to stop. I wanted to believe him, and said I did.

"I left for my work trip. I was only going to be gone a few days. When I called, he sounded fine, even upbeat. I started to hope that maybe my concerns for him had finally sunk in.

"I finished my meetings early, and found out that I could take an earlier flight home. I jumped at the chance. I would surprise him, and he would tell me how he'd been thinking about what I'd said, and that he was ready to change his ways. I built up my homecoming in my head, playing out romantic scenarios. On the taxi ride back home, I found myself getting more and more excited.

"But the moment I stepped into the apartment, I knew something was wrong. There was a mess in the kitchen—not one, but two plates crusted with cooked food. And when I entered the bedroom, well … you can guess what I found. The man who swore he would love me forever was lying in someone else's arms.

"Once the other woman had gathered her things and done her walk of shame through my beautiful home and out the door, a lot of tears and 'I'm sorrys' ensued. 'I didn't mean for it to happen!' he said. 'I went to this work party, and everyone was doing lines, and I just got carried away. It wasn't my fault!'

"I wasn't buying it. 'You cooked her *dinner*!' I raged.

"He hung his head. 'I know how it looks. But you're the one I love. You've always been the one I love.'

"As fast as I could, I grabbed some clothes and a few essentials and stormed out the door. I was heartbroken, shaking from head to toe. Some friends let me stay in their spare bedroom. Thankfully, they didn't ask too many questions. I went to work on autopilot, pretending that everything was fine.

"A few weeks later, we met on 'neutral ground,' at our favorite neighborhood café. By that time, my rage and shock had softened, and I missed him deeply. Believe it or not, I was actually convinced that we still had a future together. We were such a promising couple. We had such a beautiful life. I envisioned our meeting ending in tears and kisses and apologies.

"Instead, he launched right in. 'We're over. Finished. There's no more us.'

"*What?* 'Are you serious?' I couldn't believe what I was hearing.

"'I've had it with you trying to control my life. You're always telling me what to do, where to go, how to live my life. You're the most narrow-minded person I've ever met. Get over yourself and get out of my life!'

"I could feel his anger and coldness from across the table. *But you said you loved me, and that you wanted to change!* I thought. Then, I remembered that other woman in *our* bed, and decided to surrender.

"In a way, it was a relief. I wouldn't have to lie awake worrying when he didn't come home and didn't call. I wouldn't have to swallow my suspicions when he came home with red eyes and disheveled hair. I wouldn't have to spend so much energy caring more about him than he did about himself.

"So, I took a deep breath, and without looking at his face, said, 'Okay, then. What's next?'

"Since his name was on the condo lease, I was the one who had to find a new place to live. We agreed that I would have one week to get all of my stuff out. And that was it. It was like a door had been slammed in my face.

"He went back to work, and I went home—well, to my former home. I don't remember how I even got there. I felt helpless, lost in a gray fog. I was all alone, and I had only seven days to pack up my old life and start a new one.

"I called work, told them I had the flu, and spent the next three days hiding in bed. My boyfriend—well, ex-boyfriend, now—didn't turn up. I had no idea where he was staying, or what he was doing.

"This was not a scenario I had ever imagined for my life. What would my friends and family think of me? I'd always been the one who had it all together. How could I have let this happen?

"At the same time, underneath the screaming pain and anxiety, there was a little voice in my head that whispered, 'There were a thousand moments when you wanted to end this. You didn't. But now it's over, and you can move on and be truly happy.'

"The fourth morning was my turning point. I was trembling and weak, like a ghost of myself. But I had just four more days to get myself together and say goodbye to my old life, and lying around in bed wasn't going to help me get my suitcases packed.

"I went to the kitchen and made myself a cup of mint tea. I took a shower and put on makeup (even though I knew it would probably be cried away inside an hour), and I went outside.

"There was so much to do, but I had no idea where to begin, so I decided to walk down the hill from our building to the park. The sky was blue, the leaves had turned autumn-red, and the air was crisp and warm. The world was still turning, even though my world had imploded.

"I sat on a bench near the playground to watch the kids play. *When was the last time I felt that happy?* I wondered.

"A few minutes later, a pretty woman who appeared to be in her sixties came to sit next to me. 'Isn't it a wonderful day?' she asked. Before I could reply, she went on. 'This last year, I was hopeless. My husband had just died, totally unexpectedly, and I thought I would never breathe again. But look at what I've still got. I've got my granddaughter—see her over there, in the blue jacket?—and I have my own children, and I have my health and my home. Today, I feel happy again. I feel grateful to be alive.'

"Then, she turned to look at me. 'You don't look happy to be alive, honey.'

"I was shocked—but instead of snapping at the older woman, I found myself telling her about my breakup, and how I had to move out of my beloved home in just four days. By the time I finished, I was crying.

"The grandmother touched my arm gently. 'I know it's hard right now, but even though things weren't what you thought they were, or should be, you can still be happy. The leaves fall, but spring always comes. You're young; your whole life is a path right in front of you. Just have faith, and trust that the future is beautiful.'

"Her granddaughter came dancing toward us then, and pulled her to her feet. She smiled at me. 'Promise me you'll remember, love,' she said. I nodded as tears welled in my eyes.

"I stayed a few minutes longer, then stood up and walked quickly back to the condo. If the lady on the bench could survive the death of her lifelong mate and come out smiling, I could certainly deal with this.

"I had no idea how things would pan out, but I decided to trust that it was all for the best. Over the next couple of months, I slowly but surely built a new foundation for my life. One of my best friends had to leave her rented room, and we found an apartment together. My family and other friends were really supportive, and stepped up to help however they could. I found a therapist and began working through my emotions in a productive way. I learned a lot about why I had stayed with my ex even when it was clear he didn't want to be 'saved.'

"A few short months later, I was smiling again. Soon after that, I was laughing out loud.

"The best part of all this is that I am now in a place where I can be 100 percent honest—with myself, and with the people I love. I no longer have to hide anything or hold in my feelings.

"I also believe that the grandmother at the park was an angel sent to me at exactly the right moment. I never saw her again after that day, but I often visit the bench across from the playground, look up at the sky, and say, 'Thank you for sending her. I'm keeping my promise!'

What Is Separation–and Why Does It Hurt So Much?

Let's be honest: Separating from a partner is one of the top three most stressful events in a person's life. It's right up there with the death of a loved one and major illness. It's an overwhelming, gut-wrenching experience. This relationship you have spent so long nurturing and growing has suddenly fractured. All at once, everything is different, and all the things that you once had context for—your family, your friends, your social life, your home and belongings—feel strange and uncertain. You have lost your anchor. There is a tornado inside you, and a hurricane all around you. I know. I've been there.

Even if, like me, you were the one who took the initiative, separation is a shock to your system. If your separation took you by surprise—as it did for Isabelle in the story above—or if it wasn't your idea, it can be even harder. Ditto if you run into any unexpected secrets on your spouse's part—like if s/he has run up a lot of debt without your knowledge, has been engaged in a long-term affair, or has a child you never knew about.

Regardless of the circumstances, during the first few weeks and months after your separation you will probably go through very conflicting and often contradictory emotions. Every text message, e-mail, or phone call from your ex may hit you like a lightning bolt. Disappointment, anger, fear, frustration, loneliness, sadness, and other negative emotions may come at you like rogue waves trying to swamp your boat. If you're not prepared, they can suck you down into a paralyzing vortex of shame, panic, and helplessness. Or, worse, they can send you reeling into a spiral of anger, compulsive behavior, revenge, and self-destruction. You may wonder, "Who is this person? This isn't me!"

It's hard to function when your emotions are in chaos. That's why it's absolutely necessary to *reintroduce a sense of structure and purpose to your daily life* and tasks as soon as possible after your separation. You need to understand what's happening on a physical level, so you can do what you need to do and get through each day with a minimum of drama. You also need to take steps to care for yourself so you don't get run down and become ill.

Depending on your situation, you may find refuge in your work, or in other aspects of your life that aren't directly related to your separation. For example, in your role as an employer or employee, you might be able to function quite well—but the moment you leave work, you are thrust back into the whirlwind of legal issues, family restructuring, division of assets, or moving to a new home. Trying to live two separate lives may help you cope right now, but won't serve you in the long term. The better fix is to make a plan to navigate *all* of your life, every day—and that's what we'll learn together in this chapter.

Remember, the information I'm sharing here is not meant to discourage you, or make you feel hopeless. It's simply meant to empower you to address where you are in your life right now so you can make a plan to move forward. I won't be doing you any favors if I pretend things are all wine and roses, just as you won't do yourself any favors by wishing things were different. You need to know what's really going on before you can change it.

So now, let's dive in, and get real.

"WHY DO I FEEL SO OUT OF CONTROL?"

In order to make a plan that will help you move forward, you need to understand where you are right now—even if you don't want to look at the truth of your situation.

As I mentioned earlier, separation is one of the most challenging life experiences that a person can go through. But *why* is it so challenging? What is it about separation that is so hard for us, and makes us feel so out of control?

The true trauma of separation doesn't just come from losing our partner—although that is certainly part of it. It comes from losing our *security*. When a long-term relationship fractures, the very foundation upon which we have built our world crumbles, and our daily life and our sense of identity can feel like they are crumbling with it.

Although each person, and each separation, is unique, separation itself is common. The current statistics for divorce rates in the United States reveal that approximately 50 percent of marriages end in divorce. Rates are even higher in many European countries. Because separation affects so many, there is a lot of information out there about how to handle it. As I discovered during my own separation, only some of that information is helpful, or even accurate—but thankfully, there are some good tools and insights which can help us understand what's happening in a general sense, and apply this useful knowledge to our personal situation. One of these is Maslow's Pyramid, also called "Maslow's Hierarchy of Needs," and it sheds light on why separation can be so challenging.

Created by psychologist Abraham Maslow, this pyramid charts universal human needs from the ground level up—from survival-level needs to more intangible ones. If one or more of these needs are not being met, you will feel stressed, out of balance, and vulnerable.

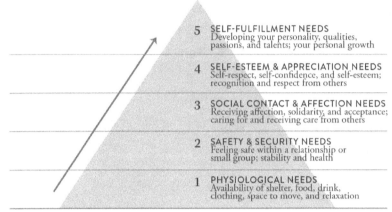

5 SELF-FULFILLMENT NEEDS
Developing your personality, qualities, passions, and talents; your personal growth

4 SELF-ESTEEM & APPRECIATION NEEDS
Self-respect, self-confidence, and self-esteem; recognition and respect from others

3 SOCIAL CONTACT & AFFECTION NEEDS
Receiving affection, solidarity, and acceptance; caring for and receiving care from others

2 SAFETY & SECURITY NEEDS
Feeling safe within a relationship or small group; stability and health

1 PHYSIOLOGICAL NEEDS
Availability of shelter, food, drink, clothing, space to move, and relaxation

Maslow's Pyramid of Needs

A separation can seriously compromise your ability to satisfy your basic needs on all levels. You may experience financial concerns, and even wonder where you will live and how you will put food on the table. You may get run down, or ill from stress. You may experience social and family shifts, including, if you have children, the opportunity to see your kids every day. You might feel isolated. You might question your own worth, and your self-esteem might take a tumble. And you might feel less able or inclined to spend time and attention on your personal growth, passions, dreams, and talents.

When you were in your relationship, things were probably relatively quiet on most levels. You may have been insecure in a couple of areas, but it was navigable. Even if you were in a relationship that was challenging—or worse, abusive—you had a known baseline from which you were operating. You knew what to expect from day to day, even if what you expected wasn't what you wanted, or what was healthy for you.

Now that you're separated, though, everything feels like it's in upheaval, and it's easy to freeze up like a deer in headlights.

In order to begin to rebuild your sense of security, take the time to analyze your personal situation according to Maslow's Pyramid and understand what you *really* need in order to function from a stable place. To assist you in this, I've created The Separation Pyramid™ (below). I've broken down each of the five Levels with a focus on the challenges of separation and the impact that those challenges might have in each area.

5 SELF-FULFILLMENT NEEDS
Not impacted in separation

4 SELF-ESTEEM & APPRECIATION NEEDS
Moderately to severely impacted in separation

3 SOCIAL CONTACT & AFFECTION NEEDS
Moderately to severely impacted in separation

2 SAFETY & SECURITY NEEDS
Severely impacted in separation

1 PHYSIOLOGICAL NEEDS
May be severely impacted in separation

The Separation Pyramid™

Level 1: Physiological needs. *Availability of shelter, food, drink, clothing, space to move, and relaxation.* Your most essential and basic needs come under threat in a separation. A great deal of uncertainty exists on this Level. As long as the roof over your head and your income are not safe and secure, you cannot function optimally. The feelings of change and loss resulting from a separation are the deepest here, and the biggest conflicts within a separation play out at this Level. For example, you may fight with your ex over who gets the house, who keeps your most valuable possessions, or how you will divide the household income and debts. If you have children, there may be conflict over where they live, and how the time, attention, and care given to them will be divided. In my opinion, personal contact with children is a primal, physiological need for most parents, and so regular time with them feels crucial.

Level 2: Safety and security needs. *Feeling safe within a relationship or a small group; stability and health.* After a separation—even an amicable one—feelings of safety and security within this Level are almost completely wiped out. The structure and sense of familiarity that were part of your relationship and your family, which gave you a feeling of safety and security, will almost certainly be gone. Others who were in close contact with you as a couple (or as a family) can also disappear, including your extended family, friends, and contacts from clubs or other associations. There's also a sense of change and loss when it comes to traditions, habits, and reference points in your agenda, such as holidays, birthdays, trips, and vacations with family and friends. Due to all the associated emotions and changes, you might be knocked back psychologically and physically. When this happens, your energy level plummets, and you don't function as well.

Level 3: Social contact and affection needs. *Receiving affection, solidarity, and acceptance; caring for and receiving care from others.* During a separation, this Level of the Separation Pyramid frequently suffers moderate to serious damage. Some of the relationships that you have carefully built up are now history. Other relationships have become problematic, at least for the time being. Your entire network of relationships is going through a period of readjustment, and you feel like you have fewer solid structures to hold on to. As a result, it sometimes feels like you have to do everything all on your own, or like everyone is against you.

Level 4: Self-esteem and appreciation needs. *Self-respect, self-confidence, and self-esteem; recognition and respect from others.* In a separation, this Level often suffers moderate to serious damage. Your self-confidence, self-respect, and ego take some hard knocks, even if you were the one who took the initiative to separate. You're more vulnerable, and therefore also more sensitive to the opinions and behavior of others. You suddenly have a new status or label, which is not always positive: "So-and-so's ex" or "The person who ran off with so-and-so." The people around you may also judge and/or avoid you.

Level 5: Self-fulfillment needs. *Developing your personality, qualities, passions, and talents; your personal growth.* At first, as a result of the separation and accompanying chaos, you may not prioritize this area of your life—but in fact, it is the only Level of the Pyramid of Needs that does not suffer any real damage in a separation. This Level belongs only to you, and therefore is *exactly* the area in which you can find the potential and resilience to unlock the art of positive separation and get your life back on track.

It is from Level 5—the need for self-fulfillment—that the art of positive separation can be accessed. When you put yourself first in the separation process, and do whatever it takes to feel positive about yourself and your new life, unlock your resilience and personal potential, and commit fully to your growth and happiness, that strong, positive energy will trickle down to support every other area of your life.

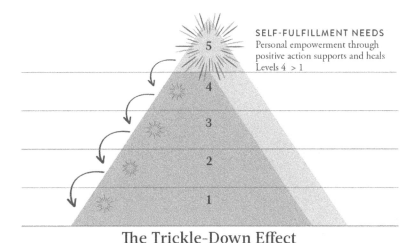

The Trickle-Down Effect

Empowered Action

▶ Your Personal Separation Pyramid™

*Note: This exercise is the best investment of time and energy you can make
for yourself right now. Sit down with a cup of tea, coffee, or water, and
give yourself the attention you deserve. You won't regret it!*

Draw your Personal Separation Pyramid to get a clearer idea of your own situation.
For each Level, note which changes, uncertainties, emotions, and losses you are
experiencing. Also write down your personal story and feelings at each Level.
Take the time to do this in some detail, even if it's emotionally painful at first.
It will quickly give you a clear picture of the changes and losses you are going
through, and give you some ideas about what you can do to minimize the chaos
in each area.

When you are finished, give special attention to Level 5. Envision yourself
standing on top of your Pyramid, surrounded by golden light. From this moment
forward, you are the beacon of strength and clarity in your own life. With this
strength and clarity, you will start taking care of yourself and performing the
tasks in your separation in a loving, caring, forward-looking way.

The Challenge Checklist–
A Personal Inventory

If you understand what's happening and has already happened, and know what's
changing and will change, it's easier to cope with your separation. Depending on
your personal situation and which phase of your separation you are currently in,
several aspects can play a role.

On the following pages, place a check mark next to any challenges that apply
to you. This personal inventory will help you understand exactly where you are
in your day-to-day life right now.

Physical and practical

- ☐ **A different daily routine.** Almost all your day-to-day activities require a different focus or routine now, from getting up and going to work to organizing your household chores and social routines. It's all up to you now—the easy as well as the hard parts.

- ☐ **Financial and legal aspects.** These may relate not only to the separation itself, but also to your children, your house, your possessions, and your debts. They may also include ongoing financial arrangements such as alimony and child support.

- ☐ **Different living arrangements.** From living together with a partner to being single—and, in some cases, from being part of a nuclear family to being a single parent.

- ☐ **Different living quarters/changes to physical spaces.** You may need to move and/or make interior changes to your home because you are no longer living together.

- ☐ **Saying goodbye to possessions.** You may lose "custody" of items to which you were attached.

- ☐ **Changes to your income and/or assets.** You may no longer be able to afford the same quality of life you enjoyed previously, either because you no longer have two incomes, or because the single household income is now split. You may also need to consider things like whether you will need to work more (or fewer) hours, whether you will have to look for work, and how your children will be provided for.

Emotional and social

- ☐ **A new future.** Your ex-partner is no longer in the picture, and neither are your shared dreams for the future. This requires some serious adjustment in your heart and mind, and perhaps some physical changes in plans, investments, or other arrangements.

- ☐ **Emotional turbulence.** Strong emotions can often surface quickly and unexpectedly, and you have to deal with them. The emotions of others—such as your ex-partner, your children, your family, and your friends—now vie for attention, too.

- ☐ **Different family situations.** You're also no longer automatically connected to two families with existing friendship and other social networks.
- ☐ **A new partner (and perhaps even bonus children).** Whether on your side or your ex-partner's, a new relationship in the midst of a separation will have a huge impact on everyone.
- ☐ **Changes and losses in relation to other contacts.** As a couple, you were part of various social groups such as family, friends, clubs etc. That will now change or even disappear. You will need to consider how you want to structure your new social life.

Health and wellness

- ☐ **Your physical health.** A separation can have a major impact on your health. As a result of stress, worry, uncertainty, changes, losses, and less attention paid to your body, you may have less energy and be more susceptible to all kinds of physical problems.
- ☐ **Your mental health.** If you have struggled with depression, anxiety, or another mental illness, the stress of separation can exacerbate it. You may also develop symptoms under intense stress that you have never experienced before.
- ☐ **Your perspective on life.** If you feel gloomy and negative, that will impact your ability to heal and move on. The same applies if you are optimistic and full of expectation.
- ☐ **Your ego, self-confidence, and belief in yourself.** In particular, you should consider how you will regain and/or retain it.

Children (if you have them)

- ☐ **Practical.** You will need to address agreements on parenting arrangements, behavior guidelines for you and your ex-partner, timetables, and financial aspects such as child support.
- ☐ **Emotional.** Your children need guidance and support in the new situation. As a parent, you now have a double role: you need to support your children as much as possible in dealing with the changing situation, while taking care of yourself and your own needs.

Stress and Needs in a Separation

A separation imposes an enormous amount of additional physical and psychological stress on you. This is true for everyone, whether you are a CEO, a builder, a teacher, a baker, a musician, or a doctor. Even if you are strong, successful, and have good friends and family to fall back on, you will feel the effects of your separation deeply. It's just a fact of life.

In addition to the stress of the separation itself, it's possible that you were suffering from increased stress for months, or even years, before the decision to separate was made. Perhaps your partner no longer loved you, or vice versa. Perhaps there were daily arguments or tensions. Perhaps there was an affair. Perhaps the loss of a job or a loved one impacted your relationship. Perhaps one of you had a major illness. Perhaps you or your ex-partner suffered from drug abuse or dependence. Perhaps there was mental or physical abuse happening. Regardless of the cause, if stress was present in your relationship before the separation, your reserves will already be weakened. This means you need to take extra care to watch out for the signs and symptoms of stress, because you are even more vulnerable to the problems stress can cause.

Now that you've completed your Personal Separation Pyramid and Challenge Checklist and better understand where your feelings of overwhelm and lack of control are coming from, it's time to look at how the disruption of your basic needs are causing stress in your life—and what you can do right away to minimize the impact of that stress on your mental and physical health.

HOW DOES STRESS WORK?

Too much stress can interfere with your day-to-day functioning and compromise your ability to deal with your separation in a positive way. It can also, over the course of weeks or months, take a serious toll on your health, or drag you even further into a negative spiral of emotional and reckless behavior.

If you are tense and stressed, your body makes extra amounts of the stress hormone cortisol. Cortisol helps you survive difficult situations, including emergencies, and propels you to take action. It's the instigator behind your instinctual "fight or flight" response. That's a good thing—and can even be life-saving—*if* the situation doesn't last too long.

However, if your stress continues over a period of weeks or months, your hormones can become unbalanced. Soon, the cortisol that helped spur you into action can overwhelm your system and interfere with your ability to function.

According to the American Psychological Association, chronic stress negatively affects every major system in your body—from your thought processes to your digestion, immune response, and even your breathing. It also affects your mood by messing with your hormone levels, making you more prone to depression, anxiety, and other serious mood disorders. There's even been a term coined for this: Divorce Stress Syndrome.

The effects of long-term stress include:

- Decreased concentration
- Decreased creative ability to solve issues
- Decreased planning ability
- Significant decrease in ability to assess your own situation objectively
- Damage to your body's immune system
- Damage to your mental health and well-being

Under stress, your decisions are made from a place of panic and urgency, rather than through careful consideration or deep intuition. This increases the risk that you will make the wrong decisions—or no decisions at all. This can create a vicious cycle of negative feelings, blame, and actions—and, ultimately, a lack of trust in yourself.

Also, you may find yourself engaging in risky or unhealthy behaviors to escape your stress, such as overusing alcohol and drugs, having unsafe flings, gambling, overworking, or other "escapist" acts.

During a separation, there are many causes of stress, some immediate, others ongoing. You identified some of these in your Personal Separation Pyramid—but the biggest of all is most likely your fear of the unknown. Your immediate future—which includes the outcome of your separation, the future of your family and social groups, your own well-being and security—is still in question. So is your long-term future—which includes your plans, dreams, and goals. This uncertainty, more than anything else, can push people in separation to make poor (or no) decisions, and become over-controlling, reactionary, or self-destructive.

You can prevent (or reverse) this trend by gaining more insight into your personal situation, the stress factors that are affecting you, and your own specific needs. Once you have this information, you will be able to use the tools in this book to create an effective action plan and reestablish your stability so you can stop sliding from one negative situation to the next and pick up the threads of your life again.

THE ANTIDOTE TO STRESS

The best way to counteract the stress of a separation is to make sure you are supported in all of the various areas where you feel vulnerable.

Adults in separation need the following:

- Empathy
- Insight
- Structure and perspective
- Support
- Good contact with friends, family, and kids (if there are any)
- Space (physical and mental)
- A healthy and strong body
- No new problems

Addressing these needs is the core purpose of this book, and I'll show you how to do this in great detail in later chapters. Still, it's helpful to get your wheels turning right away.

Empowered Actions

▶ Identify Your Stressors

What fields of stress are active in your life right now? Write about them in your notebook or in the space below.

Note: Examine the areas of home, finances, kids, health, work, future, social networks, ex-partner, etc., and check your Personal Separation Pyramid and Challenge Checklist.

My current stressors:

_____

_____

_____

_____

_____

_____

_____

_____

_____

▶ Identify Your Needs

Which of the needs on the previous page are not being met for you? (You can also reference the Personal Separation Pyramid you created in the previous section.) How can you try, right now, to start fulfilling those needs? Write your ideas in your notebook, or in the space provided.

My current needs and how I can fulfill them:

_____

_____

_____

_____

_____

_____

_____

_____

_____

_____

Your Three Tasks

Few people realize just how much hard work a separation involves. In addition to your regular day-to-day tasks and concerns, you now have to deal with your separation. In addition to all of the actual tasks and stressors that come with separation, you're mourning the loss of a meaningful relationship and a life created together.

To get through the separation and become a happy person again, you need to go through this process of mourning and deal with it seriously and consciously. You also need to tackle three major tasks which, when resolved, will help you put your separation behind you and create a foundation for your new future.

Your Three Major Tasks

1. **Settle your separation** on practical, legal, and emotional levels.
2. **Continue to function effectively on a daily basis** on both physical/practical and emotional levels.
3. **Build a foundation for your new future starting today**, not after the separation is legally and physically complete.

Getting through your separation in an empowered way (rather than as a victim or helpless bystander) will require a great deal of effort on your part. But if you understand your three major tasks, you will be able to break them down into smaller, more manageable pieces.

That said, your basic feelings of safety and security have been seriously compromised, and because of that, you will have to carry out all these tasks with one arm tied behind your back, as it were. The best thing you can do is to give yourself the extra time and space you need to accomplish each task in a way that doesn't create greater stress.

Above all, try not to blame all of your new tasks and responsibilities on yourself, your ex-partner, or a new partner. They are simply a part of your job as a person going through separation. It is not necessary—and definitely not helpful—to take out your feelings of disappointment, fear, anger, or aggression on yourself, your ex, or others. In fact, it will only entrench you further in the role of the victim, turn the separation into a battlefield, and greatly increase your risk of more unwanted problems, depression, or burnout.

Empowered Action

▶ Create an Inventory

In your journal or notebook, make a list of all your day-to-day tasks and obligations. For example, your daily tasks might include things like:

- Going to work or running your business
- Completing household chores
- Caring for your children and managing their schedules

- Caring for an elderly relative
- Running necessary errands
- Serving on volunteer boards
- Meeting with your lawyer or mediator
- Organizing financial records and meeting with your bank

Then, note how you can approach each in a positive way. Can you pair tasks together so that they feel less arduous? For example, can you follow a visit to your lawyer with a stop at your favorite café or market? Instead of lamenting the fact that your new apartment doesn't have a washer and dryer, can you combine a trip to the laundromat with a chance to catch up with a great book, or get ice cream with your kids? Bringing enjoyment into the extra work of a separation can be both fun and empowering.

The Six Sub-Processes Underlying Separation™

As you tackle each of your three major tasks, and the smaller tasks that come with them, you will begin to notice that there are layers to everything. In fact, there are six underlying sub-processes or energies which play a role in your separation as a whole, and in the three major tasks of your separation.

The Six Sub-Processes Underlying Separation

1. **Emotional**
2. **Practical**
3. **Legal**
4. **Physical**
5. **Future**
6. **Personal Growth**

These Sub-Processes may play more or less of a role in your life each day, but they are always interrelated, and they greatly influence each other. Knowing how these Sub-Processes work can give you greater strength and perspective;

when you understand what's causing a block in one area, you can choose to take positive action to open that area up and create greater flow.

Let me explain.

If one of these Sub-Processes is blocked, the entire separation process can grind to a halt. However, when you are aware of these Sub-Processes and their interrelationships, you can also understand why this is so, and take steps to correct those blocks and come into a more easeful flow in your life again.

Once you experience this mechanism you will realize that, by focusing on the Sub-Process that you are stuck in, and making use of the effective tips and tricks in this book, you can get yourself and the separation process back on track and moving forward again. It will feel like giving yourself a gift that ripples throughout your entire separation process.

Here's an example of how your six Sub-Processes can affect the course of a typical day during a separation.

In the afternoon …

You and your ex have an appointment with the mediator. Both of you are making an effort to settle the separation as best as possible, but it's a tricky juggling act.

- *Practical Sub-Process:* During lunch, you put some financial information down on paper, as requested by the mediator. You also scheduled an appointment for you and your ex-partner to meet with a kids' coach next week. Your briefcase contains some of your ex's books and personal papers, which you found in a drawer, and which you plan to return at the beginning of today's meeting with the mediator.

During the meeting …

- *Legal Sub-Process:* This is already the third meeting with the mediator, but you still haven't managed to come to an agreement regarding your shared debts and the house in which you both lived. As a result, the signing of the separation agreement will be delayed by at least four weeks.

Later that night ...

- *Emotional Sub-Process*: You feel anger rising inside you, accompanied by panic and dread. Your ex-partner had promised to deal with the debt issue and arrange things with the bank, but at the meeting, you learned that this never happened. You are sad, angry, lonely, and feel besieged. How will you deal with this debt? How will you move forward with this hanging over your head?

- *Physical Sub-Process*: Your stomach is knotted with worry and anxiety. You can't eat, and even after a full glass of wine your anxiety still has the upper hand. You can't fall asleep—and so, for the fifth night this week, you will get only four hours of sleep and wake with an enormous headache.

- *Future Sub-Process*: Still angry that no definite signing of the agreement is in sight, you refuse to give your ex-partner permission to take the kids next weekend (your weekend, by the current agreement) to their grandmother's big birthday party. Your ex-partner doesn't understand your behavior—birthdays were never an issue before—and has just about had it with your emotional ups and downs. Your refusal invites more anger and stress, and compounds the issues in the next mediation meeting. This creates even more uncertainty for you about the future of your separation, and your future as a parent.

- *Personal Growth Sub-Process*: You feel emotionally blocked and can't get over your anger and disappointment. It's unfortunate, because you almost sent your ex-partner a message later that night explaining that you were angry and disappointed because the signing of the separation agreement had once again been delayed, and that *of course* the kids should be able to go to their grandmother's seventy-fifth birthday.

The next day ...

Even though your head feels like a sponge, you still go to work. Your boss tells you—in a nice way—that you made a mistake the previous day in a proposal to a customer.

- *Emotional Sub-Process*: You can't take another moment of feeling like a failure. Your emotional response is completely over the top, and you simply stalk off. Five minutes later, your ex-partner calls to tell you that an agreement has been reached with the bank and the debt issues have been resolved, but you're still out of control and shout, "I don't feel like dealing with this right now!"
- *Future and Legal Sub-Process*: Your ex-partner shouts back, "I give up. There's no reasoning with you!" A few days later, you find a letter from a lawyer in your mailbox. The mediation is over, and the legal battle has begun.

This example illustrates the effect that a block in one Sub-Process (in this case, the Emotional Sub-Process) can have on an entire separation. As you can see, emotional blocks (anxiety, anger) can easily lead to blocks in the Physical Sub-Process (no sleep, headaches), and finally in the Legal and Practical Sub-Processes.

When blocks cause such a cascade, increased levels of stress and emotion soon follow (triggered, for example by the letter from the lawyer). When this happens, your physical and mental resilience can quickly go downhill, especially if you constantly find yourself taking the wrong actions as a result of reactive decisions. This is clearly *not* where you want to be.

The good news is that, by focusing on the block in the original Sub-Process and resolving it, you can get the entire separation process back on track quickly and effectively.

There are blocks that you can address immediately, and others over which you have little or no influence. Emotional, personal growth, and physical blocks are all under your personal jurisdiction; you can work to change your emotion regardless of the situation. You can even take preventative measures by taking care of your mind and body on a daily basis, and by taking steps to understand why you feel the way you do (for example, by working through the exercises earlier in this chapter). Other blocks, such as legal matters, may be outside your control. The best way to deal with these is to rein in your reactions and make sure that none of your other Sub-Processes become impaired as a result of a difficulty in this area.

Empowered Action
▶ Sub-Processes Quick Scan

This exercise only takes a minute. Close your eyes, take a deep breath, and scan your Six Sub-Processes: Emotional, Practical, Legal, Physical, Future, and Personal growth. Do you feel a blockage or dissonance in any of these areas (even a small one)?

Jot down any blocks you find on a piece of paper or in your journal. Now, ask yourself what action you can take to unblock this area? Where do you need to ask for help?

What Comes Next?

In this chapter, we've learned a lot about the physical, emotional, and practical elements of your separation; your stress levels and how they affect you; and how your six Sub-Processes provide an undercurrent to your daily life. You've also discovered the Personal Separation Pyramid, and how your potential for resilience and forward movement lies not in the physical security or social network of your old life, but in Level 5 of the Separation Pyramid and your potential for personal growth and self-fulfillment. Your strength and positive energy comes from inside you, and will trickle down from the top of your Personal Pyramid to give power and direction to the parts of your life affected on Levels 1 through 4 of the Pyramid, as well as to your thoughts, goals, and actions.

In Chapter Two, we will create a plan to help you disconnect from your old life in a positive, empowered way, and connect with your new vision for the future.

CHAPTER TWO

Disconnect from Your
Old Life and Connect to
Your New Future

Disconnecting from your old life is the first and most important step to embracing your new future. You can't look backwards and forwards at the same time. The power of disconnection was a major factor for my client Jane, whose divorce process began about two years ago.

JANE'S STORY

"We'd had a fight about painting some walls and windows. I was concerned because the house was getting run down and there was mold in our bedroom. It didn't bother him, though, and so although we had the money to paint (and even though I offered to do it myself), he was against it.

"This was hardly our first fight. We'd been trying to save our marriage for two years. I'd spend most of that time trying to be the wife he wanted. I'd been to counseling when he told me I should 'get over it and change my attitude.' I was becoming increasingly nervous, always feeling as though I was walking on eggshells—but we had just come back from a nice weekend away, and I had hoped that things were improving.

"I had stormed upstairs and was standing in the corridor near our bedroom. I was upset, which never sat well with him, but when he followed me up the stairs to confront me, his reaction was far worse than I could have prepared for.

"He said, 'I want you to leave this house. I do not want to see you anymore. I want a divorce. You have four weeks to pack your stuff and get out.'

"Funny, how you can feel so many things, all in a split second. My heart stopped—and at the same time, I felt like someone was drumming on it with great force. The world simply wasn't there anymore. Time stood still. I felt an inner cry, a whimper … and then, a deep silence and a gray mist that covered my mind.

"Part of me was hoping this was all a bad dream—that we would soon make up again, and that everything would be back to normal. It had happened before; once, I'd moved out for a few months, but came back when he said things would improve. But the next morning, when I saw him in the kitchen, I knew. My eyes were red from crying all night, but he didn't even look at me, or reply when I greeted him. It was if I had evaporated overnight; I had become a 'nothing.'

"He never spoke a single word to me again.

"It was so strange: one evening, we were having dinner together *à deux*, candles lit, making plans for the next summer vacation. And the next, he made his pronouncement. The shutters were closed, and there was no more future. A line had been crossed, and there was no going back.

"It was then, in that split second, that I made a life-changing decision. I couldn't rely on this man to love me anymore. I couldn't continue to believe that he would take care of me. I had to step up and take care of myself. This was serious. It was life or death.

"That moment is still crystal clear in my mind. I remember what I was wearing: blue jeans, light blue shirt, sneakers, hair in a ponytail, my favorite hoop earrings. I remember the feeling of the sun touching my hair as it streamed through the window, and the peace that came over me. It was over. There would be no more fights, no more uncertainty. No more wondering if he loved me, or didn't. He no longer wanted me to be part of his life, part of his children's lives. He did not want me anymore. I had felt this truth for years in my body, but I had closed my mind and heart to the knowing. Now, I was ready to hear and accept it.

"Trembling, I decided to take the path of Me, with myself and for myself. I had no idea what that would even mean, but I knew I had to do it.

"The house was his, the money was his. There was no arguing about it. My income over the years had gone toward groceries, flowers, vacations … I had never planned to make it on my own. I never thought I would need to. Now, all I had was my job as a creative consultant, my clothes, my car, a few other possessions, and a huge amount of uncertainty and emotion.

"I had to totally disconnect from my old life if I wanted to stay healthy and keep myself on the right track. Thankfully, I had read Eveline's book, *Je Wordt Weer Gelukkig,* and knew about the disconnection process. If I did not disconnect from my husband, I knew I would stay in his power and never build my own life.

"Disconnecting from my old life, and from him, was a process with many stages and layers. Every time something else came up, I had to find a new way to let go.

"I was angry, but my anger wasn't helping me. I knew that I had to keep moving forward to salvage my life and create a better future, but my heart didn't understand this right away. Most days, it was like I had to put on blinders the moment I got out of bed, just so I could keep moving forward, step by step, straight ahead, without looking around at the chaos that was happening.

"I had to disconnect from the house that had been my home for fifteen years. I had put care and love into every corner of it, and now it was mine no longer. I had to disconnect from my husband, who was no longer my partner, and from our future as a couple. I had to disconnect from my ex's children, since he allowed me no contact with them after the day he announced our separation. This was incredibly hurtful since I had been participating in their upbringing for years, and loved them like they were my own.

"From that day on, it was like my life was an onion. Every time I undid one layer, I found something new underneath. And each time I shed one layer of my old life, I gained a new layer of myself. It was quite beautiful, actually, like emerging from a cocoon.

"In the beginning, there was a lot of pain and emotion, not all of it rational. I won't lie: at first, I was tempted to blame my ex for everything. After all, he was the one who had wanted the divorce, but I was the one who was losing everything. There were days that I was so scared I felt like I was drowning and freezing and burning up, all at the same time—but I knew that blaming him, and giving in to those fears, would only keep me locked in a victim state. I kept seeing my practical and wise therapist, and the tools she continued to give me helped immensely. I also had my Winning Team of friends, family, and other professionals to support me through my many mood swings and low days. No matter how bad things got, I knew that I could go on.

"After two months or so, things got easier. Life was still dark, stormy, and messy, but I could see the light coming through the clouds. I refused to fall into the trap of asking others about my ex, or listening to stories about him. I removed him from my social media accounts. Part of me wanted him to be sorry that he'd ended our marriage, but after I'd fallen into that trap a couple of times (and needed days to recover) I realized it wasn't worth it. I couldn't play those games and start a new life at the same time.

"Most importantly, I learned to take time to deal with my feelings as they bubbled up. I would go into the moment and describe to myself what I had to let go, and how I felt. Then, I would open both hands and let it go with grace. Another layer peeled back, another piece of myself found.

"Around my neck, I wore three silver amulets: a dragonfly, a donkey, and a big smiling frog. The dragonfly because I was learning to fly; the donkey so I wouldn't be an 'ass' and make the same mistake twice; and the frog so that I would not try to find my 'prince' for at least another year. I knew that if I got tangled up in the excitement of a new relationship, I would stop giving this care and attention to myself. Every time I was tempted to give up, I would play with these amulets and remind myself that I was doing this for *me*. There was a happier future out there for me. I just needed to keep my arrows pointed at that target.

"Little by little, real life started to peek back in. I found a tiny apartment, a miniature home of my own, so I no longer needed to bounce back and forth between my old house and my friends' sofas. The day I moved in marked a profound point of disconnection. I decided that I was not going to waste a single moment being angry at my ex anymore. I needed to forgive him, and myself, for the marriage that did not work. I had a new home now, a new place to put down roots.

"Every day, I felt a little better, but there were still things that triggered me. I remember when, months after the breakup, I had to use a banking app to disconnect from our mutual bank account. I cried for the whole day. It was a silly, formal thing, but it really got me.

"Another powerful moment came when I sold my boat, my biggest personal treasure. I had saved for years to buy the old-timey wooden sailboat. My ex and I had spent summer weekends on the lakes in Friesland, in the north of Holland. We would stall the boat in the middle of the lake at sunset, and let ourselves be rocked to sleep by the waves. In the morning, we would have coffee and make eggs over a small gas fire pit on the deck. It hurt to sell that boat, even though she went to people whom I adore. It was like I was selling my happy memories at the same time. But the proceeds of that sale furnished my new apartment and helped me step even more into my new life.

"Now, I feel at peace with myself and my life. I know that the ending of my marriage was for the best, and that, despite all of the hard days, many good things have happened (and continue to happen) for me. I lost my foundation for a while, but I have built a new one. My goal from the start was to rely on myself—to get closer to myself, and to become proud and self-confident—and it's working! I feel creative, healthy, happy, and rooted in life. My work is wonderful, I've overcome my financial problems, and I have a cheerful group of friends and family who have stood by my side through everything. I still have moments here and there where I need to shed anger and sadness, but I'm okay with that. It's all part of the process."

***

If Jane hadn't been willing to disconnect from her old life and set boundaries around her choices, she could have easily ended up tangled in drama and negative emotion. Instead, she used her divorce as a springboard to create a new life—a life full of the things she values. Once she knew there was no going back, she made a commitment to connect to herself, move forward, and create a new reality.

When I asked her how she felt about her process now, she said, "The process of disconnecting from my old life was the strongest choice I ever made in my life.

Reconnecting to myself saved me. I was amazed at the effect. I will never lose the strength and resilience I built during those months!"

Your Disconnection

After reading Chapter One, you should have a new understanding of what your separation entails on the practical, physical, and emotional levels; what you need to do in addition to your usual daily tasks to navigate your separation; where and how you can manage your stress; and how your self-fulfillment plays a major role in creating your new, happy future. Now, it's time to take your first step toward resolving the chaos and getting your life back on a positive track.

In this chapter, we'll explore some practical steps you can take to disconnect from your old life and connect to yourself and your new vision for a happy future.

The purpose of these exercises—and the purpose of the Positive Separation Method as a whole—is to give you a practical way to plan for your own empowerment and a life beyond your separation. You *can* function effectively on a day-to-day basis, minimize your stress, and cope with the changes and losses you're experiencing. You *can* make good decisions for yourself and your loved ones. And you *can* build a strong foundation for your future.

WHAT DISCONNECTION REALLY MEANS

Disconnecting from your old partner, and your old life, doesn't mean walking away and never engaging with them again (unless you need to do so for your own safety). Your happy memories can certainly accompany you into your new life. Instead, disconnecting means unplugging yourself from any and all thoughts, emotions, activities, people, possessions, and other entanglements from your old life that no longer serve you, and creating new ones that serve your vision for a better future. When you do this, you will engage with your ex-partner in a different way—a way that is healthier for both of you.

The best way to do this is simply to take a deep breath, steel yourself, and pull the plug—in your head, and in your heart. You have to choose, finally and irreversibly, to step into an unknown future and give yourself a chance to grow, thrive, and be happy again.

At first, this will be easier to do in your head. You will start to think of yourself and your situation in a new way. You will learn to make plans that don't include your ex-partner. You will learn to dream about a future that reflects what you want.

Your heart may take longer to catch up—and that's okay. Emotions are not rational, and fear can creep in when you aren't expecting it. Despite this, it's important not to backslide, or plug in again to your ex-partner or your old life. When you do that, stress and chaos will follow.

> *Note: You must go through this process of disconnection even if you are hoping to get together with your partner again at some point in the future. You will never feel empowered if you are constantly waiting for your ex to "remember" you and the way things were, or if you keep trying to change yourself to be the person you think your ex wants. If you are really struggling with this, or if you strongly or irrationally desire to pretend that this separation never happened, you may want to consult with a psychologist or other professional. Such a person can help you through the process of disconnection in a positive way.*

Your new future starts *today*. Are you ready to meet it?

Empowered Action

▶ Make Today Your "Disconnection Day"

Take out your calendar and place a star (or another symbol that has meaning for you) over today's date. This is your Moment of Disconnection, your "starting line," the place of transition. Starting today, your task is to reconnect to yourself 100 percent. You are living your new life, not your old one.

▶ Draw Your Diverging Paths

Look at the graphic below. Visualize yourself walking down a new road—the path to your future. You are diverging from your ex-partner's road and heading off in a new, exciting direction. See yourself as strong, vibrant, and prepared to walk this new road, wherever it leads.

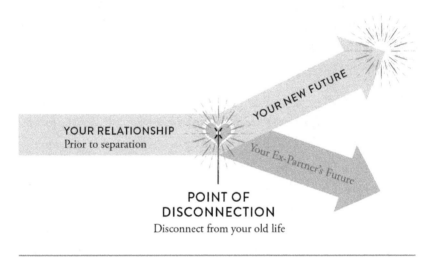

YOUR RELATIONSHIP
Prior to separation

YOUR NEW FUTURE

Your Ex-Partner's Future

POINT OF
DISCONNECTION
Disconnect from your old life

Your Disconnection Point

Now, draw your own version of your Disconnection and your diverging road. On the top road, write your name. This is your road. On the lower road, write the name of your ex-partner. This is his or her road now.

Alongside your new road, write down all of the good things you are taking with you—like happy memories, your children, and all the positive things you've learned and grown from. These things still belong to you. They are part of you, and will accompany you on your new path. You are not leaving *yourself* at your Point of Disconnection; you are simply leaving the life you used to live.

Once you have finished your list, close your eyes, take a deep breath, and see yourself stepping away from that Point of Disconnection and onto your new road. See the road opening up in front of you, like a highway into the future. Even if you can't see clearly where it leads right now, feel the possibilities for your new life.

Ground Rules for Disconnecting

As soon as the decision to separate has been made (whether it was your idea or not), your relationship becomes a closed book. There will be no more stories written about you as a couple, no more joint experiences. You now have your life, and your ex-partner has theirs.

You can think of the process of disconnection as closing the shutters on a window. When you were in your relationship, you each lived in your own house, and had your unique experiences, but there was an open window in your adjoining walls through which you shared much of what was happening for each of you. Now, that window is closed. You can no longer see through to the other side, or expect to be seen clearly.

When this happens, you are suddenly in your own house, alone. And now that you are no longer spending so much time at that shared window, many thoughts, emotions, opinions, behavior patterns, and choices will surface. You may learn things about yourself that you have never known, or realize that you had been ignoring things in your house because they didn't align with what was in your partner's house. This can feel very strange, and you may find yourself reeling from this sudden shift in perspective.

Your ex-partner is also going through this shift. That's why you may find yourself asking, "Is this really the person I knew?" You are now two separate people living in separate houses, each looking out for your own interests and feelings. You can no longer expect to understand one another the way you did when the window of your relationship was wide open.

If you are going to successfully disconnect from your ex and your old life, you need to stop trying to open that window. You need to stop trying looking at your life in the same light, and from the same angle. And you need to establish— and stick to—some ground rules that will keep you from complicating the disconnection process and the practical aspects of your separation.

Rule #1: No sex with your ex! Sex is not some kind of glue for a broken relationship, and it does not help dissolve bottlenecks in your separation. By going to bed with your ex-partner after the decision to separate has been made, you will not gain any extra influence over his or her actions and choices. Instead, you will introduce confusion and blocks into both of your Emotional Sub-Processes and complicate or prolong the entire separation process.

Rule #2: Don't rely on your ex for emotional support. Even if you end up being friends once the separation is complete, you cannot turn to your ex for comfort, emotional support, or advice during your separation. Remember, that window is closed, and your ex is going through his or her own emotional turbulence and rearrangement. Expecting your ex to "be there for you" on an emotional level is damaging for you both and compromises your ability to move forward in an empowered way. (I'll teach you more about how to do this later in this book.)

Rule #3: Don't play the victim. Even if you can no longer control or influence your ex, you *can* control yourself. This includes managing the way you feel, think, act, and engage with your ex, third parties (like new partners), and the entire separation process. Blaming your ex for your current situation and feelings is not helpful, nor does it empower you to create a better future. Same goes for basing your decisions on what your ex does, says, or feels. (Hint: Chapters Three and Four have some great tools to help you with this!)

Rule #4: Don't wait for your ex to "save" you. If you relied heavily on your ex for help with your daily tasks in the past, or counted on him/her to make you feel good about yourself, it can be tempting to let your life fall apart and wait for your ex to step in and save you—and, by extension, your relationship. This is *never* a healthy relationship dynamic, and it won't save your union now. Guilt, like sex, is not glue for a broken relationship.

Rule #5: Don't try to save your ex. Being a savior is the flip side of being a victim. This dynamic can be especially strong if your ex was opposed to the separation, or if s/he struggles with illness, addiction, or other challenges. However, it's important to put up some solid boundaries. You have your own life to manage. If you try to manage your ex's life, too, you will end up burned out, stressed, and feeling trapped.

Rule #6: Don't try to influence or control your ex. Don't try to manipulate your ex, and don't act in a way that you think will provoke a certain reaction. Manipulation might mean doing things out of spite, attacking your ex to get a reaction, or using the kids as leverage. It might also mean compromising on your principles or your future happiness to placate an angry ex-partner or avoid a fight. Instead, make choices that are best for you in both the short and long term, regardless of what your ex thinks, does, or says. (Hint: Step 2 will give you more tools to manage this.)

Rule #7: Don't try to prove yourself (even to yourself). Find safe and healthy ways to express your emotions. You are not wrong or a bad person because you're in a separation. You have nothing to prove to your ex or anyone else. Be as strong as you can be, and as vulnerable as you need to be (with people you trust).

Rule #8: Don't involve a new partner in your separation. Whether you, or your ex, or both of you have a new partner, keep your separation between you and your ex. Even if a new partner was a factor in your separation, this is between the two of you. Also, remember that you can't be plugged into two relationships simultaneously. If you don't disconnect from your ex, you will never fully be able to plug in with your new partner. (Hint: Chapter Twelve has more information on how to integrate a new partner into your life during the separation process.)

Rule #9: Don't neglect your mind and body. Neglecting yourself will only make your separation harder. Prioritize your self-care and give yourself what you need to navigate this disconnection in a healthy way—including seeking professional help if you need it.

Rule #10: Don't keep mementos. Unless they truly conjure only happy memories—and don't carry the burden of regret, judgment, or sadness—put away all of the things that remind you of your ex-partner for at least twelve months. This includes photos, objects, and even furnishings. If you still have stuff that belongs to your ex, give it back as soon as possible, and don't hang onto it to use as leverage.

Rule #11: Don't forget to grieve. You have disconnected from your ex-partner. You have unplugged from your old life, and closed the shutters on that window. You have a right to feel sad, lost, and even angry. Once you've chosen to disconnect, it can feel tempting to move on and never look back. But you can, and should, allow yourself to grieve in a healthy way—a way that doesn't involve hurting yourself, trying to manipulate your ex, or lingering in the past. You can feel sad and still make healthy decisions that will move your life forward.

Rule #12: Don't forget to be a parent to your children. The basic rule is very simple: if you're doing well, your children will also do well. The opposite is also true: if you're not okay, they're not okay. Your effort as a parent needs to go into being a calm, responsible adult, even in this stressful situation; focusing only on what you can control; processing your emotions in a positive and productive way; and taking action to create a happy, light-filled future for all of you. To navigate these waters in a positive way, you will need to apply an extra-large dose of discipline, self-control and behave in a grown-up way. If you really want the best for your kids, start using all the tools this book gives you to get into a more positive place as soon as possible, for your kids' sake as well as your own. (Check out the Golden Rules for Parents in Chapter Twelve to get started.)

Empowered Actions

▶ Your Personal Ground Rules

Write out your personal "Ground Rules" based on the rules for disconnecting I shared in the previous section. Over and above the rules I've listed above, what positive, straightforward rules will you set for yourself around your separation?

As you do this exercise, keep in mind your three major tasks in separation:

1. **Settling your separation** on practical, legal, and emotional levels.
2. **Continuing to function effectively on a daily basis** on both physical/practical and emotional levels.
3. **Building a foundation for your new future** starting today, not after the separation is legally and physically complete.

What healthy boundaries can you establish to stay grounded, reduce your stress, and move forward with the three major tasks of your separation? Once you've finished your list of ground rules, hang it in a place where you can read it often.

▶ Shutters Closed, New Window Open

Draw two houses adjacent to one another. Write your name in one house, and the name of your ex in the other. Then, draw the shared window in the connecting wall of each.

Roll down the shutter of the window by drawing a thick line, a cross, an X, or whatever you like. Then, on the other side of your house, draw a big new window where light can come in. This is your new reality, the new layout of your personal house. You might even draw a big, shining sun outside the new window! Imagine the radiance around your house now that you have a new window to see through. Breathe deeply and let this new information flow through you.

Create a Vision for Your New Future

As soon as you disconnect from your ex, your own personal future becomes the *only* future. To create a new sense of structure and a positive trajectory, it's essential for you to visualize a happy, fulfilling new future—even if you're feeling afraid to look even a few days ahead from where you are now.

The choices you make around your separation today—both positive and negative—will have repercussions for weeks, months, and maybe even years to come. If you don't have a clear vision for your future, and instead live from moment to moment in your separation, you are more likely to make bad or reactionary decisions you will regret, or get sucked into a negative spiral that could have major consequences down the line. On the other hand, your positive choices will become like steady stepping stones toward your new, happy future.

Visualizing your future in words or images encourages positive, long-term thinking, which is key to energizing yourself and getting through tough moments. Your vision will motivate and empower you, and eventually (if you spend enough time with it) become an inseparable part of all your thoughts and actions, twenty-four hours a day, seven days a week.

POSITIVE THOUGHTS DRIVE POSITIVE BEHAVIOR

When you get stuck in a negative vision of your future, it automatically drains you of energy and happiness. (Chances are you've been there once or twice already!) You no longer have something positive to work towards, and the images and thoughts in your mind's eye are not very inviting: you may see yourself alone, lonely, bitter, angry, and full of self-pity. It's a recipe for unhappiness that only compounds with time.

The good news is, you have a choice. If you choose, consciously and deliberately, to focus on a future full of new opportunities, dreams, and goals, you will change everything from your mood when you wake up in the morning to how you show up at mediation meetings.

It's a proven fact that if you replace negative or neutral plans and expectations with positive ones, your brain will adjust over time and act accordingly. Positive plans and expectations stimulate your brain to take action—and action is *empowering*, especially right now!

So, are you ready to create your vision statement?

YOUR VISION STATEMENT

Your vision is, at heart, your deepest wish for who, where, and what you want to be in the future.

In the following exercises, you will play with and expand your vision so that you can see it clearly—but for now, when you're just starting out, it can be helpful to summarize the *feeling* of the future you want to create in a single declarative sentence.

For example, your future vision might begin with "I *will* be happy again."

It's quite a general description, but serves as an excellent start for creating a personal vision because it conjures a deep feeling inside of you.

Whether you use the example above or create your own "I will …" statement, you will be exploring your future vision in more detail through the exercises to follow.

Work Out the Details of Your Vision

You can work out your vision in greater detail by:

- **Setting a specific time frame for realizing it**, and
- **Writing down several words and catchphrases** that describe the feelings, events, and goals of your new future.

For example, "I will be happy again" can be made more concrete and specific by writing, "In five years, I will be healthy, have enough financial resources not to worry, live in an attractive home, be free of major worries and tension, have a network of good friends around me, feel loved and valued, feel free and empowered, have a solid relationship with my children, and be in a new and satisfying relationship."

Here is a partial list of aspects that can make your vision of your future more concrete:

- No financial worries
- Positive financial agreements
- A good relationship with my family/friends/colleagues/children
- A job that I like
- A fine/cozy/large/happy home
- Sharing my knowledge/love
- Feeling free in relationships
- Living in peace/harmony
- Being independent
- Having more trust in the people around me
- Being more aware of my own limits
- Doing things that inspire me
- Having an attractive garden/cozy fireplace
- Going on an interesting trip once a year
- Paying down my mortgage
- Having enough time for my hobbies
- A loving/interesting/balanced new partner relationship

Your Vision: Your Daily Touchstone

Your vision of your happy future is the touchstone by which you can evaluate your day-to-day thoughts, decisions, actions, and behavior. It's a kind of mirror that you can hold up to your life, and see where you need to put your focus in order to move in the right direction.

Especially right now, when you're just beginning this process, and when things get tough or emotional, keep your vision firmly in mind. Ask yourself whether your current thoughts, actions, and behaviors are likely to help you realize that vision. If the answer is "No," take some time to step back, reevaluate, and change your direction.

For example: After a very emotional phone call with your ex, you might be seeing red. You might be thinking, "I hate my ex! His/her behavior is completely out of line, so why should I keep my promises? Why should s/he get to go to Paris this weekend with friends? Maybe I just won't pick up the kids ..."

In the moment, reneging on your agreement may seem like a great way to punish your ex-partner—but it's not your ex who is the victim here, but you and your kids. Is thwarting your ex's plans really worth confusing or angering your children, and potentially damaging your relationship with them? If you step back, take a breath, and reconnect with your vision, you will probably see that what your ex does with his/her weekend is far less important than making sure your children remain part of your happy future.

Here's a good rule to follow: As soon as a negative thought or emotion pops up, stop what you're doing and hold up your "vision mirror." If you look at the situation honestly, you will quickly get a clear answer as to how you should approach it. Follow the guidance you receive from this introspection, even if it means swallowing your pride or setting aside your desire for revenge.

If complicated or strong emotions are clouding your judgment, take a walk or talk with a sensible, trusted friend before acting on your feelings. Remember, you are not "policing" your actions to accommodate your ex; you are working hard and practicing self-discipline so you can have the happy future you envision.

Empowered Actions

▶ Write Your Vision Statement

Describe your vision of your new future in one sentence on paper. Then set a time limit to realize it, and describe it in more detail using fifteen sentences at most.

Read the sentences out loud to yourself, and pay attention to your gut feeling. Ask yourself, "Is this what I really want for my future?"

Your gut feeling should be a resounding "Yes!" with no holding back. If your gut isn't completely convinced, or if you still have some reservations about your new future, take this as a "No," and start over again.

Don't be afraid to dream big! Don't limit yourself to what you think is "reasonably" possible right now. My students and clients who do this exercise wholeheartedly and stick to their vision end up realizing 80 percent of their dreams within five years! The moment you write out your vision on paper, you add it to your subconscious mind. Once you claim it, it's inside you!

▶ Visualize Your Happy Future

Close your eyes, and imagine yourself three to five years from now. Relax, take deep breaths, and see what images come up.

Visualize yourself in a space that feels comforting to you. Your separation has receded into the past and no longer bothers you. You're now completely free. You can see yourself laughing again. You're enjoying your work, and once again find intense pleasure in the little things in life. Perhaps you can even visualize a new and loving partner. You feel relaxed and in your prime. Life is good, and you're happy.

Don't just "see" all of this. Feel it. Connect to it.

Spend some time with this "future you." Then, carry that vision and feeling back to the here and now. Know that you *can* create your vision for the future, if you stay firm in your disconnection from your partner, follow through on the goals that support your vision, and believe in yourself.

▶ Make a Collage (optional)

Cut out photos from magazines and make a collage of what your new future looks like. Your collage might include photos of sunny landscapes, mountains, the sea, smiling people, delicious dishes, your favorite hobbies or sports, or whatever else you dream about. At the center of all of these images, place a photo of a happy you. When you're done, you will almost taste, smell, feel, and hear your future in this collage. It's a future that's worth looking forward to—and worth working for.

This image will become part of you and have an effect on you, consciously and unconsciously. Hang your collage in a place where you will see it every day, and reconnect with your new life vision.

Your New Best Practice: Your Power Hour

As I shared in this book's Introduction, my Power Hour was one of the best tools I had in my toolbox during my own separation. Your Power Hour is a fixed hour that you set aside once per week to work on yourself and your separation process and check in with your vision for your new life. During this time, you will look honestly at your separation from an overall perspective with yourself squarely in the spotlight, and check on the progress you're making.

It may seem like a lot to ask on top of everything you're going through, but I promise, the Power Hour is the greatest gift you can give yourself right now. Many of my clients swear by this process, and have continued it long past the initial phases of their separations.

Reserve one hour per week in your daily planner for the next three months. Do it now! Make a commitment to yourself that this hour will be "holy" for as long as your separation is ongoing. Use your Power Hour to ask yourself deep questions, make your to-do list, and plan activities that move you closer to your goals.

Here are some questions you might ask yourself during your Power Hour:

Write the answers in your notebook or journal.

- "How am I feeling right now?"
- "What is my energy level?"
- "How are things with my children?" (If you have them.)
- "How are things for me at work?"
- "How are things for me at home?"
- "What am I focusing my energy on?"
- "Am I really working on empowering myself, or am I hiding from my reality?"
- "Have I slipped into victim mindset?"
- "Am I proud of my thoughts, words, and actions this week? If not, how can I choose differently during this coming week?"

- "What happy/comforting/fun things have I planned for the coming week?"
- "How far have I come since my separation started?"
- "What do I still need to do to get through my separation in an empowered way?"
- "Do I need extra help in any area of my life?"
- "What are my tasks for this week?"
- "What are my goals for this week?"

Working with questions like these can help you stay honest with yourself, make better decisions, plan more effectively, and move more quickly toward your new vision for life.

Empowered Action

▶ Schedule Your Power Hour

Get your daily planner, and add one hour per week for the next three months, preferably on the same day every week, to be your Power Hour.

Your Power Hour is your anchor for the week—your time to get an overview of your current life, organize your thoughts, get in touch with yourself how you are proceeding, plan and ask for the help you will need to settle your separation, and keep building on the foundation of your vision statement so you can move toward the happy future you envision.

What Comes Next?

Now that you've set a clear Point of Disconnection from your ex-partner and your old life, and created a vision for your new life, it's time to move forward to Step 2 of the Positive Separation Method, where we'll look at what you can and can't control in your separation, and how you can use that knowledge to empower yourself every day and set concrete, attainable goals so you can start moving toward the new, happy life you envision!

POSITIVE SEPARATION STEP 2

Focus on What You Can Control
(and Let Go of What You Can't)

Focus on What You Can Control
(and Let Go of What You Can't)

Now that you've taken the first steps to disconnect from your old life and partnership, to understand your separation and unique situation, and to connect to a new, happy vision for your future, it's time to start taking action to create your new life.

In Step 2 of my Positive Separation Method, you'll learn how to align your thoughts, choices, and actions with your vision for the future; stop wasting time and energy on the aspects of your current situation you cannot influence; and set attainable goals that will move you forward into your new life. You'll also make commitments to yourself that will serve as guideposts on your path and keep you from sliding into drama, victimhood, and other negative thought patterns.

This Step contains lots of helpful information about how you can master the art of positive separation in your everyday life. Once you commit to following the Method, establish your boundaries and parameters, and solidify your commitments to yourself, this actually becomes easy and natural. More, it can help you shift your perspective and energy around your separation almost immediately.

Why is it so important to focus on what you can and can't control? Well, it's a matter of *energy*.

Creating anything takes energy. Creating a new life according to your vision and goals takes a *lot* of energy. If you're wasting your precious resources fighting the inevitable, arguing about things you can't change, or wishing things were different, you will not have the strength you need to create and maintain your personal space and lift yourself up into your new, happier life.

Regaining control in your life isn't about micromanaging every aspect of your day, judging or reacting to what your ex-partner does or doesn't do, or eliminating all painful circumstances. In fact, if you try to influence things in this way, you will create a situation opposite to what you really want, which is to feel good in your life again!

Instead, regaining control means establishing sovereignty over your own feelings, thoughts, and actions, so that everything you do comes from an empowered place (and not a negative or reactionary one). This not only makes your daily life easier, but also supports you in developing and supporting your self-fulfillment at Level 5 of the Separation Pyramid.

The best way to begin exercising this sort of positive, empowering control over yourself, your time, and your energy is to examine what in your life is actually within your sphere of influence, and what is not. Once you have this information, it's easy to choose where to take action, where to be patient, and where to let go.

Once you've stopped wasting time and energy on things outside your control, you can focus on setting goals and taking actions that move you, step by step, toward your vision for a happy, fulfilling future.

Just like in Step 1, where you looked at the hard facts of your separation and disconnected from a life that is no longer yours, this Step of the Positive Separation Method is all about being honest with yourself and making commitments to work toward your own empowerment and well-being. When you can clearly see where you've been putting your energy, and how those thoughts and actions are impacting your daily life, you can kick-start your personal growth and lift yourself into a better place. Sometimes, this clear seeing is painful, especially if you've recently done things that you're ashamed of—but it's necessary if you want to move forward. After all, you can't empower yourself and lie to yourself at the same time!

Like everything else about your separation, this will take some practice and adjustment, but once you start focusing on the things you *need* to focus on—the things that are actually within your ability to influence, and which help you create a happier, healthier life—your day-to-day functioning will improve and you will start seeing real progress.

CHAPTER THREE

Steer Your Own Ship

When it comes to navigating your separation and planning your happy future, nothing is more important than focusing on yourself. When you stop worrying about or trying to influence your ex, third parties, or aspects of the separation over which you have no control, you can start to make choices that actually empower and serve *you*—both now and in the long term.

ROBERT'S STORY

Although he had been contemplating divorce himself, when Robert's wife decided to leave their marriage, it took him by surprise.

"My wife and I had three small children, all under the age of twelve. I loved everything about being a father, and since I was a successful business owner, I was able to adjust my schedule so that I could be home with my family three days a week. I loved dinners around our large family dining table. But although I was thrilled with my family, my wife and I were not happy. We had tried many times to make our marriage succeed, but things weren't working."

Robert didn't have any examples of divorce in his family, or among his close friends. When the divorce was initiated, he felt lost and confused. "I never imagined the giant emotions, the stress, the way every little detail could become a huge problem. It felt like I was living in a horror movie."

Things only escalated when the legal battles started. "My ex-wife was from abroad, and the possibility of her taking our children away was a very real threat. It took two years to settle the issues around co-parenting and time sharing. I felt like I was living two separate lives: at work, I was the calm, cool, clear-headed CEO, but outside of work I was full of stress and emotion. Not knowing if I would see my children at the end of each week blew my heart to pieces. I tried to treasure every moment with them, all the while strategically planning my actions so that my ex-wife would not get upset and take them away from me.

"I was trying to control the situation, control my ex-wife's reactions, master all of my emotions, contain my enormous fear, and say all the right things to everyone, all at the same time. I was trying to make a family home out of my new house, look after my kids, and run my business. Somewhere in the midst of all of this, I stopped taking care of myself.

"I hardly took time to eat. I did not have time to exercise. I would lie awake in my bed at night for hours worrying, or pace through my house trying to calm my nerves. I felt totally unable to disconnect from my ex, because she had such a tight grip on me through the children. I felt trapped.

Things eventually came to a head for Robert. "One evening, I was doing the laundry, preparing for the kids' next visit, when my ex-wife called. She called me names, and said that if I wouldn't do certain things for her that I could not see my children this weekend. I controlled myself on the phone, but as soon as we hung up, my heart was pounding. I was in agony.

"But, no matter what, the wash still needed to be done. One of my young daughters had spilled something on her pink dress, and I decided to try a stain remover (a new thing to me). I was so agitated that I couldn't concentrate, and … I sprayed the stuff right in my eyes!

"I was immediately blinded. I was in shock, trembling. I was alone in the house, and couldn't remember where I had left my phone, so I couldn't call for help. What if I was blind forever? What if I could never see my children again? I felt helpless with fear. Finally, I just sat down on the floor and cried.

"At that moment, I stopped pretending that I could keep it all together. I felt all of the emotions of the past few months, all at once. I faced the unimaginable grief, chaos, and frustration I'd been holding at bay, and let it all wash through me.

"After a few hours, my sight began to return. I was able to calm down, and remind myself that my life was not over. I needed to make some major changes, but I still had a future. I just needed to figure out how to approach my divorce, with all its negativity, in a new way. More, I needed to figure out how to approach my new reality, and my new life as a divorcée. If I didn't learn to swim in these new waters, I was going to drown.

"But first, I needed to get help for my eyes.

"I went straight to Doctor Vries, an older family doctor who was about my father's age. Seated behind his antique writing desk in a room filled with books, drawings, and paintings, he had an aura of great wisdom about him.

"I was his last patient of the night, and we ended up talking for a long time. He told me that he had seen the mess that grown-ups created for themselves and their children when they entered a sphere of negativity and out-of-control emotions, and that I wasn't the only one who had ever gone through this.

"'Robert, you cannot control the mother of your children,' he said. 'You cannot control the judges and the lawyers. You can only control yourself, and that must be your focus. You have to disconnect from your ex-wife and all of her emotions and actions, and concentrate on the things you can influence—like your own feelings.'

"Dr. Vries went on. 'Your roots, and those of your ex-wife, were interwoven. The basis of your existence has been blown away. The first thing you need is trust—a lot of it. You need to know that the sun will rise. The birds trust this; they sing every morning, even before they see the sun. Borrow some trust from them.'

"'The next thing you need is energy. As long as you are trying to control and influence your ex-wife's decisions, you are losing energy, and losing your grip on your own life. You are the one suffering from stress, sleepless nights, and pain. You need to become the manager of your own life again, and stop letting her decisions (or anyone else's) take precedence over your own choices. You have to focus on what you can do, and what you can influence. Because you have a future to work on, for yourself and your beloved children.'

"As he said this, Dr. Vries look deep into my eyes. He was firm and strict, and I knew he was right.

"Walking away from the doctor's office that night, I looked up at a dark sky full of stars, and felt … blessed. Blessed for my good life, and my success, blessed by my children, blessed with the wisdom and hope I had just received. I no longer felt like a victim.

"I started eating three meals a day again. I started exercising again. I made the choice only to pick up the phone when I knew it was someone who would bring me good news, or lift me up. I picked up my life in a good, healthy way. I started to trust that things would work out. And things started to change.

"It took another year, but the courts finally granted me 50 percent custody of my children. They and their mother never went to live abroad, as I had feared. I was able to spend time with them, and raise them the way I wanted.

"Ten years ago, I met a lovely woman with three children of her own. We have the greatest love I could ever have imagined, and a happy family life. We both work hard at our loving relationship, and make sure that we can both be ourselves and grow within our partnership. More than anything, we are always grateful for the life we have created.

"Sometimes, when I go for a walk on the beach, I see Dr. Vries. He is much older now, and walks with a walking stick, but he always winks at me and smiles, and I remember his words from that night in October, so many years ago: 'Trust and focus on yourself, and the rest will follow.'"

***

Everything changed for Robert when he stopped focusing on his fear of what might happen, or what his ex-wife might do, and started concentrating on his own life and making it as good as possible. This shift has happened countless times for countless people in separation—but often, it takes a catastrophe (like squirting stain remover in your eyes) to trigger it.

What I will teach you in this chapter will help you make this shift *now*, so you don't have to get to rock-bottom and climb back out again. By focusing only on what you can control, starting right now, you will waste less of your sacred energy, stay in better spirits, act more positively toward yourself and others, and start building your happy life faster.

"What CAN I Control In My Separation?"

Every separation is different, of course, but there are certain things that you will be able to control, and certain things you will definitely *not* be able to influence.

The things you can control are all related to *you* and how you show up in your life: your choices around your thoughts, feelings, habits, and actions, and how you apply those choices to the situations and circumstances of your separation.

The things you cannot influence are all related to the thoughts, actions, habits, actions, and choices of other people—in particular, your ex-partner. Trying to manipulate others' feelings, behaviors, and emotions will only exhaust, confuse, and frustrate everyone involved. Your energy is best spent on your own life and goals.

Understanding where the boundaries are between yourself, your ex-partner, and any third parties, and establishing these parameters firmly, clearly, and early will help keep you on track with your vision and goals for a happy new life. This will take some exploration, but the sooner you gain this focus and establish healthy boundaries, the better.

THINGS YOU *CANNOT* INFLUENCE IN YOUR SEPARATION

Your ex-partner's attitude, behavior, and feelings. Your ex-partner is taking a different road and creating a different life. The window between your houses is now closed, and your ex will do whatever s/he thinks is best. Each of you is now going your own way. Even if you don't like the choices your ex is making, let them go. They are not your choices.

The attitude and behavior of your family, friends, and acquaintances (or of the family, friends, and acquaintances of your ex-partner). You can try to influence the above persons or pressure them to take sides but, in the long run, such a strategy often backfires. It's better to simply focus on what you have to do, and let others do what they have to do.

The reactions from your community, coworkers, or other peers. You may feel like you've been marked as a failure, someone to be pitied, someone "back on the prowl," or "the one who ran off with so-and-so." There's nothing you can do about this. People will think what they think, and say what they say. You know the truth about yourself and your motivations, so just let it go.

How the legal and practical details of the separation are settled. How your separation is settled depends upon both you and your ex-partner, and it often involves a great deal of stress. Your ex may want to do everything slowly and carefully, or get it over with as soon as possible. He or she may even try to delay things or throw a wrench in the works. All you can do is take care of whatever is needed on your part to facilitate the process. While the wheels of law turn, focus on those aspects of your life that you can do something about.

How your kids experience your ex-partner. Children are loyal to both parents, so give them as much opportunity as possible to keep on loving both of you. Remember they must be free to feel and think as they wish, so don't try to turn them against your ex-partner, or make them "love you more."

Now, let's look at what you *can* control, and should therefore focus on. From now on, these items will be primary in your thoughts and actions. You will invest your energy and time in those areas where your efforts are useful, appreciated, and have a real effect. (Don't worry: I'll give you plenty of tools for how to do all of this in this chapter, and the rest of this book!)

THINGS YOU *CAN* CONTROL
IN YOUR SEPARATION

Your own thoughts, attitude, and behavior. Every minute of every day, *you* are the one in control of your attitude and your behavior (even if it doesn't always feel that way). Only you can choose how you think, feel, and react. Do what you need to do to stay positive and focused—even if that means making hard choices about how you engage with certain people or situations.

Your own health and stress levels. Each and every day, you can practice stress reduction and cultivate a healthy and strong body. (We'll talk more about specific ways to do this later in this book, but chances are you have a few tools for this already.)

Your role in your own story. Those who play the victim never make much progress toward their goals. In fact, they are their own worst enemies, because they don't feel empowered to work toward a new and happy future. Stepping away from the victim role isn't always easy, especially if the decision to separate was not yours, but you *always* have a choice. Even if you feel depressed and powerless sometimes, you can keep taking steps toward creating your vision and goals for a happier future.

Your own path to a new and positive future. Almost all your basic feelings of safety and security have been compromised, and you probably feel pain, anger, fear, and or chaos. So it's not all that surprising if you feel like your situation is hopeless. But even in such a situation (or rather, *especially* in such a situation), it's important to focus on your personal vision of a new and positive future. That kind of focus will help you get through your separation in the best possible shape. "I will be happy again" is your motto, guiding you in the right direction and encouraging you to take action. (If you haven't done the Visualize Your Future exercises in Chapter Two yet, go back to do them now.)

Your own physical and mental boundaries. Clearly set your own boundaries, and think about how you challenge or respect the boundaries of your ex-partner and of others. This is of crucial importance. If you find this aspect difficult, professional help can give you a push in the right direction.

Your quality of life. Aim only for the best possible outcomes for yourself (and your children, if you have them). Your main task is to fight for your own happiness—and a part of that fight is to create a comfort zone around your daily life and tasks. The best way to do this is to get rid of negative patterns and habits; I promise, this will free you up immeasurably!

The financial aspects of the separation. Make a new financial plan for yourself, including your daily and annual expenses and income, your debt (including mortgage, auto, and credit card debt), insurance policies, and any relevant benefits or subsidies. Make sure your subscriptions, bank cards, etc. are in your own name, and cancel any subscriptions or services that are unnecessary or extraneous. Finally, have your ex-partner's mail delivered to his or her new address.

Since I'm not a financial planner, I can't offer specific advice about how to do all of this, but I can make a suggestion. First, get out your notebook and write down every one of your weekly, monthly, and quarterly expenditures, including debt repayments. In another column, write out all of your sources of income. Then, consult with a professional or a knowledgeable friend about how you can make your new budget work in the least stressful way possible.

Right now is the perfect time to face any financial issues you might have, and make a clean start. Asking for help now to sort things out will save you from bigger problems down the road.

Your own actions aimed at settling the separation as proactively and carefully as possible. The vision for your happier life, which you created and explored in Chapter Two, will give you a framework to work with. Make sure that your choices are not creating more chaos, but instead moving you forward with intention and integrity.

The emotional aspects of your separation. Try to recognize and identify your emotions as quickly as possible. See them for what they are, accept them, learn how to deal with them, and let them go when necessary. Create a plan for dealing with each of the four basic emotions that are triggered during a separation: anger, grief, fear, and sadness. (We will spend more time on emotions in Chapter Six.)

How and with whom you spend your time. Surround yourself with positive and creative energy. Put yourself in circumstances of your liking, and spend time with people who you trust, who allow you to relax, and who give you positive energy.

Your recuperation time. Take time to rest and relax, deeply and completely. Rest is crucial for allowing your body to recover and deal with everything you are going through. Take time out each day to balance yourself and recharge your batteries.

Your living quarters and atmosphere at home. Make sure your home is a place you enjoy being—a place where you can rest and relax, even if you're not sure you will continue to live there. A tidy and attractive home environment has a positive impact on your mental and emotional state, and provides a good starting point for your new life—especially in these early stages of your separation.

The (physical) presence of your ex-partner in your home. Clear agreements with your ex-partner about his or her physical presence in your home, even if the house belongs to you both (or is in your ex's name), can prevent serious problems and stress. If you must share space, it's okay to set clear boundaries: for example, the hallway, kitchen, and living room are common ground, but the office and bedrooms are not.

The place where you agree to meet your ex-partner or others involved. Make sure potentially difficult or emotional discussions, arguments, etc. take place outside your home at a neutral location so that it doesn't impact your home atmosphere. In addition, emotions are much less likely to escalate and get blown out of proportion in a public space.

How you work, alone or together, with third-party professionals. If you choose to work with third-party professionals, decide for yourself if they are dealing with you and the separation process as *you* would wish. Be honest, and don't pull any punches. Are they actually helping you make progress on the positive path you've chosen, or are they just doing the bare minimum to earn their salary? Are you there because it's helpful for you, or simply because your ex-partner wants it?

How you show up for, and influence, your children. You have a great deal of influence on the happiness of your children and how they deal with the separation. Create a positive living environment for them, and make sure they can regularly spend time with their other parent, regardless of any negative emotions you may have. (Except, of course, where spending time with the other parent would be physically dangerous for them.) Reflect on how you can support them by showing up as your best self.

It was a happy surprise for me when I started focusing on the things I could control in my separation. Suddenly, I had a much longer list of things I could work with, and I was only spending my energy on positive things. This made my life during and after my divorce far easier than I expected, and gave me extra strength to cope when challenges did come up.

You, too, will notice that once you decide how you will engage with the things you *can* control, you will be able to make a plan to streamline your life and your separation and stay centered in your vision for your new life.

Undoing Blame

Before you look at and work with your personal story through the Empowered Actions at the end of this chapter, I have one more insight to share, and it's around blame.

Blame is a common emotional pitfall for anyone in the separation process, but if you don't acknowledge it from the start, it can easily lead to feelings of disempowerment and to you trying to influence your ex-partner.

CHRIS'S STORY

Chris Attwood, coauthor of the *New York Times* best-selling book *The Passion Test* and an expert in the field of human consciousness, discovered how blame shapes our experiences when he stepped out of his marriage to his ex-partner Janet Bray Attwood (whose story appears in Chapter Five). His openhearted sharing on the following pages proves that when you try to influence a person or situation, or make it line up with how you think it should be, you will only cause yourself to suffer.

"When we are going through a separation (or any other challenging time)," Chris shares, "we tend to place blame in three different areas: our partner, ourselves, or the situation. What I learned the hard way is that whenever I blame anything, I am lost in a story or a system of belief that will make me unhappy and leave me feeling less connected to myself.

"I teach people about finding their passions and getting their lives back on track. In divorce, the ability to do this is fundamentally related to our beliefs. No one outside of ourselves can make us suffer—but when we *believe* that they can, our suffering increases.

"I met Janet in a small, rural area in Fairfield, Iowa. She was a bright, beaming, effervescent personality, and very popular. I was skinny, with big, thick glasses—but of course wasn't aware of my nerdiness at the time. Janet said when she met me that I *definitely* wasn't her type.

"At first, it was just friendship, but one thing eventually led to another, and we fell into a trap of 'natural progression.' At one point, Janet—who is a very intuitive woman—said to me, 'Chris, I really love you, but I never see us being more than friends.'

"If we had both listened to our instincts, we would never have been married. But we truly did love one another, and so we ignored the signs.

"We were both deep into our spiritual journeys at that point, and although we had many moments of intimacy, we believed that we shouldn't have sex until we were married. We had two weddings: a small, spiritual Vedic ceremony, and a more traditional public ceremony with three hundred people, nine flower girls, and the works. Janet throws a great party! We spent our whole wedding night sorting through the presents and making lists of who gave us what.

"The honeymoon was in Kauai. We stayed in a gorgeous two-bedroom home next to the beach. It was a perfect, romantic setting. But when we got to the bedroom … Well, without going into any details, it was a freakin' disaster.

"Both of us were in shock. What were we going to do? This didn't work at all!

"Lots of drama ensued. I ran on the beach as hard as I could; it was the only way I knew how to deal with it. I mean, both of us had been married before; we should be able to make this work! Janet called every healer she knew, but nothing seemed to help.

"We laugh about our 'honeymoon from hell' now—but at the time, it was excruciating. After three days, we decided to give up on the making love thing and just have a good time—but when it was over, we still had to go home and make our relationship work.

"All my life, I had followed my passions and the things that lit me up. That was one of the reasons I learned meditation. But now, newly married, I fell into this concept that I had to support my wife. Instead of getting a job I loved and was passionate about, I decided to get a 'good' job with a good salary that would pay the bills and give me opportunities for advancement. This was due to a belief on my side that in order to be a 'good' husband I had to meet a certain set of criteria.

"I went through four different jobs, one after the other. All paid well. None fired my passion or made me feel happy.

"For her part, Janet was also struggling with a fundamental belief about marriage: that she needed to take care of her husband. She cooked meals, made sure the house looked beautiful, made sure that we were comfortable. When Janet would ask to buy something, I always said yes, not wanting to disappoint her. We started to fall deeper and deeper into debt. As a result, I worked harder and spent less time at home. This, on top of our nonexistent sex life, did not make for a great marriage. There were fights, angry nights, and lots of dramatic moments.

"One day, I woke up at 3:00 a.m. My body was shaking and would not stop. Janet guided me through a deep breathing practice for an hour and a half, until finally my body and mind settled down. It was a terrifying experience.

"How could someone who had meditated for so long still succumb to this kind of stress and anxiety? Well, even when you do a lot of meditation and inner work, unless you are conscious of the beliefs you hold, you can still hold a lot of stress, fear, and anxiety. I wasn't allowing myself to recognize that my beliefs about who I needed to be as a husband, rather than Janet or our relationship, were the real cause of my issues. I just wasn't there yet.

"We took courses together. We tried different therapies, studied Tantra, read books ... you name it. Once or twice a year, we tried making love again, just to see if it worked; it didn't. All that time, I believed that I needed to stay committed to our relationship for my own growth. But when Janet came to me and said, 'I've met someone else, right now he's just a friend, but I'm really drawn to him. I want to get to know him better, and I think we should separate,' I was relieved. She brought it forth with so much integrity. She would never run around with another man in secret, but she wasn't ready to keep sacrificing for a relationship that had obviously run its course.

"When I was married to Janet, I was a burdened man, with the weight of the world on my shoulders. I was miserable, not because of my marriage, but because I was so attached to my belief system. I kept telling myself that I needed to learn and grow from this—but what I really needed was to break through my own stubbornness. I had built a wall around myself that kept me from seeing what was really going on.

"Because I had a belief about how Janet and I "should" be in a romantic relationship, I had to go through five years of hell. I could have blamed Janet, or myself, or the cultural ideals that had created the beliefs that caused us so much suffering—but instead of rehashing and trying to change the past, I chose to focus on what I could control, which of course was my own feelings and my next steps.

"I delved into my tools for investigating beliefs, most notably The Work of Byron Katie. I realized where my beliefs were causing me to place blame, and where I was holding on to concepts which were not true for me, and how doing this was causing me to suffer. Once I saw how this was happening, I was able to turn things around in near-miraculous ways.

"Since we separated, Janet and I have done what many people consider impossible. We have become closer as friends than we were as partners. I've been remarried for over a decade now, and my wife and I have three beautiful children. My wife asked Janet to be their godmother, and she graciously accepted.

"Common beliefs would have kept Janet and me thinking that we were stuck: that our problems were each other's fault, and that we were in an untenable situation. We would have kept on fighting, blaming one another, and living in a hell of our own making. Instead, we had to look deeper, and go beyond blame, shame, belief, and convention to find the paths that would lead us to our passions and our destinies. We had to do this by ourselves, for ourselves, because if we didn't do it, it wouldn't get done."

***

Chris's story proves that when you are trying to influence a person or situation, or make it line up with how you think it *should* be, you will only cause yourself to suffer. Instead, look at what you can control—your own beliefs, emotions, actions, and reactions—and be honest with yourself about where you are, what you want, and what kind of future you want to create. It won't always be easy to do this, but it absolutely will be empowering!

Empowered Actions

▶ Your Sphere of Influence

Now, or during your next planned Power Hour (see page 51 for a refresher) make a list of all of the pieces of your separation, your personal needs, your major tasks, and all of the things in your life and separation that you *can* control and influence (Use the sixteen points in the previous section for guidance).

Commit to putting energy and effort only into those areas where you can empower yourself. Whenever a tough situation arises, ask yourself, "What can I actually control here?" Then, reference your lists and choose the thoughts, emotions, and actions which are most closely aligned with the life you want to live and create.

If you find that committing to this work is hard right now, don't worry. All it takes to make this shift is a bit of good, old-fashioned dedication and practice! While you acclimate to this new way of thinking, keep reading. As you incorporate all of this new information, the big picture of your happy future will become more clear, and it will get easier for you to see the reasons for letting go of things you can't influence.

▶ Tracking Your Thoughts and Actions

Write down the items you cannot influence in a notebook or journal.

1. Your ex-partner's attitude, behavior, and feelings.
2. The attitude and behavior of your family, friends, and acquaintances (or of the family, friends, and acquaintances of your ex-partner).
3. The reactions from your community, coworkers, or other peers.
4. How the legal and practical details of the separation are settled.
5. How your kids (if you have them) experience your ex-partner.

Then, under each item, create a list of all the specific aspects of this item that you cannot influence. For example, under "Ex-partner's attitude, behavior, and feelings," you might write, "How angry s/he gets about little things," or "Who s/he is dating."

Then, ask yourself, "Am I trying to influence any of these things right now? If so, why?" Journal about your feelings and what comes up for you.

Over the course of the next week, notice when you are trying to influence your ex-partner, other people, or particular situations in any of the above areas. Every time you think or take action to violate one of these boundaries, write it down in your calendar or make a note in your phone. Then, bring the focus back to yourself and redirect your energy toward the things you *can* control—like your own feelings, thoughts, and behaviors.

What Comes Next?

Now that you've identified all of the areas of your separation that you can positively control and influence, it's time to apply that understanding to your vision for your new, happy future. In the next chapter, we'll discover the Five Commitments you make to yourself when you decide to step into your new future, set goals to help you make your vision statement a reality, and devise a plan to achieve each of those goals through positive action, self-care, and powerfully self-affirming choices.

CHAPTER FOUR

Your Positive Commitments and Goals

The goals and commitments you make to yourself during your separation will carry you through whatever comes your way. Nikki, a recognized psychotherapist, sexual/marital therapist, and coach, discovered this for herself during her separation several years ago. Her personal commitments and goals gave her direction, inspiration, and resolve as she walked the road to her own vision for a happy life.

NIKKI'S STORY

Nikki met and married her second husband, Steen, when she was thirty and he was thirty-seven. "I had just moved back to my birthplace of Hong Kong after eight years of living in the U.S., and was ready for a new phase in my life. Steen and I were neighbors, living under the same roof. I was a blond underwater diving photographer who was always ready for adventure, and he was a tall, athletic Danish American with a successful business. He would come up to the rooftop gym to work out while I was catching some sun. It was like we were thrown together."

Not long after the relationship began, Nikki became pregnant with their daughter, Cleo. "We moved into a glorious family home in The New Territories, away from the hectic downtown area of Hong Kong. We had a beautiful garden with lush flowers and a swimming pool, and plenty of home help. It was an idyllic life in a gorgeous environment—as long as I was on my own with my daughter.

"Steen and I tried to make it work from the beginning, but we also felt the whole time that it wasn't working. Steen was a strong man in every respect: a successful entrepreneur used to getting his own way. He was a man who talked *at* you rather than to you. I, on the other hand, was a strong, independent, passionate woman who had my own ideas about life and what I wanted. I tried very hard to 'get it right' and be a good wife, but we clearly did not meet each other's needs. We could not connect on the same level, and had a lot of awful fights followed by amorous makeups. It was tiring, and when he was home I felt like I was in prison. Several sessions of marriage counseling unfortunately did nothing to help us.

"I moved out for a while with Cleo, but ended up coming back after a few months. My self-esteem was at an all-time low. I felt like I had totally lost myself.

"Then, one morning, everything changed.

"I was sitting in my favorite chair in the garden, reading a book called *Families and How to Survive Them* by Dr. Robin Skynner and John Cleese. The birds were singing their hearts out, and one of my cats was stroking my leg with its tail. My husband and I had had a terrible fight the night before, and I was still shaken. 'Do I really want Cleo to grow up with this?' I asked myself. "Do I really want her to witness this atmosphere where neither parent will allow the other to flourish, and where we cannot communicate in a meaningful way?"

"In an instant, I knew the answer. 'Absolutely not!'

"I realized that I had never been valued in my family of origin, and that I had been putting myself in exactly the same situation in my marriage. If I wanted my daughter to learn to love and value herself, I had to move out for good and give myself and Cleo the kind of love that my parents had never given me—the love I had never allowed myself to receive.

"I kind of looked at myself from above, as if I was floating over my body. I was no victim. I was *me*. A young mother who wanted to love and live again—

who did not count on others to organize her life, but trusted in her own soul, source, and possibilities.

"I sorted myself out in a split second. My life stood still as I planted the seed of self-love in my heart. I was the only one who was responsible for my happiness and joy, and even though I had a lot to learn, I had a good heart and was worth loving!

"In that powerful, sacred moment, I let go of any hope I had left for me and Steen, and my comfort with our current home and all the trappings of our financial and social situation. Our family of three evaporated, and became two families of two.

"From that day on, I was a different person. I busied myself with being the best mother I could be, and started thinking about what I really wanted from my life, home, and career."

Nikki had a diverse career history—underwater model and photographer, time share salesperson in Mexico, real estate agent in Colorado, diamond broker in San Francisco—but now, she felt insecure, and far less fearless than she had been in her old life. Plus, she had little Cleo to consider.

"I took responsibility for me, my life, and my daughter, but for sure I had a lot of fear under my skin. I was playing it like I was a big girl, but inside I was a trembling child. However, I couldn't let that stop me—especially since I had a real child on my hands! I had a deep desire to build something good and healthy for our future, and to create a home for us. I also wanted to learn how to create and sustain a beautiful, loving romantic relationship, and teach others to do the same. I wanted to learn the tools of Love and of Life.

"I made some strong, serious commitments to myself. The first was that I wanted Cleo to have a good relationship with her father. My feelings about him, and my frustration with his choices, couldn't be allowed to affect that. Second, I decided that I was going to be proactive instead of reactive in every part of my life, change the beliefs and habits that weren't helping me, and live with the greatest possible integrity. Third, I committed to becoming me again, and to trusting myself. I was the only one I needed, and I was not about to let insecurity overrule me. I never again wanted to hear—or feel—that I wasn't good enough. I was no one's dependent, and I wasn't going to take any crap anymore—not from myself, and definitely not from a partner!

"Within a month I was taking courses from the most renowned therapists and building my new vision for myself. I also joined a Master's program in psychotherapy. There were many ups and downs during that year, but I dipped deep into my inner reservoir of resilience, threw myself into my learning, and concentrated on growing my inner world. I wanted to blossom again, to be successful and proud for myself and for Cleo.

"Soon, there was a glow in my eyes again. I was alive, vital, maybe more than I had ever been in my life. I loved being me, and wanted to become even *more* of me.

"After graduation, I started my own practice, and soon became a successful and highly-sought-after psychotherapist and marital therapist. I felt like I was a completely opposite person to the woman I'd been before my divorce. Although I was helping couples (and feisty single ladies) with their relationships, I took this time to focus on me. My relationship with myself, my daughter, and my friends were the most important things, and they sustained me for several years.

Eventually, Nikki decided that she was ready to try to create another relationship—one that would reflect the strong, self-loving woman she had become. She built a beautiful home and asked a Feng Shui master to help her decorate it. "I told her that I had just about everything—a close relationship with my daughter, good friends, money, success, good health, and now a great home—but it was time to find my soul mate. She told me what to do, and said that once the rains had come, the river that flowed past my house would bring him to me. I spent the next few months visualizing an honest, sexy, fun, quirky guy who would not only capture my heart, but my whole soul and being."

The rains came and went, but there was no soul mate. Then, the following year, Nikki met Mike. "His father's house was just up the river from mine. It was serendipitous. In the weeks he was staying in Hong Kong, I met him three times, once in the supermarket down the street from my home. He was just getting divorced himself, and I was casually dating someone, so we swapped contact details as friends."

A year later, though, the timing was perfect. The dust in Mike's divorce had settled, and Nikki had broken up with the guy she had been dating. "He came back to Hong Kong on business, and within ten days I knew he was my soul companion. We were 'cosmic twins,' as Mike likes to put it!"

Now, with Cleo grown and studying in Colorado, Nikki and Mike enjoy a beautiful life in the Cotswolds, England. "We are all blossoming," she says.

***

Nikki focused on loving and growing herself and making strong commitments first. Only then, as the best version of herself, was she able and ready to attract Mike into her life. Her commitments to herself carried her through the tough times after her divorce, and gave her practical tools to work with as she worked to rediscover her own strength, integrity, and potential. She became someone amazing to fall in love with.

Your Five Commitments

When you are feeling insecure and on unsteady ground, or when you feel like the structure you once relied on has disintegrated, the best thing you can do is reaffirm your intention to uplift yourself and create the amazing life you want.

Your positive separation depends primarily on your own commitment to it. Like a runner tackling a marathon, your success requires ongoing training, patience, and careful management of your energy. Just like Nikki in our story, you need to know your commitments to yourself, and use those commitments to set strong boundaries. More, you need to give yourself time to adjust to your new life and way of being, and be patient with yourself as you blossom in your own time.

As we learned in Chapter Three, you cannot influence your ex's experience of the separation, or coerce commitments or behaviors out of others; you can only control yourself. The Five Commitments you will make to yourself in this section will lay an even stronger foundation for your vision for your future, help you set goals, assist you in your daily functioning, and keep you on track and in a positive mindset.

I promise: You can do this, and you will flourish!

Let's get started.

Today, right now, make the following Five Commitments to yourself and your future:

1. **"I take full and complete responsibility for myself and my actions!"**
2. **"I refuse to adopt a victim state of mind!"**
3. **"I trust in my great reservoir of inner strength and resilience!"**
4. **"I work carefully and patiently on the separation process and on myself!"**
5. **"Each day, I focus my actions on what I can do, and need to do, for myself!"**

During the coming weeks and months, these commitments will help you steer your emotions, thoughts, decisions, and actions in the right direction every single day. If you stick to them and refer to them on a daily basis, the short-term benefits will soon become evident: greater self-confidence, less stress and negativity, a clearer overview of your situation, and better planning.

Now, let's talk about each commitment in greater detail:

Commitment #1: "I take full and complete responsibility for myself and my actions!"

You are 100 percent responsible for your life, your choices, and your actions. Neither I, nor anyone else, can make this easier for you; it's all up to you. The good thing is that, by shouldering responsibility, you are no longer stuck in the problem, but have become part of the solution! (And, of course, that is just where you want to be!)

Right now, you may feel, deep in your heart, that this separation is your ex-partner's fault. In that case, you are falling into a victim mentality, and it is even more important for you to take back responsibility for your own life. (If you need support with this, seek help from a professional.)

Your happiness, joy, and success do not depend on anyone else, including your ex-partner, mediators, lawyers, parents, family, friends, or psychologists. From this moment on, give yourself permission to act independently, and to think, feel, and do what is best for you, every day.

Empowered Action: Take responsibility for your life and your separation

Say aloud right now, "This is my life, and my separation. I am the one responsible for settling my separation in a positive way and getting my life back on track again." Repeat this often over the next several days and weeks, until the words and their meaning resonate in your mind and body. (You might even write this line on a Post-It and stick it somewhere where you will see it many times every day.)

Commitment #2: "I refuse to adopt a victim state of mind!"

If you find yourself saying things like, "Why is this happening to me?" "I didn't do anything wrong!" "It's not my fault that the relationship is over," or "I have no power over anything right now!" you are slipping into a victim state of mind.

Even if you were the one who initiated the separation, you can still fall into this trap—especially if your ex has started behaving in ways you don't like, or has found a new partner sooner than you're comfortable with.

Victim mindset is one of the biggest obstacles to a positive separation. Feeling sorry for yourself can be incredibly addictive, and may provide emotional gratification in the moment, but it will get you nowhere in the long run. It will drain your energy, lead to manipulative behavior, and block you from thinking and acting in a positive and proactive way.

There are people out there who are "eternal victims." You probably know one or two of them yourself: people who have been separated for ten years, or twenty, and are still complaining about their ex-partners, their missed opportunities, and how hard their separation made their lives. Ask yourself, "Is that the kind of person I want to become? Am I willing to still be a victim to my ex's behavior one year from now? Five years from now?" If the answer is no, you need to let go of your victim mindset and take responsibility for yourself right now, today. The longer you wallow in your victimhood, the harder it will be to break free.

Empowered Action: Thoughts and feelings checklist

Fill out the following checklist to see if you have slipped into the victim mindset trap. Do any of the following feel true to you right now?

- ☐ Bad luck seems to follow me.
- ☐ Everyone seems to be working against me and my happiness.
- ☐ I frequently feel disappointed, desperate, and worthless.
- ☐ I don't want to make any definitive agreements with my ex-partner.
- ☐ I complain often to others about my separation and situation.
- ☐ I have a great many negative thoughts (ten or more each day).
- ☐ I blame my ex-partner for my situation.
- ☐ I blame other people (like my parents, siblings, or friends) for my situation.
- ☐ I share my grief with others as often as I can because I want their recognition or attention.
- ☐ There are so many things that I am simply unable to do.

If you checked any of the above boxes, spend some time considering how you can take back your power and responsibility, and see your situation differently. If you are struggling with this, reread Chris Attwood's story in Chapter Three and consider how your old, outdated beliefs may be affecting your perspective. Professional help may also be beneficial.

Commitment #3: "I trust in my great reservoir of inner strength and resilience!"

This is the pinnacle (Level 5) of the Separation Pyramid—the core of self-fulfillment. This part of you cannot be touched or damaged by anyone but you. Likewise, you are the only one who can make use of it. Therefore, this commitment is really about getting into the right mindset, focusing on your inner strength, and telling yourself that you will make a go of it, no matter what it takes. Even if you feel completely worthless in this moment, you do not need to stay in that feeling forever! By staying focused on your inner self and taking small, positive actions every day, you can unlock the energy and creativity you need to stay positive and empowered, even in very difficult situations. It also helps you block out negative thoughts that get you nowhere.

Empowered Action: Positive affirmations

While focusing on the feeling of your inner strength, say at least one of these affirmations to yourself (out loud or under your breath) several times per day:

- "I have a great deal of inner strength and resilience."
- "I'll be okay even if it takes a year to get my life back on track again."
- "I'll be okay even if I have less money in the near future."
- "I'll be okay even if I have to relocate."
- "I'll be okay even if some people disapprove of me."
- "I'll be okay even if my ex has a new partner."
- "I'll be okay even if my children have not yet adjusted to the new situation."
- "I will stay the course."
- "I'm a survivor, and no one can take that away from me."
- "I can get through my separation in a balanced and positive manner."
- "I can cope with any disappointment that comes my way."
- "I can ... (complete this sentence with an affirmation of your own)."

When the going gets rough, choose an appropriate affirmation and repeat it to yourself out loud or under your breath ten times, followed by two minutes of deep breathing. Visualize the well of your heart being filled with loving strength. Then, take a few minutes to relax.

You can also write your favorite affirmations on Post-It notes and place them around your house (on the refrigerator, in the bathroom, over your computer, in your car, etc.). Every time you notice one of your notes, say the affirmation out loud or under your breath. (Bonus points if you smile while you do it!)

Commitment #4: "I work carefully and patiently on the separation process and on myself!"

You need to have the right focus and energy to create a positive separation. By making this commitment to yourself, you are promising to work one step at a time toward creating your vision for a happy future, whatever it takes. You deserve your own careful attention and focus so you can conserve your energy and settle things as quickly and thoroughly as possible.

We often don't realize the full impact of our separations, and the energy and care they require, until years after the fact. That delayed realization can make it easier to let things slide right now, when everything feels overwhelming. But as we all know, ignoring something doesn't make it go away. If you get a splinter in your toe and ignore it, or remove only part of it because it hurts too much to dig out the whole thing, chances are it will become infected and cause even bigger issues down the line. The same thing goes when you ignore the work you need to do on yourself and your separation. Of course, your separation is bigger than a splinter, but if you only take half-measures, the result will be the same. In order to cope effectively with a life-changing event such as a separation, you need to invest all your energy and commitment. The things you run away from now will still be there later; you can't wish them away. The same applies to anything to which you do not give your full attention. Half-measures are not enough! The longer you put things off, the more heartbreak and unnecessary work you will have to do later—and potentially at a time when you feel even less prepared for it than you do right now.

This is why it's so vital to work, step by step, on embracing yourself through the Positive Separation Method and all of the tools in this book. You are your own precious gem, your own most valuable asset and resource. You are also the only one who can help you shine brightly in your own life. No one else can create the outcome of your separation for you. No one else can create your happy future for you. This is why I call it "The Art of Positive Separation": it is something *you* create.

Empowered Action: Embrace yourself and your life right now

Say out loud, "I work carefully and patiently on the separation process, and on myself. I am worth the time I am dedicating to my own growth and self-improvement. By taking this time now, I will have less trouble later. I will hold my own hand, and will be brave and caring for myself and those I love."

Then, in your notebook, jot down three things that you know you should do for yourself or your separation process, but that you don't feel like doing. What small action steps can you take today? Write those down, too, even if they're as simple as "Make one phone call," or "Walk outside for ten minutes." After you put this book down, work on them right away.

Commitment #5: "Each day, I focus my actions on what I can do, and need to do, for myself!"

If you want to leave the chaos behind you, resolve the difficulties of your separation, and take good and loving care of yourself, you need to focus and target your activities each day. In particular, you should focus on those areas where you have direct control (and stop trying to influence anything involving your ex-partner.) By focusing every day on the things you can control, taking small action steps that will move you toward the goals you will set later in this chapter, and taking the time to take care of yourself, you will not only regain a sense of perspective and control, but also feel an immediate sense of accomplishment. This helps to put you into a positive mindset and is very motivational. Matters which first seemed very difficult will suddenly seem easier. You will no longer feel dependent on your ex or your old life to provide structure for your current life and your happy future. An extra benefit here is that, as the people around you sense your positive energy, they will be more willing and able to provide you with positive support.

When I was in the middle of my own separation, I had many low days when I didn't feel like doing anything at all—least of all anything that felt like taking care of myself. But, the more time I spent avoiding the actions I knew I needed to take, the more stressed and anxious I felt. I would say to myself, "Eveline, you need to do *something* to move forward, right now." Inevitably, when I took a tiny action step to move myself forward—like making a single call, cleaning out a single drawer, or running a single errand—I immediately felt empowered and energized. (Hint: If you need inspiration around your tiny action steps, check out the Star Actions at the back of this book on page 253.)

In Chapter Three, we identified the things you can control about your separation (your own feelings, actions, reactions, and choices) and what you cannot influence (such as your ex-partner's behavior). The action steps you choose for each day should fall into that first category of things you can control. Once you start operating firmly inside those boundaries, you will be able to see your next steps more clearly, and watch your goals moving closer each and every day!

Empowered Action: Three (action) steps a day
keep the separation blues away

Right now, and each morning when you wake up from now on, make a short list of three positive action steps you can take in the next twenty-four hours to move yourself forward in your life and separation, take care of yourself, and just feel good! Again, you can use the Star Actions at the back of this book for inspiration!

Build Confidence in Yourself and the Separation Process

The Five Commitments you make to yourself are your best guarantee that, whatever the circumstances, you will deal with your separation in the healthiest possible way for *you* (and, by extension, any children involved), and that you will have the tools at hand to manage each day in a positive and progressive way.

But, as with any process, there will be setbacks—and it's during these times that it is most important to remain confident in your commitments and maintain an open, positive attitude. Remember, in a separation, you can never have it all your own way; you will always experience a certain amount of loss. But even if others criticize you or don't agree with your decisions, don't waste your energy getting down on yourself or playing the victim. Trust yourself and these Five Commitments you have made. Breathe them in every day. Get them into your system. If your self-confidence is really taking a beating, call in a third-party professional to help you work through it.

Empowered Action

▶ Incorporate the Five Commitments Into Your Daily Life

It will sometimes feel like an enormous challenge to have to respect and work with your Five Commitments each and every day, plus deal with everything else that's happening. There will be times when you simply want to throw in the towel. Stay committed! It's certainly no disaster if you skip a day—but if you do, get back into the rhythm as soon as possible. Your Five Commitments are your beacons in the dark, the lifelines you can hold on to no matter what happens. Being worthy of your own trust is truly the best way to welcome your new future with open arms.

Morning ritual

Repeat your Five Commitments to yourself each morning as you stand in the shower or do your morning routine. Think about the best way to comply with your commitments over the course of the day. Do you expect to face a difficult moment during the day? Think about how you intend to deal with it. In the evening, look back to see if you succeeded. If you did, be proud of yourself. And if you didn't, expect that the next day will be full of new opportunities!

Formulate Practical Goals

Once you have made your Five Commitments to yourself, take some time to let them sink in. Let them become part of your new life, and the new you.

Once you feel like you're strong in your commitments, your next step will be to formulate specific, practical goals that support you in honoring those commitments, and that move you toward your vision of your new, happy life.

Studies have shown that people who don't know where to begin don't begin anywhere. They remain in a limbo state, always looking for that crucial starting point, but never establishing a concrete destination or building momentum. That's why it's so important to focus on specific and concrete goals during this period of your life. Like your Point of Disconnection and your vision of your new future, your goals will motivate and empower you, and will soon become an integral part of your thoughts and actions, twenty-four hours a day, seven days a week.

When you set positive goals for yourself, you are saying to yourself, "My new life starts here, and these are the steps that will lead me toward it." These goals give you a sense of purpose and direction—a trajectory to follow. By consciously formulating these positive goals and associating them with a specific time frame and concrete activities, you make it clear to yourself that you're starting a new chapter of your life. In that new chapter, you will invite new ideas, skills, decisions, and encounters to reinforce and solidify your vision for your future.

Without goals (and the actions you take to fulfill them) to support it, your vision is no more than a daydream. You will function better and take more positive action if you have a target to aim at.

In this section, we are going to create several goals which will support your vision for your future. (Hint: Your Five Commitments will help you reach those goals!) In my Method, all goals must be associated with a specific time frame and concrete activities. You want your goals to feel attainable and actionable—like plans, not wishes.

First, we will create a Focus Goal for the coming year to give you inner direction and motivation. Then, we will define your Personal Goals, which are smaller steps you will take to focus your energy more effectively and help you feel uplifted. By the time we are done, you should see your way clear to the next phase of your personal journey.

But before any of that can happen, you need to let go of your old goals.

RELEASE YOUR OLD GOALS

You began this work when you consciously disconnected from your old life in Step 1 and started on your new path to a happy future. Now, go deeper. Write down all of your old, outdated goals and dreams on a piece of paper, and consciously let go of them with an appropriate ritual. (For example, let them literally go up in smoke.) This will give you a sense of closure with regard to your former life, and allow you to start fresh with your new goals.

You may or may not have been conscious of your old Focus Goal, but it was probably something like "I want to create a happy life and relationship with (ex-partner's name)." This goal is no longer valid or attainable. Your ex-partner and the life you created are no longer the focus of your goals and dreams. The window between your two houses is closed.

Your old Personal Goals are likewise outdated, especially if your Personal Goals were things like, "I will keep my relationship together no matter what," "I will keep my emotions to myself," or "I will be ready to help whenever s/he needs me." Again, these goals might not have been conscious, but they were still agreements that you made with yourself, and they need to be cleared out before you can start fresh.

On the other hand, you may have some Personal Goals which are not related to your ex-partner, and which fully support your new vision for your life. These might include things like, "I will earn the degree I've always wanted," or, "I will write a book this year." Other goals can be modified to align with your new life and vision. For example, "We will go on vacation to our usual beach destination this year" could turn into, "I will go on vacation to a fabulous new beach destination this year."

Getting rid of your old Personal Goals and replacing them with new ones prevents you from encountering any confusion about what actions to take, and when.

YOUR FOCUS GOAL

Now that you've disconnected from your old life and have started fresh, it's time to identify and set your Focus Goal.

Your Focus Goal for this year should be something like:

*"I will get through my separation this year as a positive
and balanced individual."*

This is an excellent target for all your arrows. It is the Focus Goal I used in my own separation, and the one I encourage my clients to use. The Positive Separation Method we are exploring together in this book is also fully focused on this goal.

Write your version of your Focus Goal in your daily planner on your Disconnection Date. Commit to your goal starting right now. Mark your calendar for one year from your Disconnection Date. By this date, you will have realized your Focus Goal. The core process of your separation will be over (even if the legal processes are not yet wrapped up), and you will be ready to continue toward your new, happy future.

Yes, it really is that simple. You are now that arrow, pointed at a target. You are in flight toward your goal. Nothing can stop you unless you let it.

YOUR PERSONAL GOALS

Next, we'll define your Personal Goals, which will help you focus your energy, thoughts, and actions in the coming period. These Personal Goals will serve as a source of energy and motivation for you to take action and realize your vision of your new happy future. They should be in line with your Focus Goal, and help you take baby steps toward that bigger target.

You can choose from the list of Personal Goals defined below, or create your own. Either way, your goals should feel light, happy, purposeful, and most of all, *possible* to you. Some Personal Goals can be realized within a day or a week, while others will take longer. Regardless of time frame, however, the idea of fulfilling each of your goals should energize you.

Tips for Formulating and Realizing Your Personal Goals

- Start each goal with "I will ..." and not "I want to." Remember, these goals are promises you are making to yourself.
- Define several goals that will make your (daily) life more enjoyable.
- Formulate and work out your goals in more detail whenever possible. (Hint: This is a good way to use your Power Hour!) They will then be

more in tune with your personal wishes, dreams, and vision of your future.

- The more specific and concrete your goals are, the easier it is to also define actions and activities that will help you realize them.

- Don't work on too many goals at the same time. For example, start by working on your Focus Goal together with five short-term Personal Goals and two or three longer-term Personal Goals.

- Don't change your goals too quickly, since that only confuses matters. If, after some time, a goal turns out not to be feasible and is taking up too much of your time and energy, simply put it aside; you can always go back to it later. You can also formulate a new goal or modify the old one to make it more realistic.

- If, after a while, you have realized some of your Personal Goals, congratulate yourself! Then, set new goals to direct your energy and keep yourself in motion along your new path.

Suggestions for Personal Goals

Practical short-term goals (daily/weekly/monthly)

- This week, I will change my telephone number.
- This week, I will clean up my contact list. (Phone, e-mail, Facebook, and Twitter.)
- Within three weeks, I will change the locks on my house and give a reserve copy of the key to a few good friends.
- Tomorrow evening, I will cook my favorite meal instead of eating takeout.
- Within two months, I will have my upstairs floor repainted.
- Within two weeks, I will have all the paperwork related to my separation neatly organized and filed away.
- Within two weeks, I will have ten large garbage bags filled with excess clothing and household items removed from the house. (Hint: You can find great tips for this in Chapter Eleven!)

- Within two weeks, I will return all my ex-partner's stuff (childhood pictures, books, CDs and other significant memorabilia and personal things).
- In the coming week, I will not display any angry behavior towards my ex-partner.
- This week, I will make a good plan (together with my physical therapist) to deal with my back pain, and join a gym to get some exercise.
- This week, I will read three chapters from *Happy Again! The Art of Positive Separation.*
- This week, I will not watch TV or go online after 8:00 p.m. (Except on Saturday, when I will watch my favorite program at 10:00 p.m.)
- This week, I will clean up and reorganize my desk.
- This month, I will visit my GP to make sure that the medicines I'm taking are all compatible with one another.
- This month, I will walk or bicycle for one hour each day, regardless of the weather.
- This month, I will cook a meal for my three oldest (school) friends, who I haven't seen for several years.
- This summer, I will take an exciting trip. I will start planning this trip in the next couple of weeks. (Hint: If your budget is limited, get creative. Housesitting is a great option!)
- This month, I will pick up my old hobby (motorcycling, choir singing, horseback riding, knitting, tango dancing, blacksmithing) again.
- By the end of the year, I will have a flower/vegetable garden.
- This coming autumn, I will do something for the seniors in my neighborhood.

Long-term Personal Goals

- I will create peace of mind at home.
- I will live in a comfortable and lovely home environment (even if it's very small).
- I will have a healthy and strong body.

- I will get through my separation in good mental, physical, and emotional shape.
- I will ensure that the transition for myself (and the kids) to a new location goes as smoothly as possible.
- I will strengthen and deepen my relationship with my kids.
- I will maintain as good a relationship as possible with my ex-partner (and/or his or her family members and friends).
- I will follow a course or training program that supports my growth.
- I will find a different job that is more suitable for who I am.
- I will learn more about myself and my emotions and actually benefit from this difficult period of my life.
- I will learn how to relax.
- I will not repeat the same mistakes in my next relationship.
- I will become more open and aware as a person.
- I will accept and love myself the way I am.
- I will be the best possible example for my children about how to deal positively with a major life transition.
- I will work on creating a loving co-parenting situation with my ex, so my kids can benefit from both of us as they grow up.

YOUR MINI-GOALS

These are not part of my long-term Method (as they don't really give any long-term structure) but are incredibly helpful in emergencies. If, on any given day, life suddenly seems too much to take, you can make mini-goals to get through the day. Simply divide your day into blocks of one to two hours and list your tasks.

- Eat breakfast
- Get the kids off to school
- Get to work
- Eat lunch
- Go outside for half an hour for fresh air and exercise
- Pick up kids
- Cook dinner

- Watch my favorite TV show
- Take a hot bath
- Go to bed early with tea and a book

You can also create miniature general goals to help you set boundaries and honor your commitments to yourself, such as:

- I will not pick up the phone unless the caller is someone I know and like
- I will spend no more than 30 minutes on social media today
- I will not open my computer after dinner

Write your mini-goals on a piece of paper or in your daily planner. You don't need to use them all the time, but on difficult days, organizing your day with a series of mini-goals can help you feel like you're on top of things, and motivate you to keep going.

GUIDELINES FOR DEFINING YOUR FOCUS GOAL AND PERSONAL GOALS

1. Set a Time Limit for Each Goal

For each goal, write down a target date or time by which you think you will be able to realize the goal. If your goal will not be accomplished today, write the target date in your daily planner.

Moving toward several goals at the same time means that you will have your work cut out for you, so be realistic in setting your time limits. Be wary of setting yourself up for failure by expecting instant gratification. For example, it isn't really possible to achieve a healthy, strong body in thirty days if you've been sedentary for ten years—in such a case, six months to a year is a more realistic time frame—but it *is* possible to create a diet and exercise plan for yourself within two weeks.

At first, try to set goals that you can realize within a relatively short period of time, especially if you're still caught up in the turbulence of the separation process. Goals that can be achieved in a day, or in a week, are easier to organize and stay focused on than goals that take months or years to reach.

A time frame of one year is appropriate for your Focus Goal. If you stick to the Positive Separation Method and really work at it, you will have made lots of progress after a year, and be ready to set a new Focus Goal and embrace your new future with a new and more empowered outlook.

If you don't succeed in realizing one of your goals by the target date, give yourself a few extra days or weeks to get it done. In order to avoid disappointing yourself, however, don't postpone or delay things too often. Reaching your goals is part of your commitment to yourself and your new life.

2. Set Healthy Goals, Not Unhealthy Ones

Healthy Goals = A Healthy Future.

Healthy goals are those that move you toward greater stability, happiness, and joy in your life. They support your security in each of the five Levels of the Separation Pyramid, align with your Five Commitments, and connect you with yourself. All of the suggested goals we've explored thus far are positive goals.

Unhealthy goals are those that rely on someone else's actions or feelings, or set up your happiness as a consequence of an event. Unhealthy goals might be goals like "Get my ex to love me again," "Make sure my ex knows that dumping me was a bad decision," or "Show my ex that I'm not worthless." These kinds of goals directly contradict your Five Commitments, your Focus Goal, and your vision for a happier future. More, they are focused on things over which you have no influence, and so go against the boundaries we set in Chapter Two.

When in doubt, ask yourself, "Who is at the center of this goal? Who does it really benefit?" If the obvious answer is not "Me!" then that goal is not a healthy one for you right now.

3. Make Each Goal as Concrete as Possible and Link It to Specific Actions

The better you can describe your goal in concrete terms, the better your chance will be of realizing it. Dreaming or wishing for your goal to be realized will not have much effect if you're not taking action to create results. For each goal you set, prepare a concrete plan with specific steps and actions. Know the what, where, when, how, and why. Will you need specific help to realize this goal? If so, seek out that help. Will you need to plan extra time in your schedule each week? If so, get out your planner and assign that extra time now. What can you do to realize your goal, where and when? Make a concrete list of actions under each goal so you know what you have to accomplish to get there.

In all stages of your goal-setting and goal achievement processes, *action* is the catalyst for change.

4. Link Your Focus Goal with Your Personal Goals and Action Steps So Your Actions Feel Cohesive

Your action steps will support your Personal Goals, and your Personal Goals will support your Focus Goal.

Here is one example of how that might work:

Focus Goal: "I will get through my separation this next year as a positive and balanced individual."

Personal Goals:

- I will turn off my computer each evening after 8:00 p.m., and I will try to do so for a period of one month.
- This week, I will print and frame five photos of my family and friends to remind me that I have supportive, loving people around me.
- In the next two weeks, I will sort out all of the paperwork required for my separation, organize it, file it, and respond as necessary to any correspondence.
- I will get up early once a week to go fishing/walking for a period of two months.
- Within two weeks, I will apply for membership in the club I intend to join.

- Within six months, I will have my entire home cleaned up and reorganized (including my tool shed).
- This coming autumn, I will plant new bulbs in the garden.
- In the coming year, I will work on and improve my health and physical fitness to the point where I feel just as energetic and fit as I did five years ago. I will create a concrete plan for this within one month.
- I will create a situation in which my children will have the opportunity to live happily at my ex-partner's home as well as my own home. During the coming six months, I will work on laying a good foundation for this to happen.

Actions (for one day):

- Go walking for 20 minutes.
- Sort out the shoes in your entryway/hallway.
- Call the club I intend to join and ask about the application process.
- Make a healthy lunch.
- Answer four e-mails related to my separation.
- Print three photos.
- Turn off my computer by 8:00 p.m.

Empowered Actions

▶ Formulate Your Goals Within One Week

Spend some time today, this weekend, or during your next Power Hour to release your old goals, formulate your Focus Goal, and create any Personal Goals that support your Focus Goal. Each week, set one or two new goals, especially once you start checking realized Personal Goals off your list!

Don't rush this process. Take the time to do it properly, and make sure each goal feels exciting and attainable to you. Remember, these goals, along with your vision and your Five Commitments, are the basis for your future progress and happiness!

Here's how to go about this goal-creation process:

- **Write down your Focus Goal and five to eight Personal Goals in your notebook.** If it makes it easier, you can use my Focus Goal as your own for now. Don't make a long shopping list of goals right now; you'll only overwhelm yourself. Begin each goal with "I will …" and specify a time limit.
- **Define the action steps for each goal.** Describe everything you will have to do, in small steps, to complete each of your goals. (Hint: If you need help with this, a life coach can be a great resource.)
- **Define where you need help** from friends, family, or professionals to meet your goals.
- **Schedule your action steps and the completion date for each goal** in your daily planner.
- **Work a little bit each day** to take action and move toward your goals.
- **Chart your progress** in your notebook or planner during your Power Hour each week.
- **Compliment yourself each time you achieve a goal.** If necessary, link further actions to a specific goal to make sure you complete it in the time you allotted.
- **Be kind to yourself.** If you discover for some reason that you will be unable to realize one of your goals, don't get down on yourself. Just be honest about what's happening, and if necessary modify your goal and action steps, or simply remove your goal from your list and set a new one that you feel motivated and energized about.

▶ Affirm Your Goals Every Day

On a loose sheet of paper, write out your vision statement for your happy new future, followed by your Focus Goal and your Personal Goals. Put this paper in your wallet or purse. Read the entire sheet out loud to yourself at least twice a day for the first week, then once per day after that.

What Comes Next?

Now that you've solidified your commitments to yourself, set goals that support your vision, and created a plan of action to realize those goals, it's time to move on to Step 3 of the Positive Separation Method: Empower Yourself and Reconnect to Your Core! This Step is all about doing the inner work and taking daily action to stay aligned with your Five Commitments, goals, and life vision so that you can master the art of positive separation and stay on track in your new life.

POSITIVE SEPARATION STEP 3

Empower Yourself and Reconnect to Your Core

Empower Yourself and Reconnect to Your Core

The Separation Pyramid™ we worked with back in Chapter One made it clear that your underlying support structure was seriously compromised by your separation. Your familiar and trusted framework for stability largely disappeared, and the platform from which you operated your daily life felt weakened.

You've already done some very important initial work. Together, Steps 1 and 2 of the Positive Separation Method helped you discover how you can rebuild your sense of stability, continuity, and empowerment. We've walked through how to create your vision, and how to focus on what you can control. We've made your Five Commitments, and learned how to set attainable goals on which you can take action every day. You may already be putting many of these powerful strategies into action, and seeing happy results!

Now that you have the tools to get the daily chaos under control (at least to some degree!), we can focus even more on the most important factor in your separation: *you.*

Level 5 of the Separation Pyramid—the layer representing your personal growth and fulfillment—is still the best place to put your energy from this point forward. The work you do to further your personal growth will start to have an even more noticeable "trickle-down" effect into the four lower Levels of your Pyramid than it did in Steps 1 and 2; if you stay in your positive zone, and work diligently with the tools in this Step soon, you'll start to see an even bigger positive impact in every area of your life, security, and happiness.

Step 3 of the Positive Separation Method is all about your inner health and well-being. As we work through this Step together, we will work to connect you with the core of who you are as a person, and rediscover the alignment and confidence that may have been damaged in your separation. More, I will share some powerful tools to deal with any lingering chaos, uncertainty, and victimhood inside you; remove any potential blockades to forward motion; and help you choose a Winning Team to support you and help you keep your positive progress going!

Your inner strengths and qualities will provide you with enormous joy and momentum in the weeks and months to come. You will work on identifying and using your Positive Inner Drivers (Positive IDs), managing your mindset, tapping into your inner source of energy, passion, and purpose, and building your Winning Team of friends, family, and experts. In combination, these will help you restore your damaged feelings of self-confidence and security, and empower you to feel whole, fulfilled, and happy again, wherever your new life takes you.

CHAPTER FIVE

Your Positive Inner Drivers

Every person—no matter where they are in life—has Positive Inner Drivers. Your Positive Inner Drivers (or Positive IDs, for short) are the strengths, qualities, talents, and core values that form your essence as a person. They represent your inner potential, and can be extremely useful in turbulent times because they are a lifeline to the core of who you are and how you want to live your life.

JANET'S STORY

Janet Bray Attwood, coauthor of the *New York Times* best-selling book, *The Passion Test*, rediscovered her connection to her Positive IDs while recovering from a breakup that, quite literally, burned her.

"After my husband Chris and I got divorced, I met a new man. He was a friend of Chris's, and seemed like a wonderful guy. I'll call him Charlie. We ended up living together. I felt like he was the one. 'This is it!' I told myself. At that point, I had been practicing transcendental meditation for many years, and it was exciting for me to be with someone who understood my practice, and was on my level. I was sure he was 'the one.'

"A year after we had been living happily together, I decided to go to India to enjoy some much-needed Ayurvedic health treatments. Charlie sent me off with a big kiss and a wish for my perfect health. I thought to myself, 'He is so amazing for me.' Finally, I felt totally loved and supported.

"While I was in India, the Ayurvedic master who ran the clinic brought in two seers, people with really profound psychic abilities. 'Do you have any pictures?' they asked me. 'Sure!' I said, pulling out my cell phone. 'Here are my friends Marci Shimoff and Debra Poneman. Here are my brother and sister, Mickey and Johnny, here are my dogs. And here—'

"The seers stopped me in my tracks. 'Who is this man?' they asked.

"'That's my boyfriend, Charlie.' I proudly replied. 'Isn't he gorgeous?'

"Without missing a beat, one of the seers shouted, 'This man is having multiple relationships.'

"Immediately I stopped breathing. 'No!' I replied. 'Not Charlie!'

"I was stunned. Here I was, on my third day in India and with six weeks still to go, and I got this bomb dropped on me. My heart was beating so fast I thought I would die. 'These seers must be wrong,' I told myself. 'I love him, and he loves me.' But the seed of doubt had been planted.

"I decided I would just do my Ayurveda and wait until I returned to the U.S. to say anything to Charlie. I was sure the seers got it all wrong. Charlie was going to be furious with them when I told him!

But when he picked me up from the airport, I knew immediately that something wasn't right. My sweet Charlie, standing next to me as we waited for my luggage, felt like he was hardly there. The silence between us was deafening. This new feeling of awkwardness was debilitating. There was absolutely no connection between us. My heart was broken.

"When we got back to our house—the home we'd shared for more than a year—I asked Charlie, 'Is there something you need to tell me?'

"'No,' he said, trying to look normal. 'Everything is fine.'

"'Charlie … please tell me the truth. Are you having an affair?'

Acting shocked, he immediately denied having any kind of relationship while I was away. I wanted so much to believe him, I wanted the seers to be wrong, I wanted my sweet love to be as I thought he was—as I'd always known him to be—but although I tried to block thoughts of his betrayal, my feelings were screaming the opposite.

"'Are you having an affair?' I asked again.

"'No!' he shouted. 'What is wrong with you? Why are you so paranoid? I hate this. I'm leaving.'

"And with that, he stalked out.

"I felt horribly guilty. Was I wrong? Were the seers wrong? Oh my God, what was I doing to poor Charlie? Was this the end for us?

"Then, as all things hidden eventually do, the truth came to light. My computer broke down while I was in deadline on a project. Charlie had an extra computer at work, so I called him and asked if I could borrow it. He said he'd bring it home after work.

"The moment I opened the computer, I knew the evidence of Charlie's affair was somewhere hidden on this machine.

"'Don't go there, Janet!' I said to myself, as I swiftly perused the folders. 'You know it's not your business.'

"Shaking, I clicked on the folder marked 'family.' There they were: love letters to women he'd said were just friends. Some of the women were close friends of mine.

"Shocked and heartbroken, I closed Charlie's computer and called the dogs to go on a walk. I had to plan my next move. My life depended on it.

"Later, I sat on our porch, waiting impatiently for the moment when I would hear Charlie's key turn in the door. It was one of those beautiful Midwest evenings: blue skies, chirping birds flying overhead.

"When he finally arrived home, unable to wait a moment more, I blurted down the deck stairs, 'Charlie, I know. I have evidence. Please, love me enough to tell me the truth. Are you having an affair?'

"'No!' he screamed.

"'Oh, really? Then how do you explain this?' Shaking, I pulled up the files I'd found on the computer.

"Furious that he had been caught, Charlie turned on his heels and ran for his car. His tires screeched angrily as he sped away.

"That was the last I heard from Charlie for a whole excruciating week.

"'How can I salvage this?' I asked myself over and over again. Finally, I called and asked Charlie to please come home and talk to me.

"As we stood in the kitchen, arguing loudly, I was also heating water for tea. Not paying attention to what I was doing, I picked up the kettle, tripped over my own feet … and spilled boiling water all over myself.

"'Help me!' I screamed. The pain was worse than any I had experienced in my life. Charlie quickly responded, peeling off my jeans. 'Should I call an ambulance?' he asked.

"'No, just help me to bed.'

"Having an aversion to hospitals, I decided I could manage on my own. Little did I know how hard it would be to manage that much pain. For days, I couldn't even pull a bed sheet over myself. I couldn't do anything but lay there and try to fight the agony.

"More than just the physical pain, I was dealing with the pain in my heart. Charlie and I hadn't resolved anything before my accident. I was still carrying so much grief, and so many unanswered questions. Heart pain, burn pain—they blended together into one giant sea of hurt.

"Then, about a week in, a miracle happened. Instead of fighting the pain, I totally surrendered. I fell into the pain. I surrendered to it, feeling it fully … and then, suddenly, I was through to the other side. I was immersed in blissful peace. For a while, I vacillated back and forth: pain and bliss, pain and bliss. I realized that as long as I resisted, I was going to stay stuck in the pain. The only way to undo the pain was to give myself over to it, 100 percent.

"In the weeks that followed, I went back and forth between anger and surrender. Things got harder when I found out that Charlie had taken up with a friend of mine—but I started practicing the ancient Hawaiian forgiveness prayer, Ho'oponopono. I also used The Work of Byron Katie, an amazing process to undue any limiting beliefs about myself and others. In a few weeks, my feelings about my relationship with Charlie had totally shifted. I realized that the only person to forgive was me, and that Charlie falling in love with my friend had nothing to do with me. Lastly, and most importantly, everything I needed was already inside me. There was nothing outside of me that needed to be fixed, morphed, or healed.

"During this time, my ex-husband Chris and I were working together on an e-book called *From Sad to Glad: Seven Steps to Staying Open in the Midst of Change*. It was hard; I was still slipping into anger, lashing out with words. 'How can you still be friends with Charlie?' I asked Chris one day. 'You can't trust him!'

"'Who would you be without that thought?' Chris asked me.

"I thought for a moment. Finally, I replied, 'I would be the Janet I love.'

"'So, what's the turnaround of that statement, *I cannot trust him?*'

"'I cannot trust myself.'

"'And was there a time in the relationship when you couldn't trust yourself?' Chris asked.

"Then, I remembered. When Charlie and I decided to move in together, he stopped me on the porch, just outside our front door. 'Janet,' he told me, 'I just want you to know that I am not 100 percent sold.' And, instead of telling him to come back when he was ready to offer the love I needed and deserved, I thought to myself, *It's okay. He will love me. I know he will.*

"Charlie had told me that day, back at the beginning, what was going on—I just hadn't heard it. I had walked right into this. By blaming him, I was denying my own role in what I had created. I needed to forgive him, and myself, if I wanted to move on.

"I also needed to reconnect to my own positive qualities—the qualities that had gotten buried in all my pain and anger. I had to do my inner work to come back to the beautiful feelings that were always inside of me: hope, harmony, joy, and the truth of life. I had to—literally—tell the whole truth to myself about what really happened and walk through the fire of my own discomfort to get back to myself.

"Two months after Charlie and I broke up, my inner work had paid off. I had no remorse, no unhappiness, no jealousy; I felt all was good and as it should be. I invited Charlie and his new girlfriend (my friend) over for Thanksgiving dinner. I was truly able to celebrate their happiness, because I had rediscovered my own happiness inside of me. I wasn't holding on to my victim story, or playing the 'poor me' card. I had everything I needed inside myself.

"As you practice with your tools of inner connection, you become more courageous. No one is born knowing how to do this, and it can be scary at times to face yourself. You just have to tell yourself, 'I am going to know myself.' Don't get me wrong: it was awful to be rejected like I was, and massively painful to be left for someone twenty years younger. Coming back from that was like digging myself out of a grave, but each step forward helped me grow in courage, and I finally got to the point where I could truly let it go.

"So, the question isn't 'What has happened to you.' It's 'Are you creating the world you want to create? Or, are you creating the world you don't want to create?' This is your choice."

Get to Know Your Positive Inner Drivers

Janet needed to reconnect to her Positive IDs—the beautiful qualities within herself—in order to move on and heal her body and spirit. Once she did, forgiveness and a new life were waiting for her on the other side.

In the same way, you can discover and connect to your own Positive IDs to empower yourself during your separation and along the road to your new, happy future.

Working with Positive IDs is one of my favorite parts of the Positive Separation Method—not only because it's fun to discover more about who we are and what we value, but because it reveals the beauty of who we are in a new way, and how we can make use of our personal greatness in a concrete and results-producing way.

If you take the time to really get to know them and work with them, your Positive IDs will act like road signs along your path to a new future. As long as you pay attention to where they're pointing, you will never lose your connection to yourself and your vision for a happy life.

By using your Positive IDs to analyze who you really are and uncover your sources of positive motivation in daily life, you are much less likely to be distracted by the negative emotions and reactions of others. You can simply make use of the strength and potential already present inside you (for example, courage or a sense of harmony) to settle your separation as positively as possible and approach your new future with a sense of anticipation and optimism. Your Positive IDs are a great free source of energy to "keep your motor running" on a daily basis, as long as you keep them deliberately in the limelight!

WHAT ARE YOUR POSITIVE IDS?

Many of your Positive IDs have been part of you since you were a child. They are part of your innate makeup as a human being, and are as unique as your fingerprints. They can serve as a source of enormous energy, power, and internal connection—but before you can unlock their potential and work with them, you need to figure out what they are!

To do this, ask yourself two key questions:

- **"What motivates me to take action?"**
- **"What makes me feel good?"**

Because your Positive IDs are closely intertwined with your inner motivation and your natural comfort zone, they are powerfully connected to the core of who you are.

For example, daily tasks that are aligned with your inner motivation will feel easier, and you won't waste energy fighting to overcome internal resistance or uncertainty. And when you have to do things that don't feel like they line up with your Positive IDs, you can reframe them in your mind so that they do! For example, if you love being organized, you can reframe filling out bank paperwork as setting one area of your life in order.

If you respect your personal comfort zone—the place where you feel aligned and happy with who you are, and can act accordingly—you will feel like your feet are firmly planted, no matter what is happening around you.

Note that your personal comfort zone has nothing to do with your habitual "comfort zones" or your established status quo. Just because things have always been a certain way doesn't meant that that way is best for you. For example, if you are accustomed to being put down by your ex-partner, that doesn't mean that being put down all the time needs to be acceptable in your new life! Remember that you can stretch yourself outside of what you're used to without contradicting your Positive IDs or the place of balance within yourself.

DISCOVER YOUR POSITIVE INNER DRIVERS

It's time to find your Positive Inner Drivers!

Place a check mark next to any and all words that you feel apply to you—that motivate you to action, or that feel connected to your personal sense of joy and comfort. Place an exclamation mark next to the words that, without doubt, describe your positive essence.

You'll notice as you read that some terms overlap or are similar. The exact term you choose will be the one that resonates most strongly with you. You may even feel an inner lightness or "gut reaction" to your Positive IDs! If you can't find a word you're looking for, just add it to the list!

One more note: Be careful of choosing Positive IDs that you *wish* applied to you, but don't. This isn't about changing yourself, but about embracing yourself *exactly* as you are. If you find yourself wishing that you had a particular quality or set of qualities, put a smiley face next to that word to show that you value it—but don't waste time feeling guilty that that quality isn't at the top of your list of core strengths!

A

☐ Abundant
☐ Accepting
☐ Action-oriented
☐ Acquisitive
☐ Adventurous
☐ Affectionate
☐ Ambitious
☐ Assertive
☐ Attentive
☐ Authentic
☐ Authoritative
☐ Autonomous

B

☐ Balanced
☐ Beautiful
☐ Believing
☐ Brave
☐ Brilliant
☐ Builder

C

☐ Caring
☐ Careful
☐ Certain
☐ Charitable
☐ Cheerful

☐ Child-oriented
☐ Collegial
☐ Comforting
☐ Communicative
☐ Compassionate
☐ Companionable
☐ Comradely
☐ Concentration
☐ Confident
☐ Connected
☐ Convincing
☐ Cooperative
☐ Courageous
☐ Courteous
☐ Creative
☐ Curious
☐ Calm

D

- ☐ Daring
- ☐ Decisive
- ☐ Dedicated
- ☐ Deep
- ☐ Development-oriented
- ☐ Discovery-oriented
- ☐ Direct
- ☐ Disciplined
- ☐ Domestic
- ☐ Driven
- ☐ Dutiful

E

- ☐ Effective
- ☐ Effervescent
- ☐ Efficient
- ☐ Emotional
- ☐ Empathy
- ☐ Energy
- ☐ Enjoys life
- ☐ Enthusiasm
- ☐ Entrepreneurial
- ☐ Equality-oriented

F

- ☐ Fair
- ☐ Family-oriented
- ☐ Feeling
- ☐ Financially secure
- ☐ Flexible
- ☐ Frugal
- ☐ Focused
- ☐ Forgiving
- ☐ Friendly
- ☐ Free
- ☐ Fun

G

- ☐ Generous
- ☐ Giving
- ☐ Good listener
- ☐ Grateful
- ☐ Growth-oriented

H

- ☐ Happy
- ☐ Hard-working
- ☐ Harmonious
- ☐ Healthy
- ☐ Helpful
- ☐ Highly-sensitive
- ☐ Honest
- ☐ Hopeful
- ☐ Humorous

I

- ☐ Impulsive
- ☐ Independent
- ☐ Innovative
- ☐ Inquisitive
- ☐ Integrous
- ☐ Involved
- ☐ Irreverent

J–K–L

- ☐ Joyful
- ☐ Kind
- ☐ Knowledgeable
- ☐ Light
- ☐ Loving
- ☐ Loyal
- ☐ Lucky

M

- ☐ Merry
- ☐ Mild
- ☐ Mindful
- ☐ Moderate

N

- ☐ Nature lover
- ☐ Neat

O

- ☐ Open-hearted
- ☐ Open-minded
- ☐ Orderly
- ☐ Organized
- ☐ Original

P

- ☐ Passionate
- ☐ Patient
- ☐ Peaceful
- ☐ Perfectionist
- ☐ Performer
- ☐ Perseverant
- ☐ Pioneering
- ☐ Playful
- ☐ Positive
- ☐ Practical
- ☐ Precise
- ☐ Predictable
- ☐ Problem-solver
- ☐ Professional
- ☐ Punctual
- ☐ Pure

Q

- ☐ Quick-witted
- ☐ Quiet

R

- ☐ Recognized
- ☐ Relaxed
- ☐ Reliable
- ☐ Respectful
- ☐ Responsible
- ☐ Restful
- ☐ Risk-taker
- ☐ Results-oriented
- ☐ Robust
- ☐ Romantic

S

- ☐ Satisfied
- ☐ Self-aware
- ☐ Self-development-oriented
- ☐ Self-disciplined
- ☐ Secure
- ☐ Sensitive
- ☐ Sets limits
- ☐ Simple
- ☐ Sober
- ☐ Sociable
- ☐ Solid
- ☐ Sound
- ☐ Spontaneous
- ☐ Sports-oriented
- ☐ Stable
- ☐ Strong
- ☐ Structured
- ☐ Subtle
- ☐ Successful

T

- ☐ Technologically-inclined
- ☐ Thrifty
- ☐ Tidy
- ☐ Traditional
- ☐ Trusting
- ☐ Trustworthy
- ☐ Truthful

U–V

- ☐ Urban
- ☐ Useful
- ☐ Visible
- ☐ Visual
- ☐ Vulnerable

W–Z

- ☐ Warm
- ☐ Warmhearted
- ☐ Willing
- ☐ Wise

Which words did you immediately reward with an exclamation mark? These words probably best describe your essence!

Now, choose your top five or ten words from the list of those you marked. Take your time, and make sure to choose only those IDs you feel deeply connected to. These represent your core traits and values—the things that make you the amazing person that you are. In the coming weeks and months, you will be able to shine a spotlight on your Positive IDs and use them to lighten your load with regard to your separation and life in general. They will serve as a source of inner comfort and motivation, both of which you will put to very good use in the weeks and months to come.

MY POSITIVE IDS

The following IDs will help me in the coming year by guiding me in a positive direction and making me happy again:

√ _____

√ _____

√ _____

√ _____

√ _____

√ _____

√ _____

√ _____

√ _____

√ _____

Positive Drivers Vs. Negative Drivers

Your Inner Drivers—the feelings, beliefs, and associations that push you toward action—can be either positive or negative.

The difference between the two is that Positive IDs are directly related to who we are, and who we have always been inside. Negative IDs are directly related to what we've learned (or have refused to learn) in our lives.

Examples of Negative IDs include victimhood, blame, unworthiness, jealousy, aggression, and anger. When we are tapped into our Negative IDs, we will make poor choices which do not reflect or lead to the happy life we really want. More, those choices will work against our vision, goals, Five Commitments, and Positive IDs.

No one is born a victim. No one is born feeling unworthy. We *learned* these things at some point—which means that we can also *unlearn* them.

When you start to work with your Positive IDs in a meaningful way, you will begin to see your Negative IDs as less powerful in your life. You will also see how your Negative IDs contradict your positive ones, and how letting them go can help you become more connected to your core essence. For example, if you have a Positive ID of "strength," how can you be a victim at the same time? How can you be happy and compassionate and yet act aggressive and angry? How can you be a "problem solver" and yet blame others for your problems? The answer is, you can't! When you see your Positive and Negative IDs side by side, it will be easy to choose which one will move you toward your new, happy life, and which will keep you stuck in a spiral of unhappiness.

One note on this: Uncovering your Negative IDs isn't about creating guilt or blaming yourself for the past. It's about empowering you to live by and with your Positive IDs even more strongly! So if you find Negative IDs that make you feel bad or sad, don't focus on them. Just make a commitment to yourself to let them go, and work with only your Positive IDs from now on!

Inner Drivers Vs. Temporary Drivers

In addition to being either positive or negative, many of your drivers may also be temporary—meaning, they have been caused by your separation and your need to acutely defend your interests. Unlike your Positive IDs, these temporary drivers are not an essential part of who you are, but are determined by your present circumstances.

Your Temporary Drivers might include things like "Find a stable place to live," "Make X dollars this month to cover my household expenses," or "Find one hour a day to spend quality time with my children." As soon as a result has been obtained or your interests have been secured, the Temporary Driver associated with that interest disappears. For example, if you find adequate accommodations, when you are once again financially secure, or when you establish a healthy schedule for co-parenting, you will no longer be pushed toward action by that particular driver, and your attention will switch to some new aspect of your situation.

Temporary Drivers are things you feel an enormous need for right now—such as settling your living situation—and as such can be extremely motivating in the short term. They may also be related to the Personal Goals we worked with in Chapter Four. Your Positive IDs, on the other hand, are always with you. Not only do they serve as a permanent reservoir of personal strength, they also can help define and enhance how you show up in your new life, and how you strive to create your vision of a happier reality.

Put Your Inner Drivers to Work

Now that you know what your most important Positive IDs are, how can you put them to work in your separation process and the path to your new future?

Your Positive IDs are energies that you can put to use in various ways at any hour of the day. They can be reminders of your most positive qualities when things get challenging. For example, if you are having a tough week and experiencing challenging communications with your ex-partner, you can remind yourself, "Trust and caring are two of my most powerful Inner Drivers." Then, you can ask yourself, "How can I apply trust in this situation? How can I apply caring?" When you apply your Positive IDs in conjunction with your Five Commitments, your goals, and your vision for a happy life, you will see the best path forward, even in uncomfortable situations.

In the coming weeks and months, regularly check in with yourself as to whether you are still aware of and using your Positive IDs to your advantage in your thinking and behavior. (Hint: Your Power Hour is a great time to do this!) If you notice that you are not fully using your Positive IDs, take the time every day for at least a week to reconnect with them so you can stop working against yourself and wasting energy, get back in your comfort zone, and ride the wave of your own positive energy.

Once you've embraced and worked with your Positive IDs for a while, you will notice that they have started to become an integral part of your thinking and behavior. You may also notice, sooner than you think, that you feel more "like you" than you ever have before! This is because your thoughts and actions are more in harmony with your essence and your inner core—and that harmony can, with care and tending from you, carry through the rest of your lifetime!

Your Buried IDs

Here's an extra piece that really helped me along the way. Did you notice during the earlier exercises that any of your Positive IDs had become a bit … clouded? Meaning, you resonated with the words strongly, but couldn't find a lot of evidence of that particular ID in your life? That may be because that Positive ID has been *buried*—by your ex-partner, your relationship, or your own choices.

Perhaps, although you love to throw parties and spend time with groups of family and friends, socializing was not appreciated in your past relationship. Perhaps being ambitious or adventurous was simply not acceptable. Perhaps you stifled your caring nature out of frustration, or stopped trusting as a means of self-protection.

My personal Positive IDs are action-oriented, effervescent, family-oriented, creative, highly-sensitive, harmonious, and problem-solver. Knowing that these qualities were at the heart of my values and choices helped me greatly during my separation. The more I put them in the spotlight and referred to them in my daily decision-making, the more connected to myself I felt. Soon, I also uncovered two buried IDs, adventure and joy. Once I got those two qualities on the podium with the others, I was able to rely on them to counteract the turbulence of the separation process.

So, take some time to look at your list again. If you have uncovered any buried IDs, write them down, and pay extra attention to them for the next few weeks. Doing so will help you cultivate a deeper inner relationship with yourself. From now on, there is nothing stopping you from connecting to these facets of yourself; you can begin to enjoy them and benefit from them in full.

Empowered Action

▶ Work with Your Buried IDs

Write down any IDs that you feel had been buried in your former life. Then, think of a way to engage with each of those IDs in a fun and creative way this week.

For example, if one of your buried IDs is "sociable," schedule drinks with friends or attend an event in the next seven days.

Buried ID: _____

Action: _____

Buried ID: _____

Action: _____

Buried ID: _____

Action: _____

Reconnecting to these neglected parts of yourself will not only help you feel better and more empowered, but will also help you reach your goals and create your vision for your new life faster and more easily!

What Comes Next

The Positive IDs you selected are attuned to your core essence. By making full use of your Positive IDs as well as your Five Commitments, you will be better equipped to step into a positive and empowered mindset and create a caring and effective Winning Team using the tools and information in the next two chapters. Once your whole mind, heart, and soul are connected to the truth of who you are and what you value, you will have a very solid foundation to work from in the coming year!

CHAPTER SIX

Manage Your Mindset, Change Your Experience

B efore we launch into our discussion of mindset and emotions, I want to share a special story from my friend and mentor Marci Shimoff.

MARCI'S STORY

When Marci told me the story of how she dreamed of finding her soul mate, and how she courageously shifted her mindset to both survive a breakup and strengthen a friendship, my heart lit up with sparks. She turned what was one of the darkest periods in her life into one of the most transformational and positive. Here is her beautiful story of courage, trust, and friendship.

"I had wanted to be married since I was a little girl.

"One of my earliest memories is lying in my cozy little bed with a dream in my heart to be with my beloved. I would peek out the window to see the beautiful dark sky with its sparkling stars, and every night I would pick out one star as my 'wishing star.' Every night, I wished with great belief that I would meet my Prince Charming—my life partner, the person with whom I could share my dreams and create a beautiful, romantic life of love, friendship, and deep connection. It was my heart's deepest desire.

"I was only five or six years old, but I *knew* that someday my dream would become a reality.

"In my twenties, I had wonderful relationships, but I knew that none of the men I dated were my true life partners. Then, along came Bob—and my heart was cracked wide open.

"I met Bob when he interviewed me for a job. We had a nice rapport, and he hired me as his marketing manager. We really liked each other as colleagues and friends. Then, on one fateful weekend trip, we also discovered a deep love for each other, which ended up growing into a relationship that was full of fun and deep, loving connection.

"I appreciated Bob's humor, his values, and his perspective on life. I really loved him. But there was a problem: I knew Bob was not the life partner I was supposed to be with—the one I'd dreamed about when I wished on my wishing stars. And I sensed that, if I stayed with him, I would not have the space to find my true Prince Charming.

"So, we broke up—not because anything was wrong with our relationship, but because I wanted to be with my true life partner. It was a drive that came from someplace deep inside. I missed Bob immediately, but I knew that was part of the game. I'd have to let go and move on if I wanted to be open to my dream.

"Letting go got a lot harder when, two weeks after our breakup, Bob fell in love with another woman. My world came crashing down. The pain was unbearable. I didn't want to be with him—but I didn't want anyone else to be with him, either! My rational mind knew that this wasn't reasonable, or fair—but matters of the heart generally aren't, are they?

"To make matters worse, the woman Bob had fallen in love with was a good friend of mine. Holly was a wonderful woman, but I was so jealous that it felt like my heart had been pierced by a dagger.

"My life went into a tailspin. Even though Bob no longer worked at the company where we'd met, I was a wreck at work. I went out of my way to avoid driving by her house, although it was smack in the middle of my usual commute; I didn't want to see where he and Holly were sharing their new life together. When I got home each day, feeling overwhelmed by my hurt and pain, I would curl up in a ball in a corner of my bedroom and cry for hours.

"The degree of pain felt bigger than the circumstances warranted, but I couldn't talk myself out of the hurt. I felt as though I would never be happy again. I had sunk into the deepest, darkest place in my life, and I didn't know how to climb out.

"Friends tried to console me. My parents were so worried that they offered to fly across the country to make sure I was okay. The pain went on and on for what felt like an eternity. It was actually about three months.

"Then, one morning I heard a knock at my door. I glanced out the window and was shocked to see Holly. She was the last person I wanted to see on my doorstep! I very nearly didn't open the door, but then she said, with great compassion, 'Marci, you need help. Please, let me in!'

"In that split second, I made one of the most important decisions of my life. I decided to hear her out.

"We sat down at my kitchen table, and I made some tea. 'Marci,' she said, 'You are in a funk. You have so many blessings in your life, but you're not seeing any of them! So every night for the next twenty-one days, I want you to write down three things that you're grateful for.'

"Now, keep in mind, this was in the 1980s, well before most people had ever heard of a 'gratitude practice.' But I was so desperate to get out of this awful place I'd fallen into that I would have tried anything. I agreed to do what Holly had asked.

"That night, I struggled to come up with three things for which I was grateful. What I ended up writing was: *I'm thankful that I ate lunch today. I'm thankful for the sun. I'm thankful for my arms and legs.*

"As the days passed, my list-making became easier. I started noticing again the beauty of life. I remembered that I did, indeed, have a lot of things to be grateful for.

"By the end of my twenty-one days, even Holly—the friend who'd 'stolen' my love away—made it to my gratitude list.

"Holly gave me another gift as well. She said, 'Marci, you need support! We are going to form a woman's support group. We will meet every week to support each other in our dreams and goals.' Now, *that* was a real stretch—but I agreed to be part of the group we formed of six women.

"In the beginning, I hated hearing about Holly's great life, and about how in love she was with Bob. But the more time I spent with our sisterhood, and the longer I continued my gratitude practice, the more my life felt like it was back on track.

"I continued to meet with that support group for ten years, until I moved to a new city. I still count those women among my closest soul sisters.

"By changing my mindset from one of pain to one of possibility, I took a leap into the unknown. I was finally able to let go of my pain around Bob and reconnect to my dream of finding my *real* soulmate. A number of years and a few relationships later, I finally did meet Sergio, my Prince Charming. He didn't appear on a white horse, but in the gravel parking lot of a retreat center. Still, it didn't take long for me to know that he was the one I'd been waiting for.

"And what happened to Bob and Holly? Theirs is a great story, too. They married a year after they started dating. I was an honored guest at their wedding, and wholeheartedly wished them all the good in the world from my seat in the front row. Over the last thirty years, I've witnessed them raising their beautiful daughter and sharing a wonderful life together. They are part of my soul family, and our friendship is for life. Sergio and I visit them whenever we happen to be in the same town.

"For me, gratitude was the fast track to healing. Shifting my mindset from one of loss to one of gratitude gave me my life back. It returned me to who I was, and what I really wanted from my life. If I hadn't gone through my breakup with Bob, I might never have learned these lessons so strongly.

"Nowadays, when I look up at a beautiful night sky filled with stars, I still pick one and smile. But now, they're not my 'wishing stars'; they're my 'gratitude stars.'"

Manage Your Mindset

Mindset is all about perspective. It's about how you see yourself, your life, and the world around you.

When you're in the midst of a painful separation, your world can seem to close in around you, just like it did for Marci. Your pain and hurt can send you into a tailspin—and, unless you consciously choose to do things to move yourself out of that dark place, you can get stuck there for months or even years.

I have already given you several tools in this book that can help you shift your mindset and pull yourself out of your pain. Your vision for a brighter, happier future; your Focus Goal and supportive Personal Goals; your Five Commitments, and your Positive IDs can all provide a foundation for your positive, empowered mindset. They're like the columns that will hold up your dreams for your new life, and give you a safe, solid place to go when you're feeling lost and alone.

In this chapter, we'll learn how to deal with your emotions in a positive way using your vision, goals, commitments, and Positive IDs as tools and guides. If you dive into this work with your whole heart, knowing that you have nothing to lose except your pain, you will make great strides toward being happy again and building your new, empowered life on the other side of your separation.

DEALING WITH YOUR EMOTIONS IN A POSITIVE WAY

As we learned in Marci's story, our emotions around separation aren't always easy to deal with. They don't even always make sense! Whether you initiated the breakup or not, you may find yourself swamped by pain, panic, anger, loneliness, or sadness.

No matter what you're feeling, it's important to start dealing with your emotions as soon as possible. You might be able to put them off for a time while you deal with the physical tasks of your separation, but you can't stay busy and avoid your feelings forever! If you want to get through your separation in a balanced manner and fulfill your Focus Goal of getting through your separation as a whole, positive, empowered person, you need to address what's really happening.

Denying or ignoring your feelings about your separation is completely senseless. The longer you delay in dealing with your emotions, the more difficult it will become. Systematically suppressing your emotions can even result in a pressure cooker effect. Don't go there! You may think you're being very clever by coping so well day to day, but you're really building an emotional bomb that will explode in your face when you least want or expect it. Suddenly, out of nowhere, for a completely trivial reason, you will simply lose it in front of your kids, at work, or somewhere else.

Or the bomb can go off *inside* your body and mind. When this happens, you might become run down, weak, or ill. Or, you might try to block out your emotions via drugs, alcohol, overeating, excessive time on the internet, unsafe or excessive sex, or working too hard. These escapist tactics just pile one problem on top of the other—and while they might make your emotions go away in the short term, they don't resolve them.

Even if it doesn't result in an explosion, delaying requires an enormous amount of energy and creates mountains of extra stress. Your mind may be miles ahead of your heart, and the facts on the ground may go even faster, but before your heart can feel true love and happiness again, it first needs to heal itself of the loss and pain of separation.

Now, I want to be clear about something here: recognizing and engaging with your emotions is NOT the same as giving into a victim mindset or allowing your ex-partner's choices to have power over your life. You can feel pain without being victimized by it. You can be sad about what has happened without letting sadness become your whole life. To deal with your emotions positively, you need to find the balance between expressing and releasing them in a healthy way and letting them take over your life.

Dealing with emotions is a complex process. Every separation is unique, and everyone has his or her own way of coming to terms with it. But there are guidelines, tips, and practices that can help you a great deal in doing so during the coming period—and I'm going to share them with you in this chapter.

If you need help processing and accepting what's happening, or your emotions feel too big to deal with on your own, it's vital for you to get professional help. (I'll share more about how to do this in Chapter Seven, where we'll meet your

Winning Team. For now, just know that you don't have to do it alone, and asking for help is better than getting stuck!)

In the next section, I'll share with you my personal tips for dealing with the challenging emotions of your separation in a positive, empowered way so you can move on toward your new, happy life.

POSITIVE WAYS TO MANAGE YOUR EMOTIONS

Draw a Line

The first step in dealing with difficult emotions is to recognize the lines that separate the past from the present, and the present from your future.

You already marked the date in your calendar when you went through your disconnection process in Chapter Two. You've drawn a line and crossed from your old life into your new one. Now, it's time to draw the same firm line again, this time across your emotions.

Whatever the reasons behind your separation, they are no longer important when it comes to the present moment. What's done is done, and reviewing the sordid details of what happened to cause your separation won't change the facts on the ground. In order to move forward, you need to acknowledge and accept where you are right now, not waste time wishing your "now" was different.

Acknowledge What You Feel Right Now

Now that you've put the past in the past, you need to acknowledge and accept what you feel right now, in this moment. Recognize and explicitly identify all of your emotions to yourself whenever they arise. What are you feeling in your heart and body?

If you confront your pain, fear, anger, and other challenging emotions without looking away, they will stop sneaking up on you and knocking you around when you least expect it.

All emotions want to be seen, felt, heard, and touched; the difficult ones are no different. They need you to *engage* with them, not shut the door in their faces. To do this in a healthy way, you first need to learn how to tune in to your emotions and not block them out. That means feeling them when they arise, and giving yourself the time and space to let them flow through you. Once the storm is over, you can realign your mind and heart with your vision, goals, Five Commitments, and Positive IDs, and take each day as it comes.

This process has its ups and downs. At times, you might feel very intense emotions which disappear quickly, only to resurface later. You can also switch between positive and negative/challenging emotions extremely quickly. Don't deny them or push them away. Especially avoid telling yourself that it's "wrong" to feel what you feel. Instead, look at all of your emotions clearly, and see them for what they are.

There are two types of emotions: positive and negative. These aren't separated by whether they are "good" or "bad," but rather by how they affect the way you function in and relate to yourself, your vision, and your life.

Positive emotions are those like enthusiasm, pride, satisfaction, joy, affection, comradeship, solidarity, love, safety, harmony, relief, and freedom. These emotions are enjoyable; they lift you up inside. They help you feel stronger, more resolved, and more empowered.

Negative emotions, on the other hand, are those like panic, anger, hate, jealousy, confusion, concern, (excessive) anxiety, loneliness, sorrow, guilt, disappointment, grief, regret, fear, and shame. Negative emotions drain your energy—and, like positive emotions, they can produce physical responses. You can stiffen up (from fear or panic), start shaking (from nervousness or anger), feel hot or cold, or feel powerless or paralyzed. You may feel your throat tightening, or have the urge to fight or take flight. You may feel like you need to scream or fight to release the pressure inside of you.

Most of the time, we focus on our negative emotions because they feel the most powerful. But for our purposes here, I want you to feel and notice all of your emotions equally, without judging them. Only then can you make a solid plan to deal with the negative emotions in a helpful, healthy way, and make more room for the positive ones to take their place.

Of course, there are situations when it's not appropriate to just let your emotions flow. For example, if you find yourself in a very difficult situation while at work, in public, or with your children, holding back until you're in a safe space to process your feelings—such as your home, your therapist's office, or with a friend—can be a positive thing. When you feel challenged, or like you're about to explode, employ the age-old practice of counting to ten in your head. Or, simply excuse yourself to take a breather until the storm has passed.

Dealing with and working through your emotions, especially in the beginning, is hard work, but it also brings a great sense of relief. When you practice your coping mechanisms regularly, you will no longer feel like you are being "stalked" by your painful feelings. More, by dealing with your emotions instead of hiding from them, you will give up the struggle of refusing to accept your new situation; in doing so, you will immediately feel lighter, freer, and stronger.

Give It Time

Time plays a big role in your healing. The coming days, weeks, and months will put much-needed distance between you and your ex-partner that will change your perspective, soften your feelings, and bring important new insights.

Most people need between two and four years to completely resolve the emotions around their separation. Don't let this number scare you, though. Instead, embrace it. You are on a journey; you don't have to resolve everything at once! The hardest part of the journey is in the first couple of months; after that, it's still an uphill climb, but it no longer needs to feel like a daily battle.

Of course, some people (like those "eternal victims" we talked about in Chapter Four) hang on to their old emotions forever—but you don't want to do that! The key to letting time do its work is to let yourself feel what you actually feel each and every day instead of dredging up negative or difficult feelings from other days and reapplying them. Sooner or later, you will notice that it actually takes work to stay as angry or sad as you once were. Don't do that work, even if it feels righteous or validating! That's a victim strategy. If your emotions become less strong with time, that's a wonderful thing: it means you're making more space for new, positive feelings to come into your life!

Follow the Uphill Model

I created the Uphill Model™ based on the ideas and insights of grief specialist Elisabeth Kübler-Ross.

Basically, the process of coping with, processing, and resolving your emotions around your separation is like climbing a hill. Sometimes, you will gain a lot of ground quickly. Sometimes, you will need to stop and rest. And sometimes, you will backtrack, backslide, and revisit the same place several times before you start walking upslope again. But as long as you keep in mind the ultimate pinnacle of the hill—your personal future—you will keep moving steadily upward, because that is the only possible path toward a new and happy future!

Each phase of your Uphill Journey is characterized by specific feelings and behaviors. Each partner in a separation goes through these phases differently. You may find yourself in a different phase than your ex-partner—but don't let where your ex is on the hill affect your progress. All that matters is that you keep climbing at your own pace, day by day, step by step … and eventually reach the top!

PHASE 7: A new future full of opportunities

PHASE 6: Building self-worth & independence

PHASE 5: Acceptance & letting go

PHASE 4: Pain & grief

PHASE 3: Awareness & recognition of truth

PHASE 2: Bargaining, hoping to turn the clock back

PHASE 1: Denial, disbelief

The Uphill Model™

Empowered Actions

▶ Draw Your Line

Go back to the date on which you committed to disconnect from your old relationship and old life. (See Chapter Two.) Take a look at what you wrote there, or the symbol you drew. Take a few minutes to just sit and breathe. Then, ask yourself, "What is different on this side of the line? What steps have I taken? What have I accomplished?"

Then, draw a new line to separate yourself from any lingering attachments to your past. Imagine yourself letting go of your feelings of regret or "what if," and starting fresh from where you are right now. If it helps, you can draw an actual line on your floor with chalk (or cut a line from a piece of newsprint), and step over it to symbolize leaving your old life and attachments behind. Once you cross that line, you have stepped into your future—and the only place to go from here is upward!

▶ Get to Know Your Emotions

For at least two weeks, write down every emotion you feel, every day. Pay equal attention to both positive and negative emotions, and track the effects that each emotion has on you physically.

Then, ask yourself, "What is the healthiest way to engage with each of these emotions?" For example, you might take more time to connect with and reinforce your positive emotions, and give yourself extra alone time to process your anger and sadness. Schedule your actions in your planner so you don't put them off!

▶ Listen to Your Mind, Heart, Body, and Soul

During a quiet moment, take out your notebook. Let go of your conscious thoughts and let your body relax. Feel what your head, heart, body, and soul have to tell you. Write down everything that comes to the surface, floats by inside you, or weighs you down, including any physical pain or discomfort.

Use this knowledge to prioritize the feelings and emotions that you want to address through your actions (which we'll look at in the next section).

▶ Trace Your Uphill Journey

What stage of the Uphill Journey do you think you are currently in? (Hint: It might be more than one!) Take notes, and write in your journal about how you feel right now. Focus on how much progress you have made, and make a list of actions you can take to move yourself to the next stage.

If you like, you can also think about what stage of the Uphill Journey your ex-partner is at. This isn't because you need to take action on your ex's behalf; it's simply a way to get clarity and find compassion for what may seem like inexplicable behavior. Remember, you cannot pull the other person to catch up (or pull them back to where you are) so that you are both in the same phase. All you can do is focus on your own progress and present position, and on the actions that you need to take to cope with your separation and proceed further on your new path.

When I was on my own journey through separation, I actually drew my hill, complete with flowers, grass, trees, animals, and a cozy shelter near each point along the journey. I pictured myself climbing the hill at my own pace, stopping to drink from the streams, sitting on benches, eating a piece of Toblerone (my favorite chocolate), or taking a nap in the nearest shelter when I needed to rest. This personalization of the Uphill Journey helped my journey feel less stressful, and more like a climb toward a new, happy life full of promise and adventure.

Coping in Action

Identifying your emotions and letting them flow is only one stage of the process. Now, you need to create a plan of action for coping with your emotions in real time, and making progress each day toward where you want to be. (Hint: This is where your vision, goals, Five Commitments, and Positive IDs come in handy!)

Coping in real time can be hard at first, and you will definitely have some uncomfortable moments, mishaps, and all-out explosions. But the more you practice your coping skills, the faster you will be able to recover your equilibrium.

Here are my seven Coping Steps to help you process your emotions in real time.

Coping Step 1: Pay Attention

There is a close link between your ability to cope with the emotions of your separation and your ability to settle the practical and legal aspects of the separation. (Remember the Emotional Sub-Process from Chapter One?) If you become blocked emotionally, the entire separation process will quickly grind to a halt. However, if you cope with your emotions and work through them, all of the other Sub-Processes will get a boost.

So, pay attention to where your emotions take you each day. Sometimes, simply noticing where you are and what's happening is enough to make a difference.

Coping Step 2: Identify and Describe Your Emotions Immediately

It may sound strange, but your emotions are your allies, not your enemies. When you examine them with curiosity and an open mind, you will learn more about yourself and your behavior, and be able to make choices that help, rather than hurt, your separation process and your vision for your future.

Even if you only have the time and space to jot a few lines in your daily planner, write down all of your emotions. Describe them exactly. This process alone will have a calming effect. Then, reflect on your emotions immediately, or later in the day when you have more time. This will help you to make adjustments in your actions and thought patterns if necessary.

Coping Step 3: Express Your Emotions in a Healthy Way

I can't say it enough: It is unhealthy to bottle up your emotions! Find ways to express your emotions in a healthy way that releases them gently and gives you space to heal.

This expression might be hard for you at first, and might even feel unnatural. For example, if you're normally a "tough guy," chances are that nothing will help you more than a good, long cry. If you're a "people-pleaser," venting your anger in a constructive way can be hugely empowering. And if you're inclined to seek solitude, talking to a trusted friend, family member, or therapist can be amazingly helpful and give you new perspective.

You can also vent your emotions through activity. Go to the gym, take a walk in nature, or play sports. If you're working out alone, you can also use your workout as "bonus time" to reflect on what's happening inside you.

Finally, take up a hobby that channels your emotions in a helpful way. Feeling angry? Sing heavy metal karaoke! Feeling sad? Paint a picture that captures your emotion. Whatever means of expression you choose, if it releases emotions inside you, you're on the right track. If you're not sure what creative venture might help you, take a class to try something new!

Coping Step 4: Relax!

How can you process your emotions in a healthy way if you barely have time to breathe? Give yourself time every day to relax, retreat, and disengage from your daily activities. Take a bath. Get a massage. Curl up with a good book. Take a long, quiet drive through the countryside. Whatever makes you feel calm and at peace and helps you to replenish your inner strength will help you through this process of coping.

Coping Step 5: Find Helpful Resources

As you may have guessed, I'm a huge advocate of seeking professional help from therapists, social workers, and other trained professionals during your separation. But you can look for inspiration from other resources, too. For example, reading the right self-help book can spark major insights and help you shift your perspective. You could also read inspiring stories from others who have gone through the process of separation (or any other challenging life event), watch movies that inspire you, or join a support group—whatever helps you feel great!

Coping Step 6: Focus on Your Successes

You have done a lot of amazing things in your life. Just because you are feeling at a low point right now doesn't mean that you have become less capable, successful, or accomplished. Take thirty minutes or so to reacquaint yourself with your successes, and bask in the knowledge that you have done some pretty great things.

Your successes could be any accomplishments that have meaning to you. For example, passing exams, having great friendships, having children, earning a degree, having a great job (now or in the past), helping in your community, caring for an elder, participating in a bike race, knowing how to build a website, reading a book every week … all of these things are accomplishments. If it helps, look at old photos, newspaper articles, trophies, or other memorabilia to remind you of your accomplishments. Sit with your own greatness until you feel it sink in—and remember that you're not done doing great things!

Coping Step 7: Push the Reset Button

No one else is going to go digging around in your mind and heart to build a new foundation for you. It's your responsibility, so you're the one who has to pay attention and push the reset button when your negative emotions are pushing you in the opposite direction of your vision.

Use your vision, goals, Five Commitments, and Positive IDs as reference points. Read your vision out loud. Review your Five Commitments and renew your dedication to yourself and your happiness. Go back to your Positive IDs and work with one at a time. Remind yourself of who you are, what you really want, and where you want your life to be. Then, say, "I will deal with this, because I committed to my vision for a happy life."

Empowered Actions

▶ Make a Plan to Deal with Your Emotions

Read the Coping Steps once more. This time, make notes for yourself about where, when, and how you can take action on each of these Steps. Write down which methods of coping seem the best for you, and which you want to investigate further. Then, write down three small action steps you will take to move yourself in the right direction today. Schedule your activities in your planner so you aren't tempted to let days go by!

▶ Find Additional Resources to Help You Cope

Depending on your situation, you may need more assistance with coping with your emotions. If this is the case, I encourage you to seek professional assistance from a therapist, psychologist, medical doctor, or other qualified professional. You can also look into the work of emotional separation expert Katherine Woodward Thomas, author of *Conscious Uncoupling: 5 Steps to Living Happily Even After*. As I mentioned in the Introduction, her work is a perfect complement to the Positive Separation Method and may help you go deeper into the emotional undercurrents of your separation process.

▶ Connect with Yourself

This week, set aside some time to connect with yourself and your emotions, and ask yourself, "What do I truly need to feel supported and stable right now?" Then, take some time to research and reach out to the professionals, resource centers, and others who will give you what you need to stay on solid emotional ground.

What Comes Next

After the work we've done in this chapter, I'm sure that you have some great ideas and techniques for managing your mindset and dealing with complicated emotions. You may also be feeling a little overwhelmed by the enormous task of identifying, processing, and coping with your emotions. It's okay. Take it easy on yourself, move forward one step at time, and ask for help when you need it.

You don't have to do it all alone. In fact, you shouldn't even try!

In the next chapter, I'll show you how to create your Winning Team so that you have constant support and encouragement in all areas of your life, and properly-equipped people to turn to when managing your mindset and emotions becomes more than you can handle on your own.

CHAPTER SEVEN

Create Your Winning Team

When I was still in the middle of my own divorce, I discovered why creating and relying on a Winning Team of friends, family, professionals, and resources is so important to Positive Separation. Just a few days after I created my vision for a happier future at that canal-side café (a story I shared with you in the Introduction), I met an acquaintance on the street. Her children went to school with my own kids, and we had chatted on a few occasions. Having heard about my divorce through the social grapevine, she asked how I was doing.

That was a low day. I'd had a vision of my happier future, yes, and taken some steps toward creating my positive commitments to myself, but I was still feeling frustrated, stuck, and very vulnerable. I hadn't yet disentangled myself from the whirlwind of emotions I was feeling. Plus, I was lonely. So when my acquaintance invited me to lunch at a nearby brasserie, I said yes.

As the rain poured down outside, I talked to my sort-of-friend about what was happening in my life and my divorce. I cried a bit (okay, a lot), and, in my need to vent my bottled-up emotions, ended up sharing some of the most intimate details of my private life.

Afterward, once I was drained and had no more words, I stared at my plate in horror. "What have I done?" I asked myself.

The issue wasn't that I was vulnerable, or even that I had gotten emotional. There's nothing wrong with crying on someone's shoulder. But what I had ignored in my need to unburden myself was how I felt about this woman, my casual acquaintance.

You see, this woman was not the kind of person I would want (on any other day) to have access to my personal information. From my mouth to her ears, and from her mouth to the ears of anyone who would listen, I knew that the deep, vulnerable secrets I had shared would soon be spreading like wildfire through our whole social network. I was terrified.

Usually, I have a nose for indiscretion, and I avoid sharing things I don't want spread around. But after suppressing my emotions for so long, they had just bubbled up and taken over. As a result, I felt like I had broken one of my most sacred promises to myself.

Thankfully, nothing terrible resulted from my emotional outpouring that day (although it caused me stress for weeks afterward as I blew the incident up like a balloon in my mind). There wasn't any backlash from my friends or acquaintances. Maybe they all let the woman's stories go in one ear and out the other, or maybe my fears of her gossiping were never actually warranted.

The positive outcome of this incident was that it planted a seed in my mind—and that seed grew into my Winning Team and the teachings I will share with you in this chapter.

I realized that there was an important lesson here for me: I needed to find steady, positive, discreet, nurturing people I could rely on when I was having a tough day. I needed to talk to people who cared about me on a regular basis so that I could prevent the kind of emotional eruption that had led me to share intimate details about my former marriage with a near-stranger whom I knew I couldn't trust. More, I needed to find professionals who could help me manage the challenging feelings that sometimes clouded my judgment and prompted me to make unhealthy or unhelpful decisions.

That night, after the kids were in bed, I lit some candles and reflected on what I needed to do in order to create the support system I needed and prevent another emotional blowout like this one from setting me back or diverting me from my focus on my happy future. Immediately, I flashed back to my student days. I was in my final months of study to obtain my Master's degree in law, and had just broken up with my boyfriend of two years. I'd been kind of a wreck then, too—but even at such a young age, I was also aware enough to know that I needed support from different people to get through this tough time. I remembered, vividly, how my family, friends, fellow students, teachers, and counselors each contributed to my healing and success in their own ways. A few months later, after graduation, I threw a celebratory dinner to thank them all.

Now, at forty, I realized that I needed to create another support net for myself—a Winning Team of friends, family, and professionals—if I wanted to heal and move forward.

I drew a circle with myself in the middle. Then, around that picture of myself, I wrote the names of everyone I thought would support me, my growth, and the best interests of my children. I wanted different things from each of these people: constructive advice, good laughs, shoulders to cry on. I wanted to find people to exercise and be active with, and people who would give me the kick in the pants I needed when I started to get down on myself. Most of all, I wanted to partner with people who were also aiming to create a happy future for themselves and everyone around them.

I realized that I also needed a professional family therapist who would understand the feelings and needs of my children during this process, and a different psychologist who could help me manage my own emotions; I was lucky enough to find Annelies and Willem, who became my staunch allies. Emma, my lawyer, and Edwin and Ruud, my accountants, were also part of my Winning Team, and helped me sort out all the details that had once felt so overwhelming.

With so many people to turn to, I never felt alone again. And because I had different people to fill different needs in my life, I never needed to rely on any one person too heavily. Soon, it became easy and natural to ask for help when I needed it. There were still hard days, but I never had to face them by myself, and I never again suffered the consequences of keeping everything bottled up inside of me.

Choosing Your Team Players

Once I formed my Winning Team, I no longer had to face my separation alone—and neither do you. You can and should seek help, knowledge, support, and love from others, but before you can do so in an empowered way, you need to *organize* that help.

The heat of an emotional moment (or worse, an actual crisis), is *not* the time to worry about who to call or who will give you the best advice. During those times, your judgment is not as sound as it usually is. You're not looking at the big picture. The last thing you want is to let your need for help create more negativity and drama.

Sometimes, in the thick of a separation, you can feel like you're drowning. Like I did that day in the brasserie, you will then reach out to whomever is closest, and hang onto them as tight as you can, hoping they will keep you afloat. As I discovered, this is not always the best idea, because the closest available person is often not the person who is best prepared to give you the support you really need.

Worse, when you reach out blindly, you may run into resistance from the very people you are asking for support. Some jealous or spiteful people will treat your separation as "payback time." Others may simply be too close to the situation to offer the help you need.

Even when it comes to the people who genuinely want to help, it's important to maintain balance. Try not to ask too much of any one person in your life. When others feel overloaded by your needs, they will step back—and there's nothing worse than feeling rebuffed by someone you care about when you're already lonely and vulnerable!

The solution to all of these issues? Your Winning Team.

Your Winning Team believes in you! Its members support you 100 percent, and are willing to go the extra mile for you. They have a positive attitude toward their own lives, as well as yours, and always deliver on their promises. From them, you can receive structure, comfort, energy, motivation, and wisdom.

A Winning Team is not just a loose collection of well-meaning friends, colleagues, family members, and others who love and support you. It's a network of people whom you hand-select to create a protective group structure around you as you go through your separation. Each person on your Team serves in a specific role or function for a period of three months (a time period which can be extended if mutually agreeable), and is chosen for his or her key qualities and abilities to carry out certain tasks.

Creating a Winning Team is one of the most practical and useful tools in the Positive Separation Method, and one of the biggest steps you will take in mastering the art of positive separation. Knowing that you are surrounded with people you can rely on provides a huge energy boost, and gives you an anchor when things get stormy. The results it produced for me—and that it continues to produce for the people I work with—are amazing. All it takes to create a Winning Team that works is a little bit of planning, clear sight, and defined boundaries.

FAMILY, FRIENDS AND YOUR WINNING TEAM

Everyone in your life will react to your separation in his or her own way. Some will react positively and supportively, and others negatively, angrily, or just plain incomprehensibly.

For example, family ties are often strengthened during a separation. You might find that your brother is suddenly there for you, your mother makes life easier for you on a daily basis, your aunt helps take care of your kids, and your financially-savvy uncle helps you figure out your financial situation. If this is happening, accept such help graciously, even when it's not easy to do so. You need all the help and support you can get right now!

Unfortunately, the opposite situation is also common. Some family members may not understand your decision, or may condemn you for your choices. They may be jealous of your new "freedom," or still harboring negative emotions about their own separations. They may be judgmental, gossipy, or just plain patronizing. Remember that you cannot influence their behavior; you can only control what *you* do in response to it. Try to adopt a neutral attitude, avoid getting sucked into negative discussions. If this is too difficult, try to avoid all but the most necessary interactions for a while, until you feel strong enough to deal with them.

Friendships, like family relationships, can go one of two ways in a separation. Some friendships become stronger, while others turn antagonistic, or simply disappear. The loss of your relationship is also, in a way, a loss for your friends, so this can also be a confusing and emotional time for them as well. I know that sounds crazy, but it's true. Your friends are used to relating to you as part of a couple, and when you are no longer paired, it requires your friends to make a mental shift around the relationship.

For shared friends, a separation can often be especially difficult, since they often don't know how to react or whether they should take sides. Remember that, during your separation, you are bound to be extra-sensitive, and certain friends' reactions to your situation might be more painful than expected. If this happens, just keep focusing on yourself and what you have to do, and remain confident that the friendships which really contribute to your life, happiness, and well-being will emerge from this time even stronger than they were before.

The bottom line is, you should not allow your relationships with friends or family to disrupt your progress or undermine your vision of a positive future. So, if you find yourself battling to keep negative behavior at bay, or feel drained every time you have contact with your family, a certain friend, or a particular group of people, try to maintain a safe distance. Avoid arguments, even if you feel like you're being treated unfairly. You don't need any additional drama right now. Instead, express your frustrations to people who you trust, and with whom you feel safe—the people who ultimately will become members of your Winning Team.

HOW TO CHOOSE YOUR WINNING TEAM

Putting together your Winning Team is a serious business that deserves a great deal of careful thought. It will require you to look honestly at the people in your life, and evaluate your relationships with them based on key criteria. I think it's best to do this in a single sitting, so set aside two to three hours to set up and connect with your Team members as soon as your schedule allows. (Hint: Connecting in person or by phone is best!)

Your Team consists of roughly four to eight people. Some of them will be personal Team members, people with whom you have an emotional bond and whom you trust with certain aspects of your life, emotions, and separation process. The rest of your Team will be made up of professionals whom you can rely on and who have your best interests at heart. (You may already be working with these professionals; if not, find and connect with them as soon as possible.) You should trust your entire Team implicitly, and know for certain that they will deal with your information, emotions, and needs in a confidential, trustworthy way.

Personal Team members

Professional Team members

Your Winning Team

Chances are, you already have some ideas about who should be on your Winning Team; these are the people and professionals who are already offering you constructive support, guidance, and care. Then, there may be people you want to include, but aren't as sure of. Don't let guilt or obligation get in the way of your selection process. Your best friend will stay your best friend, and your mom will stay your mom, even if they aren't the right fit for your Winning Team.

Start your planning with a blank page, and assign Team positions based on who is the best fit for the role, not who you feel you *should* ask. Remember, just because someone in your life doesn't make your Winning Team (for any reason) doesn't mean that they shouldn't be part of your life, or even part of your separation process. It just means that you will not rely on them for any of the specific tasks or support mechanisms you have assigned to your Team members. In other words, the love and support non-Team members offer is a bonus!

Here are some guidelines for choosing the members of your Winning Team:

Ask yourself, "What do I need?" In which areas do you most need support? Are you looking for a reassuring voice, someone to make you laugh, financial expertise, a realistic and objective perspective, an accountability partner, a workout partner, positive energy, coaching, or mentorship? Should this help be private, professional, or both?

Make a list of all the areas where you want to receive support, physical, mental, emotional, practical, and professional.

Make a list of potential Team members. Include trusted friends, family, colleagues, and professional resources you already have.

Assign a specific function to each Team member. If you don't have someone to fill a specific need (for example, if you want to work with a trained psychologist and don't currently have one), note that you need to find that person.

Contact your potential Team members. As soon as your schedule allows (preferably within the next three days), call your potential Team members to explain the idea of a Winning Team, and ask them if they want to be part of yours. Explain the specific task you want to assign to them, and set a specific timetable for your work together. (In my experience, three months is a great start.) For example, you could say, "Alice, would you like to be my positive energy partner? This means that I want for us to check in once a week for three months, and for you to help me reframe things in a positive way. I will also call you when I need positive reinforcement at other times during the week. Do you think you can step into this role for me?"

Describe how you intend to deal with your separation, based on your vision for your future, your Five Commitments, your goals, and your Positive IDs. Share the steps you have already taken to move forward in your new life—such as disconnecting from your old relationship, creating your vision, setting goals, and identifying your Positive IDs—and which you still plan to take. Talk about the emotions you find difficult to deal with, and the things that are the hardest for you. Your Team members will then understand how they can give you the help you need.

Understand each Team member's role. Your personal Team members are there to support you emotionally and practically, each in their own way. Your professional Team members are there to offer expertise and help you solve particular problems. Commit to honoring the role each of your Team members has agreed to. (In other words, don't ask your financial consultant to talk with you about your emotions, and don't ask your "positive energy" Team member for financial advice!)

Keep your Team members updated on your progress, and regularly ask them for feedback.

Always be honest with your Team members. That's the only way they will be able to really help you. If at any point you realize that you are not receiving what you need from one of your Team members, or that you simply aren't working well with that person, don't be afraid to speak up and find someone else with whom you connect in a more positive and helpful way.

PERSONAL TEAM MEMBERS

Here are some examples of Winning Team positions that you might fill during your Team creation process. Remember, this is all based on what *you* need! Don't worry about getting it all in place on the first try.

If you find out down the road that you need support in a new area, just open up a new spot on your Winning Team.

Your Personal Team members might include:

The comforter. This person is your big, strong shoulder to cry on—the person with endless patience, the perfect listener who understands that you need somebody to whom you can tell your story, even if it's for the hundredth time.

The sensible one. This friend offers practical advice and constructive criticism, and always keeps you on course (even when you feel like jumping in five directions at once). S/he will push you forward on your positive path, and offer reliable, straightforward wisdom and feedback whenever you need it.

The positive energy partner. This friend is the one who always sees the light at the end of the tunnel, and can reframe any situation in a positive light. Call on this person when you're having trouble seeing the blessings in a situation and need a new perspective.

The communications director. This is an honest and level-headed person who will look at all of your important e-mails and letters before you send them to your ex-partner or third parties. This person can save you a great deal of grief by intercepting reactive or impulsive communications that you might later regret, and can keep you from engaging in passive-aggressive tactics or victim behavior. This person should be willing to look at things several times over the course of each week.

Note: Evenings and nights are danger zones to send anything to your ex, your lawyer, or anyone else directly involved in your separation. This includes voicemails, text messages, e-mails, and images. Promise yourself—and your communications director—that you will only send such communications in broad daylight, and only after checking in!

The pick-you-up Team member. This friend is someone who makes you feel better as soon as you think of him/her. With this friend, you should only do fun things that give you positive energy. Make an agreement that, when you see each other, you will spend no more than fifteen minutes talking about your separation.

The numbers whiz. This person is someone who's good with money, budgets, and planning. Start with an intensive session to go over where you are now and address your concerns about budgeting. Then, once a month or so, ask this person to help you go over your bills, budgets, and financial plans to be sure you're staying on track.

Note: This person does not need to be a financial professional, just someone who is good with money and who can help you make positive everyday decisions. You will want to include professional financial advisors on your Team as well.

The role model. This person is your source of inspiration in dealing with your separation and with life when things get tough. They have been through their own life dramas and setbacks, and are now living the kind of life you want to live!

Note: This person can be someone you know, or a public figure. If you know them personally, ask if they will act as your mentor—but always stick to what they can teach you about moving upward!

The fitness buddy. This Team member motivates you to continue to work out and stay in shape (or to start doing so), even if you really don't feel like it. They might come with you to the gym, yoga and meditation classes, or on outdoor hikes. Whatever activities you do with this person, they should feel nourishing to your body.

The hobbyist. With this friend, you almost never talk about your separation. S/he simply takes you along to all kinds of activities related to your shared hobby.

The companion in adversity. This person is also going through a difficult personal situation. S/he could be a friend, a colleague, or a member of a support group. You encourage each other and have similar goals—namely, getting through your situation in the most positive and uplifting way possible. You share advice and practical tips.

Note: Be careful not to let your talks with your companion in adversity turn into blame-and-shame sessions. Always stay focused on moving forward, not looking back. If you feel like this person is taking energy away from you instead of helping you build yourself up, s/he may not be the right fit for your Winning Team at this time.

As you create your Winning Team using the roles above (or designing your own), be very clear about each person's role. Try not to let those roles get mixed up, or ask anyone to take on more than what they've agreed to. Also, remember that not everyone in your circle needs to be on your Winning Team, and you can allow any Team member to go back to being a friend with no special job at any time.

People Who Should *Never* Be Part of Your Winning Team

No matter how much they want to help you, the following people should *never* be part of your Winning Team during your separation. Having them on your Team will only cause complications, lack of clarity, and extra drama for you.

Your children. Even if they are adults, your children should not be involved in the emotional or physical details of your separation. Don't burden them with your emotions and physical tasks, and don't discuss your separation with them any more than is necessary or comfortable for both them and you. Most importantly, don't discuss your ex-partner with them unless it relates directly to their own health, safety, or situation. (For more on how to support your children in separation, see Chapter Twelve.)

A new partner. Your Team members are there to help you get through your separation. Your new partner (if you have one) is part of your new life and your new path, and is there to help you build your new future. Involving your new partner in your separation will likely introduce negative energy, which will make things harder for you in the long run. (You can find more information about how to integrate a new partner into your life in Chapter Twelve.)

Negative helpers, status-quo helpers and attention seekers. *Negative helpers* give you the feeling that they are, intentionally or unintentionally, working against you. They make promises—like promising to make you dinner, pass on the phone number of a talented professional, or take you out for a fun evening over the weekend—but don't deliver. They tell you that you can always depend upon them, but when you need them, they're never there. They tell you that you can trust them, then spread stories behind your back. In short, they block your progress. Stay away from them!

Status-quo helpers, such as your father, mother, siblings, or friends, may want to be useful but aren't able to help you progress toward your vision and goals. They themselves may be disappointed or upset by the entire separation, or may simply be afraid of the change that your separation is bringing. Or, their idea of "helping" might be less than helpful to you (like the friend who wants to go to the bar three times a week). You can love and have fun with your status-quo helpers, but don't rely on them to help you move forward.

Finally, *attention seekers* feel that they have been unlucky or treated unfairly and deserve better in life. They try to make every situation about them, and only want to hear about your situation insofar as it gives them an opportunity to complain about theirs. If you don't help them or do what they want, or if you don't take their advice or join in their plans, they become obstinate or angry. Don't waste your energy trying to please an attention seeker. Right now, you need to focus on yourself!

If you are having trouble separating any of the above people from your process, ask yourself, "What is this person providing that is helpful and positive in my separation? Is there someone else who could give me what this person is giving, but in a more positive and uplifting way?"

PROFESSIONAL TEAM MEMBERS

Professional Team members are exactly what they sound like: members of your Winning Team who have professional experience or expertise in a certain field related to your health and wellness, the practical and judicial aspects of your separation, or both. These people provide you with information and practical help in settling your separation and functioning on a day to day basis. They become part of your Winning Team as soon as you ask them for assistance.

You may already be working with one or more professionals such as lawyers, doctors, therapists, or others. If you feel like they are genuinely helpful to you, invite them onto your Winning Team. If not, find different people to work with who will help you stay on your positive track toward your new life.

Your Professional Team members might include:

- A lawyer
- An experienced mediator
- An experienced coach
- One or more financial experts (such as accountants, financial planners, investment advisors, or pension consultants)
- One or more health professionals (such as your general practitioner, other physicians, psychologists, psychiatrists, physical therapists, etc.)
- One or more child experts (such as social workers, education specialists, child psychologists, family coaches, etc.)
- One or more helpers from other institutions such as your church, local charities, or other institutions

There is a stigma in some social circles about obtaining professional help, especially in the areas of mental health, physical health, and support for children.

However, receiving good professional help right from the start can be crucial for a positive settlement of your separation and for getting yourself and your life back on a positive track. Don't be afraid to utilize whatever resources are at your disposal. As long as you connect with and trust the professionals you choose to help you, they will be indispensable members of your Winning Team.

At the same time, you must always remember that *you* are responsible for dealing with your separation and settling it in all areas, including physical, mental, and emotional. You can't delegate this responsibility to a professional. Weekly therapy sessions will avail you nothing unless you do your own inner work the other six days!

Professional Team Members from Your Work Setting

During your separation, it's very important for you to be able to continue functioning effectively at work. Work provides you with financial security and a sense of structure, and also gives you something to think about besides your separation.

It's a good idea to inform your employer about your separation, in confidence, as soon as possible after the decision to separate has been made. After all, the major changes you will be going through in your private life are bound to have an effect on your work, and there will be practical and legal matters that you will sometimes also need to deal with during working hours. Ask about any options available for additional job-related support, so that you can take preventive action if necessary. By doing so, you will avoid being "secretive," and also reduce your risk of job underperformance or absenteeism.

Examples of work-related Winning Team members might include an HR officer, staff welfare officer, company psychologist, company medical officer, or any other professionals contacted via your employer.

If you do choose to add someone from your work environment to your Winning Team, be sure that this person is able to help you in the specific areas you need, and that they are able to maintain confidentiality without causing conflict in their obligations to your employer.

Tips for working with Professional Team Members:

- **Specify what help you are looking for.** Be clear about what kind of support you need, and the number of weeks or months you think you will need it for.

- **Don't expect a professional to be there for you on a 24/7 basis** (unless you're dealing with a mental health emergency). Your separation is part of your professional Team member's work schedule.

- **Talk about the specific things you find difficult, and the challenges you are facing.** By doing so, you avoid receiving cookie-cutter solutions, and allow each of your Team members to shine in his or her own expertise.

- **Discuss the costs beforehand.** During your first conversation with a professional, ask explicitly about the potential costs involved, and ask for monthly invoices and updates. If you are working with health professionals, be sure that your insurance covers the services you plan to use—and if it doesn't, that you are comfortably able to pay for those services. (Hint: You can also reduce costs by reducing unnecessary emotional phone calls, e-mails, and office visits. Remember, you are engaging professional time and resources, so every minute costs money.)

Empowered Action

▶ Make Your Winning Team

Set aside about two hours for this exercise.

Make yourself a cup of tea or coffee, and get out your notebook. Reread the guidelines above for selecting your Personal and Professional Winning Team members, and select the people you want to be your support structure in your separation.

Remember, you'll want to choose four to eight people to be Team members, including the professionals you plan to work with. Don't rush this exercise. Think carefully about the people you are inviting to be part of your Team. After all, your Winning Team is your best investment toward your happy future!

What to Do in a Crisis

In the coming months, it's possible that, despite being surrounded by your excellent Winning Team, you will go through a crisis moment. All the lights seem to turn red at the same time, nothing seems to be working anymore, and you feel like you're in freefall.

Going through a crisis period is nothing to be ashamed of; it happens at some point to all of us. But, like a hurricane or a tornado, both the crisis itself and its aftermath can be made easier by having a solid "emergency response" plan in place.

When you're in a crisis situation, sometimes it feels harder to ask for help and delegate tasks than to try to handle it all yourself. You can end up feeling alone and overwhelmed, even though you have a great Winning Team, simple because you don't have the energy or time to tell them what you need from them.

While things are calm, speak to your Winning Team members about a plan for crisis situations. For example, you might tell your personal Team members that, if any of them receive a text message or phone call from you with an agreed-upon code word (or simply the word "help"), that person will immediately take the lead in providing you with short-term emergency support. You can specify the support beforehand so that no delegating needs to be done in the moment. Also, if support is needed in more than one area, Team members can coordinate amongst themselves (be sure that everyone has the relevant phone numbers and/or e-mail addresses of other Team members).

Here's an example of how this planning worked for me. On one really bad day, I was full of anxiety and just couldn't seem to get it together. I reached out for help, and within a few hours my comforter friend showed up with flowers and cooked a meal for me and the kids. My lawyer phoned, and helped me reframe my emotions on a letter I had received earlier, and my family coach made room for me in her very full schedule so we could meet up the next morning. Thanks to the help of my Winning Team, I was back on track and brimming with love and gratitude in less than twenty-four hours.

When you set up your emergency response system in this way, you can always count on the fact that someone (or many someones) will be available whenever you need help, with minimal effort on your part.

What to Do When You Don't Have Enough People to Fill Your Team

One of the common issues I hear from my clients is that they don't have enough people living close by—or enough people in their lives, period—who can act as members of their Winning Team.

There are many reasons why you might not have enough people in your inner circle to make up a great personal Winning Team. Perhaps your closest friends are too involved in your separation to be objective. Perhaps you've recently moved to a new city and don't have your usual support system around you. Or perhaps you simply don't have a broad social circle. Not to worry: you can still create a successful Winning Team for yourself!

If your personal Winning Team doesn't feel well-rounded, see where you can fill in some of the roles with professional Team members. Instead of workout buddy, consider a personal trainer. Instead of a hobbyist, find an instructor. You'll get many of the same benefits—and meet new people in the meantime!

You can also reach out to support groups for help, especially if you don't have someone to turn to for comfort and a shoulder to cry on. You may even find new friends and mentors through such groups. However, be careful of groups that repeatedly let you fall into the victim trap, or that spend more time rehashing the past than looking to the future. You need inspiration more than commiseration right now!

More Ways to Work With Your Winning Team

Getting Feedback

Once a month, ask your Winning Team members (private and professional) for suggestions on how to deal with matters more effectively. Ask them if they have any practical advice, suggestions, or actions that might help you approach your separation and daily life in an even more positive way.

If you get feedback that you're not happy with, don't slide into victim mode. Your Winning Team member isn't attacking you; s/he is trying to help! For example, if your sensible friend says that you're exhibiting victim behavior, try not to get defensive, or write him/her off for "not supporting you." Instead, ask yourself, "Why did this feedback bother me? What do I not want to see or acknowledge about myself right now?" Same goes when your "numbers whiz" suggests that you might be spending too much money right now given your budget and the uncertainty of your situation. S/he has an objective viewpoint that you don't share right now, and is trying to help you prevent a financial meltdown.

Most of the time, when you react to feedback, it will be because of situations like those described above, where you are momentarily unable to see the merit in the advice given. However, if you truly feel like a Winning Team member is giving you non-constructive feedback, or doesn't have your best interests at heart, feel free to ask them to step down.

Above all, your Winning Team should be a network of positive, helpful, and growth-oriented processes. If it feels otherwise for you, make the necessary changes so that you are getting what you need.

Gather Your Winning Team for a Celebration!

At some point, you will feel that your separation is behind you. When that happens, express your appreciation to your Team members by giving each of them a small gift, or by inviting them all to get together. It's a good way to officially and positively mark the end of a difficult period in your life while acknowledging all that your friends, family, and professional Team members have done for you.

Empowered Actions

▶ Team Mapping

Draw a picture of your Winning Team. Start with your own name (or a picture of yourself) in a circle in the center of a blank page; then, add your Winning Team members with their assigned functions in a circle around you. Keep a copy of this diagram at home and at work (if you work outside the home). That way, if something comes up with regard to emotions, planning, focus, or other issues, you can quickly see who you need to call. Notice how having this diagram helps you feel more supported and prepared.

▶ Make a Plan to Deal with Your Emotions

Read the Coping Steps in Chapter Six once more. This time, make notes for yourself about where, when, and how you will receive support on each of these Steps. Decide which of your Team members can best help you with each Step, and how. Add this information to your plan of action.

▶ Schedule Daily Check-ins

Plan to connect with at least one member of your Winning Team each day, or in conjunction with appointments when you will need their support. Schedule these check-ins in your planner so you don't let them slide by. For example, you might talk to your therapist on Tuesdays, your exercise buddy on Wednesdays, your "hobbyist" on Thursdays, your "comforter" on Fridays, your "positive energy partner" on the weekend, etc. This gives you something to look forward to each day, and makes sure no single Team member feels overwhelmed.

What Comes Next

Hooray! You have come a long way toward empowering yourself, reconnecting to your core, and establishing a solid support system that will carry you through your separation and beyond!

Next, we will enter Step 4 of the Positive Separation Method, and focus on all of the ways you can care for your heart, mind, and body in the coming weeks, months, and years. Combined with the planning and emotional work we've already done and the knowledge you've gained so far in this book, these strategies will support your daily functioning and help you connect even more deeply to who you are, feel better each and every day, and ultimately create your happy, healthy, positive life!

POSITIVE SEPARATION STEP 4

Take Loving Action to Care for Yourself

Take Loving Action to Care for Yourself

Congratulations on coming this far! You've done some hard work, and taken solid steps toward creating greater structure and support for yourself in your separation. Step 4 of the Positive Separation Method is really all about celebrating you, honoring your connection to yourself, and gaining a deeper sense of commitment to your balanced and positive new life.

You've already created (or are on your way to creating) a framework to manage yourself through the first phases of your separation and your new life. In Steps 1 and 2 of the Positive Separation Method, we learned how to rebuild and create a sense of stability, continuity, direction, and empowerment. In Step 3, we connected with the truth of who you are through your Positive IDs, set some parameters around your mindset, learned some healthy ways to process strong emotions, and created your amazing, supportive Winning Team.

Even if you haven't fully implemented the tools, exercises, and skills in Steps 1 through 3, there's no better time than now to get into a daily routine of self-nourishment so that you can stay aligned, balanced, healthy, and on track as you move through the weeks and months to come.

Step 4 of the Positive Separation Method is less about the kind of personal growth work we did in Step 3, and more about practical actions you can take in your physical world to nourish and sustain all aspects of yourself. In this Step, you'll learn why a positive environment is critical to realizing your vision and goals for your new life. I will share some tools to help you integrate self-care and personal nourishment into your daily and weekly plans. You'll learn why taking care of your physical body, clearing out clutter and baggage (both tangible and metaphorical) from your environment, and prioritizing time for you to actually relax are key to keeping your energy levels and spirit elevated so you can grow stronger every day in this new life you're creating.

This work is vital to mastering the art of positive separation because when you give your mind, body, and spirit what they need to thrive and grow into your new, happy life, you will have even more energy and stamina to keep making that "uphill journey"! It's all about loving your body and moving through the coming days, weeks, and months in an empowered way.

Remember, this process is all about honoring yourself in this phase of your life, and creating the new life you envisioned in Step 1. If anything I suggest feels overwhelming to you right now, don't worry; you can always take it in smaller chunks. The goal of Step 4 is not to burden you with extra tasks and to-dos, but to help you comfort yourself during challenging times and create a new framework for your life that will provide you with the most energy, joy, and support possible, every single day.

Are you ready to dive in?

I thought so! Let's go!

CHAPTER EIGHT

Your Positive Environment

Your Positive IDs, Winning Team, and new, hopeful mindset are important resources that will help you through the turbulence of your separation; give you structure, focus, and support in times of chaos; and keep you centered in your positive vision for your future. However, you won't be able to use any of these assets to their fullest capacities if your everyday environment—including your home, your routines, and the body you live in—are full of pain and negativity.

SOPHIA'S STORY

My client Sophia discovered the power of a positive environment when she broke up with her fiancé. By taking care of herself, her body, and her space, she created a sanctuary for her own renewal.

"Jim and I fell in love in an instant," she says. "We didn't want to spend a single day apart, and moved in together almost immediately. For the first time in my life, I had really opened up to a man. He was my greatest love, and I fell unconditionally into his arms and into his life.

"For months, I was feeling and looking radiant. My friends and family were all so happy for me. My grown children would visit us on weekends and holidays, and loved him nearly as much as I did. His own kids felt just the same. For a long time, it felt like an ideal situation.

"I don't know exactly when it changed, or what happened. Things were not as beautiful as they looked, but I couldn't admit it. I was so much in love, and so much wanted Jim to be the man I thought he was when we met. I went along with whatever he wanted, and made choices that I knew were not right for me just to keep the peace. I thought maybe there was something wrong with me—that I wasn't seeing things clearly, and that if I just tried harder, everything would be okay. But no matter how hard I tried, things continued to deteriorate.

"Tensions built up. We kept up appearances with friend and family, but I was miserable. I put on weight. I was perpetually stressed out. We tried couples' therapy, but we were just on different frequencies. No matter what we did, we couldn't seem to get on the same page.

"One day, after a week of awful fights, I stood in front of the mirror and really looked at myself. Was this the woman I remembered myself to be—the woman who loved to live, to laugh, to create? When had I become so small and sad? When was the last time I had really smiled? Was my love for Jim as big as I thought it was, or had I just become frightened to live on my own? I didn't have any answers—but I felt a new fire in my heart, a burning desire to get back to myself.

"Shaken, with tears flowing down my cheeks, I went out to the garden, where he was reading the newspaper. 'I'm leaving you,' I said. 'I'm going to pack my things, and in two weeks, I'll be gone.' He protested, and got really upset. But I had let him influence my decisions for too long. He was not going to have any say over my life anymore.

"I didn't know where I would go, but even the shed at my parents' house was better than where I was. I had made my decision, and that was final.

"I didn't give myself time to think. An hour later, I had packed a bag and was on the road to my parents' house. On my way there, I thought back on the many challenges I had faced in my life. Partway through the two-hour trip, my tears evaporated, and I was able to get a clear picture of my situation. I had decided to leave Jim because I wanted to take care of myself. That meant that I needed a plan—but where should I start?

"My parents were loving and caring, and didn't ask too many questions. Before going to bed that night, I did a search for information about breaking up, and came across the Positive Separation Method. I scheduled coaching time with Eveline, emailed my clients to let them know I was taking time off from work (I work as a freelancer), and sat down to figure things out.

"The way I saw it, I needed a roof over my head, a car, daily structure, love, companionship, and space to work on my emotions. Well, first things first!

"I found a sweet little cabin for rent on the Veluwe, in the eastern part of Holland near the forest. I could move in within a week! It was a far cry from the luxurious home where I'd lived with Jim, but it was a perfect sanctuary for me in the midst of so much uncertainty.

"I spent the next two weeks driving between Jim's house and my new home. Clothes, hobby gear, and household items went into my tiny car, one by one. Every time I unpacked a load, I went through a little ritual. I washed all my clothes before hanging them in the cupboard. I polished all my shoes before putting them away. I cleaned all my gear and kitchen items. It was like I was washing off my old life and all the negative feelings attached to it.

"I created my Winning Team the week after I announced my separation. I really needed to talk to wise people, especially during those first few months. My trusted friend agreed to take the job of advisor, and I felt so grateful for her honest advice, even when it was hard to hear. She kept my focus pointed like an arrow at my future. Another friend sent me funny and sweet messages every day; I loved reading them when I woke up. FaceTime was really helpful to me, too; since I was alone in the country, it was great to see familiar, smiling faces every day.

"Despite my empowering choice to separate from a relationship that wasn't working, and despite the amazing love and support of my Winning Team, my self-worth was at an all-time low. My actions looked like those of a confident, grown-up woman, but inside I felt scattered and scared, like a little girl left alone in the dark. I've always been a small person (I'm five-foot-three) but for the first time ever, I felt like a little mouse, too small to stand up in my life.

"In the beginning, I felt so miserable all alone in my new cabin that I thought I would choke. It was as if there was a big stone on my heart. Lying in the dark, I felt panicked and powerless—like a ghost of myself.

"I decided to focus on taking care of my body. It gave me structure, something to hold on to. I bought fresh flowers for my kitchen ever week. I kept my house warm and cozy, and only wore comfortable clothes. I started eating healthily again, and made the act of preparing each meal a kind of meditation. As I chopped vegetables and fruits, I focused on every little motion and let my negative emotions drift away. It was so much easier to eat well now that I was on my own again. I hadn't realized how often Jim and I ate too much, or too late, or in a rush. I tried to get more sleep, wake up on time, and get plenty of fresh air and sunlight. Although work did give me much-needed structure, I had to resist the temptation to bury myself in work or stay at my computer all day!

"I also made more time to engage with my creative self, a part of me I had neglected while my children were living at home and when I was living with Jim. I looked for classes to fill my free time, and looked forward to seeing people in a social setting. I loved telling my Winning Team about my 'adventures,' like what I was making, the models I had to draw in class, the sculpting and painting techniques I was discovering, and my new Tai Chi moves.

"Part of taking care of myself was cutting off communication with my ex. For many weeks, Jim tried very hard to get me back, but I knew that I couldn't get swept up in that drama. I blocked his telephone number. I stopped following him, his family, and his friends on social media the day I moved out. I thanked my 'family in law' for their love and friendship, and asked my own friends and family not to engage with him until the storm had passed.

"As I took care of myself physically, I also let my emotions take center stage, and started 'studying' myself. Why hadn't I taken better care of myself? Why hadn't I left the relationship when I first realized things were not right? How had I ended up feeling so trapped? I had betrayed myself, and I needed to understand how and why if I wanted to keep it from happening again. I realized that I had been avoiding many strong emotions for a long time. Now that I had created a positive, nurturing environment for myself, I needed to live through all of the negative emotions I'd been ignoring, and embrace them so I could move on.

"Grieving and letting go happens in phases. You're not just going to be 'over it' in three months, or six months, or whatever. You need to give yourself the time you need, and not force it. You need to get back all the parts of yourself that you let slip away.

"It took time for me to return to myself, but because I concentrated on structuring positive circumstances for myself, my 'recovery' went much quicker than it otherwise might have. In the beginning, I really had to plan it. It would have been very easy to slide downward. But the more I stuck to my commitments to myself, kept looking after my body and my heart, and made my life as wonderful as it could be under the circumstances, the easier it all became. It was a total package.

"Now, I have a much better understanding of what is good for me, and what is not. That process started with forgiving Jim, forgiving myself, and forgiving us both for creating a relationship that didn't work out. We both did the best we could under the circumstances. I've learned to cherish the happy memories, and learn from the rest. That is really precious, because it means I will never go back to where I was before. I have returned to myself, and that makes me proud. My future is radiant and promising—and although I am still only five feet three inches small, I know I can once again stand up to anything that comes my way!"

***

Setting up positive circumstances was Sophia's key to unlock her new life. The more she took care of her body and maintained a positive environment, the easier it was for her to process her challenging emotions in a healthy, supported way. She's truly a wonderful example of how this Step of the Positive Separation Method can set the tone for your new, happy life!

Positive Thoughts + Positive Actions = A More Positive Life

Regardless of what you're dealing with right now, you, too, can create a positive environment for yourself to bolster your energy, give yourself space to rest and relax, and protect you from any outside negativity related to your separation. As simple as it may seem, this energy-boosting is a key component of my work, and of the Positive Separation Method. The moments of positivity you experience throughout your day will keep you as energized as possible, and make you more receptive to new thoughts, opportunities, and people (as well as more resistant to thoughts, opportunities, and people that are negative or unhelpful to you).

Many studies have shown that a positive mindset is very energizing, but it doesn't happen by itself. You have to work at it in a focused and proactive manner.

THE INTERNAL PROCESS: POSITIVE THOUGHTS

You can influence your own thoughts to a large degree, perhaps even more than you think. In a separation, it's common to have negative thoughts—and there's nothing wrong with that. However, if you allow those dark thoughts to keep circling endlessly inside your head, you will waste a great deal of valuable energy on anger, fear, sadness, and other negative emotions. This will, in turn, create stress, which (as we know) can have major physical impact, and can prompt you to lash out in ways that you will later regret.

The longer the life cycle of a negative thought, the more likely it is to impact you in a negative way. That's why, when you notice one, it's important to gently set it aside and replace it with a more positive thought.

Sometimes, we aren't even aware of our negative thought patterns, because our negative thoughts sound like the same thoughts we've always had. If this is the case for you, it's a great idea to take the time to notice and write down your everyday thoughts. That way, you can evaluate which are helpful to you, and which are not.

Positive thoughts lead to positive feelings and positive actions. Negative thoughts lead to negative feelings and negative actions. This means that your thoughts can either be your greatest ally or your worst enemy during your separation. Yes, your thoughts have that much power! Every negative spiral, every regrettable action, and every emotional obstacle can be prevented, or at least minimized, if you can keep your negative thoughts from taking over.

Identifying and changing your negative thoughts takes time, patience, and practice—but the more you do it, the easier it gets. Soon, whenever your mind is heading for negative territory, you will feel it, and be able to intercept it before it even gets there!

THE EXTERNAL PROCESS: POSITIVE ACTIONS

Creating an enjoyable and positive environment for yourself is not only necessary, it's also fun. It stimulates positive thinking and encourages positive feelings.

You don't need to move to a new city, renovate your home, or spend a lot of money to create a positive environment for yourself. All you need to do is create small pockets of positivity in your everyday routine—moments that make you feel good and that encourage positive thoughts and grateful feelings. These pockets will then expand to displace the shrinking pockets of negativity.

You can also focus your attention on transforming (or at least neutralizing) potentially negative situations (which lead to negative thoughts and actions). Either you can try to avoid such situations altogether, or you can try to link them to positive situations. For example, if you're expecting a difficult meeting with your ex, plan to follow it up with a more positive experience, such as watching a film with a friend, enjoying a cup of coffee in a favorite café, or taking a stroll in the park. Then, when you look back on that day, you will remember the loving care you took for yourself, instead of only negativity and drama. If you can't find a way to link a negative situation with a positive one, at least try to even out the dose of stress you'll be receiving that day; for example, you could go to the gym before your meeting so that you are calmer and more balanced in the stressful situation.

Thinking about your contacts and relationships with the people in your life can also be helpful. Take note of what effects the people in your life have on you. After spending time with them, do you feel uplifted and energized, or depressed and drained? For now, try to minimize your contact with those who don't help you create positive moments, or who drain your energy.

Empowered Actions

▶ Revisit Your Five Commitments

In Chapter Four, you made your Five Commitments to yourself. When you get distracted by negative thoughts, refer back to these Commitments and read them aloud to yourself to reaffirm them. Staying true to your promises to yourself is a great way to keep your mind on a positive track.

▶ Track Your Thoughts

Every time you have a negative thought, make a mark on your hand with a pen. As soon as a positive thought comes by, cross it out. At the end of the day, tally how many negative thoughts you were able to change—and congratulate yourself!

▶ Create Positive Associations

Look at your calendar for the next several weeks. Are there meetings, events, or other commitments that you anticipate will be negative or stressful? Schedule other, positive events as "links" to these stressful ones as soon as possible. (Also, alert your Winning Team that these times may require some extra love and support!)

▶ Identify the Positive and Negative People in Your Life

When making your plans for the week, note which engagements you are looking forward to, and which you are dreading. Just like you did when creating your Winning Team, consider how each person in your life makes you feel. Try to minimize contact with those who don't help you feel like you're moving forward.

TAKE SMALL STEPS TO CREATE POSITIVE CIRCUMSTANCES EVERY DAY

Each day, create "pockets" of positive energy for yourself. You can do this in small ways or big ways.

Small and Simple Positive Pockets

- **Read the newspaper** in the morning sun.
- **Go for a walk outside**, rain or shine (30 minutes is enough to reset your energy).
- **Notice how nature greets you,** even in the city, with trees, flowers, birds, and sunshine.
- **Take a new road home** from work, instead of your usual route.
- **Check out a coffee house** or restaurant you have never been to before.
- **Buy freshly-baked rolls** for breakfast (or make them yourself).
- **Put fresh flowers on your table,** and make sure to pause and smell them when you walk by.
- **Carve out time each week** for your favorite (or new) hobby.
- **Have coffee or tea with a positive friend** on your lunch break.
- **Make a favorite treat** that you loved as a child.
- **Make a "happy table" in the corner** of your living room or kitchen. Fill it with flowers, a happy picture of yourself, candles, talismans, or anything else that makes you smile and feel good.
- **Listen to your favorite songs** at full blast (and maybe dance, too)!
- **Take a long, leisurely shower** or bath.
- **Put on your favorite clothes**, even if you have nowhere particularly special to go.
- **Stop to pick wildflowers** on the roadside.
- **Prepare an elaborate breakfast** or dinner for yourself, and take the time to enjoy every bite.
- **Get out some old photo albums,** and look at pictures of yourself when you were smiling and happy. Connect to that feeling of joy.

- **Turn on some lights** (inside and outside) before you leave the house so you will feel welcomed when you come home.
- **Take a long walk on the beach,** in the forest, or underneath the full moon.
- **Light candles** around your home.
- **Put a bottle of "positive water" in your fridge.** Each day for a week, speak a positive thought to it. Then, drink it! (If you're curious about this method, check out the work of Masaru Emoto and how emotion affects water.)

More Positive Pockets

These pockets require a little bit more time and commitment, but the rewards are well worth it!

- **This coming weekend, do something that you've wanted to do for a long time**—like seeing a film, going on a hiking trip, or taking a pottery or cooking class.
- **Call a friend you haven't seen in a long time** and make plans to have dinner or go on an excursion.
- **Take a day trip** to a town or city you haven't seen before.
- **Repair three things at home** that need fixing.
- **Bow out of an obligatory engagement** that you don't want to attend (like a birthday party or work gathering) and treat yourself to a spa day, day trip, or new experience instead. (Don't feel guilty; you can send a card and a gift in the mail, or ask a friend to bring it for you!)
- **Tidy up your house** and open all the windows for a while, even if it's winter. You'll feel better and your house will feel fresh.
- **Create one clutter-free room** in your house where you can go to relax.

Eliminate Negative Moments and Circumstances

Negative moments create a great deal of unnecessary stress in your mind, body, and spirit. If you allow it, one negative moment can ruin your whole day! That's why, while you're practicing your new, positive mindset and building your internal defenses against negativity, it's vital to minimize your negative moments and circumstances as much as possible.

Here are some ways to minimize or eliminate negative moments in your daily life. Do them as soon as possible!

- **Put away all photographs, music, artwork, and trinkets that remind you of your ex-partner,** in-laws, or friends who generate negative emotions for you.

- **Un-follow your ex-partner and his or her family and friends on social media.**

- **Turn off your smartphone, tablet, and computer for at least a portion of each day.** Instead, devote the time you would usually spend browsing on social media or reading e-mail to creating a positive pocket from the list above!

- **Reduce the chaos in your home environment.** Even little things like turning the heat up, adding a warm blanket to your couch, or clearing up the messy paperwork on the dining table can make a huge difference.

- **Stop sending negative e-mail messages, text messages, and social media posts.** When you broadcast negativity, it comes back to you! If you need to let off steam, call a trusted member of your Winning Team and vent your feelings in private.

- **Don't listen to stories or gossip about your ex-partner** or your ex's friends, family, or new partner. Your curiosity can quickly become a negative trap!

- **Avoid social situations where your ex is also present.** If you can't do so, remain friendly, but don't engage in any conversation about your separation. (Bonus: When you keep your commitments to yourself during these trying situations, you will feel amazing afterward!)

- **Don't listen to others' separation stories unless they actually uplift you.** Feel free to shut down negative people, even if they are trying to offer well-meaning advice.

- **Don't try to convince others in your "tribe" to turn against your ex, or start a shared "breakup app."** Your separation is between you and your ex, no one else. Keep the conversation positive and constructive.

- **Let go of hobbies, classes, contacts, and other time commitments that no longer make you feel positive.** Being a slave to your obligations is a sure way to create negative thoughts!

- **Don't waste time searching the internet for information or stories related to separation, divorce, breakups, cheating, or anything else.** Don't even read tabloid articles on celebrity breakups! If you really need to find a particular resource—such as a new lawyer—stick to sites that can give you fact-based recommendations, and stay out of chat rooms.

- **Don't grill your kids about the time they spend with your ex-partner.** Instead, concentrate on enjoying every moment you have with them.

Empowered Actions

▶ List Your Positive Actions for This Week

Right now, or during your Power Hour, choose ten actions (or create your own) from the "positive pockets" lists, and schedule between one and three actions per day in your planner. Do this every week for at least one month. The fact that you are arranging positive moments in your planner and thoughtfully monitoring your schedule will give you a sense of added structure and direction, and keep you focused on yourself, your vision, and your positive growth.

▶ Commit to Positive Changes for the Coming Year

Take a blank notebook, a pen, and your daily planner, and find a quiet place to sit down. Reserve at least an hour for this exercise.

Then, ask the following questions to help you discover how specific moments, situations, and persons affect you, and how you can make the changes necessary to eliminate as many negative moments as possible from your daily life.

- **"Which situations and people stress me out?"** Write down every situation and person you can think of that brings you down, makes you angry, or stresses you out. Be honest with yourself, and make as complete a list as possible. (Hint: This list is a work in progress. You can always add to it in the coming weeks if necessary. If you need more guidance, refer to the information on "negative helpers" in Chapter Seven: Your Winning Team.)

- **"How can I avoid the situations and people on my list, or deal with them differently?"** Create an alternative positive or neutral situation for each list item. For example: If you have a negative coworker/friend who always wants to spend your lunch hour complaining, start saying no to lunch with that person. If you have a nosy neighbor who is always asking questions about your separation, keep a big smile on your face when you leave the house, wave hello, and keep walking quickly. If you dislike the cashier in a certain shop, go somewhere else. If you can't think of a way to change the situation, ask members of your Winning Team for advice. Remember, practice makes perfect. You're learning to use your emotional radar in a whole new way—a skill which will serve you for the rest of your life!

- **"Which situations and people make me feel relaxed and happy?"** Make a new list of people—both on and off your Winning Team—who uplift you and help you feel positive. Make a separate list of situations— places, conversations, activities—that also make you happy. In the coming weeks, keep both lists close at hand. Try to spend more time with these people doing these things. (Hint: Use your Power Hour to schedule time for these activities!)

- **"What difficult appointments and situations do I expect in the near future?"** This exercise is really important, and will help you greatly in the coming months, so don't skim over it! Take out your calendar or planner and look at your appointments. Are there any negative appointments that you can simply avoid without causing problems? For those you cannot avoid, is there a way you can shorten their duration or otherwise make them less stressful? Or, can you pair negative moments with positive ones—like meeting up with a friend, or taking some "Zen time"—as we learned in the previous section?

- **"Are there any dates coming up that I know will be challenging for me?"** If you are dreading certain dates—like holidays, birthdays, your anniversary with your ex, vacation weeks, etc.—you can build up a lot of stress and negativity inside. Yes, these days may be challenging when they happen, but you can alleviate a large portion of your stress around them by starting your planning right now, even if the events themselves are months away. For example, if your birthday is coming up in six months, start making plans for a weekend getaway, or invite a friend to spend the night so you aren't waking up alone. If you're dreading spending Christmas or Hanukkah alone or at home with extended family, make plans to volunteer at a homeless shelter and invite others to join you. On your old anniversary, schedule something that makes you feel pampered and appreciated, like a nice meal with friends, a spa day, or a road trip. The more you can turn a day you're dreading into a day you're excited about, the easier it will be to get through with a positive mindset and lots of energy!

- **"Are there any upcoming engagements where I can bring a friend for support?"** You don't have to do this alone! If there is a wedding, party, work event, or any other engagement on your calendar, ask a friend to come along for moral support! This will keep you cheery, give you someone impartial to talk to, and help you have a good time regardless of who else is there!

▶ Create a Daily Gratitude Practice

Remember Marci's story from Chapter Six? Her daily gratitude practice allowed her to flip her entire outlook on both her breakup and her life. A similar practice can also help you create a positive environment for yourself and steer clear of lingering negative thoughts.

Keep a small notebook on your bedside table. Before you go to sleep each night, write down three things for which you are grateful. They might be small things—like hearing your favorite song, or receiving a stranger's smile in the café—or they might be bigger things, like when the painter worked three hours later than scheduled so you could move into your new flat by the weekend, or when your boss took you to lunch on a day when you needed moral support. As long as your three daily items bring a smile to your face and make you feel warm and grateful inside, they are enough.

If you know you will need an extra boost during a hard day, bring your gratitude journal with you to work and appointments. Open it and read it whenever you feel yourself starting to slip into negative thoughts.

You can also get creative with this. For example, my client Jane (whose story appeared in Chapter Two) kept her gratitude notes in a kangaroo cookie jar from Australia. Every time someone said or did something nice for her, she wrote it on a slip of paper and put it in her jar. When her self-confidence was low, she would open the jar and read about how blessed she was!

What Comes Next

Now that you know how to plan and create small positive moments for yourself in your daily life and take care of yourself during challenging times, we will explore more ways for you to take care of your body, mind, and spirit, and bring more happiness and fulfillment into your world. In the coming chapters, we'll talk about ways to take care of your body, spruce up your personal space, and create pockets of deliberate relaxation so that you become stronger and more positive every day!

CHAPTER NINE

Healthy Body, Healthy You

When my friend Heather enters the room, you immediately see a strong, beautiful woman with a healthy glow. When she smiles at you, you feel as though you are instantly accepted into that strength and grace. This is a rare gift, one that she cultivated even more during her separation, when she started caring for herself in a new way, and found the strength to blossom into the brilliant butterfly she is today.

HEATHER'S STORY

"I was married at twenty-two," Heather told me. "That was the culture I grew up with in Utah. Although I wasn't from a hardcore religious family, there was a lot of pressure to marry and 'settle down.' I had a few boyfriends in high school and college, but felt that romance was something that only happened in the movies.

"When I met my husband-to-be, I thought, 'He's a nice person.' He had a lot of qualities I looked for in a man, and still does. His family was lovely and supportive, and I adored his parents. We didn't have the romantic connection, but since I'd never found that with anyone before him, I didn't think it actually existed.

"Even in the beginning, we never talked about our deep feelings. That was perfectly okay with me; I didn't know that a deep emotional connection was something I needed, or even wanted.

"We were married for fourteen years and had two lovely boys together. In that time, I also created a huge career in retail and became the family breadwinner. Next to my kids, my job was the love of my life.

"We moved to a lovely home in New Jersey, and on the outside, life was great. Deep down, I had the feeling that something was missing—but I didn't know what it was. When my unhappiness rose, I just pushed it down and went on with my day. Work was the perfect cover-up; I could always find something to occupy my time and energy. I told myself that I had a wonderful, down-to-earth husband who was a great father—so what did I have to complain about? So what if we weren't mushy romantics?

"Then, one night, it all fell to pieces.

"If you haven't guessed this about me already, I was a bit of a rule follower. I always did what was expected of me. It was part of what made me so successful at work. This also meant that I always knew how to behave, especially in social situations. Being calm and controlled was my ground rule. So, although I usually indulged in one or two cocktails at work parties, I never allowed my control to slip … until one night when the CEO of my company was in town.

"My heart still skips a beat when I think about it. For whatever reason, I let myself have far too much to drink that night. I went from reserved professional to social butterfly, happily partying and dancing and chatting with everyone. In the midst of this good time, I saw one of my girlfriends deep in business talk with our CEO. *So serious*, I thought. As I floated by the two of them, I put my hand on the CEO's shoulder and said to him, 'Tell my girlfriend she looks gorgeous in that dress. Isn't she beautiful?' And off I glided.

"You might think that this wasn't a big deal … but to me, it was a *huge* mistake. Never in my career had I made such a giant social blunder. When I woke up the next morning and remembered what I'd done the night before, I had a personal breakdown. I'd worked my whole life for this wonderful career, and now I might have ruined it by acting like a drunken idiot in front of my CEO.

"I had a sudden vision of myself cast out, with no more career, no more prospects. What if my boss fired me? What if no one else would hire me since I was such an embarrassment to the organization? Any day now, I could go from corporate hotshot to stay-at-home mom, decked out in my apron as I cooked and cleaned and gardened … What would happen to my independent, hardworking spirit? I felt totally helpless.

"To make matters worse, I couldn't even face my fate right away, because we had scheduled a family vacation the following week. I had days and days with nothing to do but wallow in my panic and paranoia. I tried to talk to my husband about what I was feeling—about being scared of losing my job, my career, and everything that made me who I was—but after so long avoiding our deeper feelings, we couldn't really communicate about it. He brushed it off. No, he brushed *me* off.

"In fairness, I couldn't be angry with him. I mean, I'd never asked for emotional support before, so how could he be prepared to give it? Given how well he knew me, he probably didn't even think I needed it. But on that vacation, I felt so alone, so lost inside. Our kids were having a blast at Disney World, and all I felt was … raw.

"It was the first time I'd truly needed this kind of support, but I knew it wouldn't be the last. Could I really see myself living this way at age fifty? Sixty? Seventy? Living without any emotional connection? I didn't think I could.

"When I got back to work, it was as though nothing had happened. No one said a thing. I didn't get in trouble. But the seed had been planted, and I started questioning everything about my life. Why was my job so important to me? Was I using my work to avoid looking at a marriage that felt dead on the inside?

"I became more and more unhappy. Whenever I had free time, I went walking for hours. I didn't want to be at home. In the end, I went to a therapist, who helped me deal with my limiting beliefs and come to terms with the fact that I wanted a divorce. I had been telling myself things like, 'He hasn't hurt you. He's a good man. He doesn't deserve this.' 'If I divorce, I will ruin my kids' lives forever!' And, my personal favorite, 'It's selfish of you to want more than you already have.'

"The therapy helped me to see that I didn't have to live my life the way I'd been told I *should* live it. I could live the way I wanted to in my heart. I didn't want to cause my husband and sons any pain—but I couldn't continue to live like I had been. I was awake now, and there was no going back to sleep. I couldn't keep chasing the bigger house, the new car, the promotions and vacations, reaching for happiness that was always just out of reach.

"It took me some time to make the final decision to divorce. When I finally told my husband, he was in shock. Naturally, he wanted to stay married. Life was going well for him, and he didn't feel as though he was missing anything. But I had made up my mind, and in the end, he could only agree. We made plans for co-parenting and living arrangements, and set out on a journey toward new and separate lives.

"I never expected what divorce would really bring me. I hadn't seen the big picture at all. I don't think anyone can. I had gotten married so young—and now, here I was, on my own for the first time in my life. I experienced a lot of personal chaos that had nothing to do with the separation itself. I had married a good man who, despite his sadness at our split, continued to be a good man, and I had lovely in-laws who were still supportive and gracious.

"No, the chaos came from the change in my daily life. I was in unknown territory. My world had been turned upside down, and I had nothing to hold on to. I was on my own, as open and vulnerable as a child—and yet, I was still parenting my two children. What the heck did I think I was doing?

"I threw myself into my job even more than I had before. I attacked weekends single-mindedly, trying to get as much accomplished I possibly could with the time I had, certain I was making progress. The feelings I got when I completed a big to-do list helped to hide the other feelings, the ones I wouldn't let myself feel.

"I had thought I would deal with my divorce in the same controlled and predicable way I dealt with everything else in my life, but my feelings were raw. For the first time in my life, I struggled with insecurity and a fear of the unknown, self-doubt, the fear of everyone judging me … they kept me on edge. I felt like a failure. I—who considered myself so smart, successful, and worldly-wise—had avoided doing the right thing for myself for *fourteen years*! I wanted a do-over—but at the same time, I knew I couldn't play the victim. I needed to get my act together and put some of that famous competence to work creating a happy future for me and my kids.

"In the months leading up to the divorce, I had already lost a lot of weight. Now, I was a physical wreck. I was focusing on calorie counting (because at least I could control that), I was totally stressed out, and my energy was fading by the day.

"This was not the happy future full of possibility that I had envisioned.

"One day, standing in front of the mirror, I took a good, long look at myself, and made my second life-changing decision. What I was doing to myself wasn't right. I couldn't fool myself into thinking I was okay any longer. I needed to take care of myself if I wanted to make it through this in one piece.

"I had never belonged to a gym in my life, but I decided that I needed to start taking care of my body straight away. I started working with a personal trainer and eating healthfully. I quickly fell in love with fitness. My workouts gave me the structure, personal space, and 'me time' I desperately needed.

"As I climbed thousands of steps on the Stairmaster, I cried buckets of tears. Step by step, I climbed—and I knew that this was how I needed to approach my new life. Little steps, one at a time, every day. This was the way to my happy future—but I couldn't try to control the process. I had to trust myself and the universe.

"Looking after myself gave me more confidence. Working out helped me sleep better, which made my daytime hours easier. I started setting new goals for myself. Since my husband was resistant at first to moving out of our house, I decided to find an apartment in the city where I could stay on my 'non-parenting' days. I was over the moon. This was a place totally for me. It was *mine*! I decorated it exactly the way I wanted it. I updated my wardrobe. I bought a new car—not a practical family vehicle, but the car *I* wanted. I stopped thinking and talking about what I 'should' do, and started doing only what felt right and good to me in the moment.

"I was a brand new Heather—a Heather who didn't put herself last. I still had a lot of work to do on the inside, but I was taking back my life. If I wanted to succeed in the next phase of my life, I couldn't be the same person I had been for the last fourteen years.

"One night, I was getting ready to go out with my girlfriends. I had a fabulous red dress on (no more conservative 'Mom' clothes for me!), and when I caught a glimpse of myself in the mirror, I thought, 'Wow! Is that me?'

"I walked up to the mirror and said to my reflection, 'I don't know you that well yet, but I know where we are going. We are heading into a happy future!' I took a picture of myself smiling into the mirror, and thought, *This is how I want to show up in the world!*

"Throughout all of this, my ex-husband and I stayed committed to creating a positive environment for our kids. Both of us agreed never to talk negatively about the other parent, and we stuck to that promise. Of course, there was a lot of adjustment, and there were moments where I felt guilty for focusing so much on myself. But in the end, the positive changes I made in my life, and the efforts I made to take care of myself and my body, paid off. My kids got a mother who followed her intuition and inner guidance to become happy, and they quickly picked up on this positive energy.

"Now, three years after my divorce was finalized, I feel like a better and happier mother and woman. I have a life that feels balanced. No part is of me is suffering. I really take care of myself, and my kids feel it. Although I still keep strict boundaries, I have much more patience. I no longer waste time doing things I don't want to (like cooking perfect homemade meals every night); instead, I enjoy my time hanging out with them and showing them what a happy person who expresses her feelings looks like.

"I am loving life today because I feel connected to myself in a way I never have before. I feel like I found a well of happiness inside of me, and I can share that happiness with my friends, family, and the whole world."

A Healthy Mind in a Healthy Body

Does any of this sound familiar?

You're making mistakes at work. You can't focus on a book for more than three pages. You can no longer remember a simple shopping list, and you forgot the key in the front door yesterday. You always feel tired, and often indulge in an extra glass of wine or beer in the evening. You eat too much, or never feel hungry. You're angry, over-emotional, or just plain overtired, and your temper regularly seems to get the better of you.

If so, it's more than just emotional stress. It's your body trying to get your attention!

Your body, like your mind and heart, has a lot to endure during a separation. When you neglect it, it can go downhill very quickly.

I have experienced this myself. Out of the blue, about two years after my separation, I landed in a depression. It came as a complete surprise. I knew I was juggling too many plates, but I was a single mom trying to take care of my work and my household, and at the same time create a new happy future for myself and my children. In the midst of all the to-dos, I forgot to pay attention to my best friend, my body.

I am very sensitive to medications, so I had to find alternative ways to keep going. I discovered that getting out of the "gray mind" trap began with taking proper attention to the health and well-being of my body. I started applying the same positivity and dedication I used in my divorce process to caring for my body and mind. I started taking long walks outside; ate three healthy meals a day (whether I felt hungry or not); booked sessions with my personal body awareness coach, Hans; made sure to get plenty of sleep; and generally payed greater attention to the feelings my body was sharing with me. These relatively simple things gave me direction in my quest for healing.

Giving proper attention to your body is critical if you want to get through the next year (and beyond) in a well-balanced fashion.

If your body is not getting what it needs to function optimally, you will not have the energy and stability you need to navigate your life on a daily basis, let alone stay emotionally balanced. The good news is that, although you may feel like a wreck just now, you can start focusing the right kind of attention on your body today, right now. If you do, you will feel much better within a few weeks— and you will then have a very important instrument at your command.

A strong and resilient body fills a very important role. It's the "home base" from which you function on a day to day basis, regulate your emotions on a physiological level, and execute important actions in your separation. This isn't just conjecture: research has proven that if your body is healthy and strong, you will deal more effectively with your stress, emotions, and disappointments. You will also have more strength and confidence to draw from as you work on your happy future.

Maintaining a strong, healthy body doesn't mean that you have to go to the gym every day, eat only carrots and lettuce, swear off chocolate, or stop enjoying your nightly glass of wine. It simply means prioritizing the kinds of physical care and activities that make you feel stronger and better-cared-for, and that help you release the physical effects of stress. These activities can be bite-sized (taking just five or ten minutes each), or longer. Either way, adding these care elements to your day will give you structure and help you feel empowered, just as they did for Heather in the story at the beginning of this chapter.

THINGS THAT GENERATE STRENGTH AND ENERGY

The following is a partial list of things that can help you build and generate strength and energy. Some are simple, while others require a bit more effort.

Place a check mark next to those items that you are already focusing on, or that you want to focus on. During your weekly Power Hour, add the activities you've chosen to your calendar so you don't let them slide. With a little focus and dedication, they will become integrated parts of your daily routine.

- **Eat regularly and healthily.** Don't put your faith in vitamin pills or "meal replacers," no matter how convenient they seem. Your body needs real, healthy food now more than ever before. Eat three meals a day (including a good breakfast), with healthy snacks in between, and eat something you *really* enjoy once a day (even if it's not "good for you"). Meals that you prepare yourself are much better than fast food or take-away meals. The more time, love, and attention you personally devote to your meals, the better. Bonus: Eating together with people you love— like your friends, family, and Winning Team—is a real energy booster!
- **Get enough sleep.** A shortage of sleep reduces your ability to concentrate and makes you irritable. Create whatever conditions you need to get a good night's rest. Stop dealing with matters related to your separation (e-mails, letters, telephone calls, and text messages) at least two hours before you go to sleep. Make your bedroom a sacred space. Don't watch TV, play with your smartphone, or work on your computer in bed. (If you can't resist looking at your phone, leave it in another room and get an old-fashioned alarm clock instead.) Make sure your bedroom is neat

and tidy, and keep the window cracked open for fresh air whenever possible.

- **Breathe deeply.** Conscious deep breathing is a powerful and effective tool for releasing stress in charged moments. When you feel tense, tight, or stifled, stop what you're doing, and take several deep belly breaths to recharge your system. Imagine that you are breathing in peace and light, and exhaling stress.

- **Enjoy daylight and fresh air every day.** Even when it's cloudy or raining, try to spend at least 30-60 minutes outdoors every day—no excuses. This helps your body to produce stress-combating hormones. Try it for just one week; you'll be amazed at the difference it makes!

- **Meditate.** Meditation is a great way to reduce stress, clear your mind, and calm your emotions. It can also add extra structure to your day if you practice at a certain time each morning or evening. Check out meditation apps or courses in mindfulness training near you.

- **Exercise or play sports regularly.** Especially during a tense separation, exercise is a wonder drug. Getting exercise every day, preferably outdoors, is as important as eating, drinking, and sleeping. Scheduling exercise as a regular part of your weekly rhythm also adds structure to your days and weeks. And playing sports is an ideal way to meet new people and get back in the social swing of things.

- **Schedule "chill times."** Quiet periods for chilling out between your daily activities allow you to restore your energy and reduce your stress level. Schedule two or three shorter chill periods (10 to 20 minutes each) every day, as well as two longer ones per week. (Hint: Chilling out completely requires a bit of practice. Chapter Ten deals with this in more detail.)

- **Laugh and have fun.** A healthy dose of humor can help you reduce your levels of stress and tension. Now and then, just forget about the difficult period you're going through, call on your "pick-you-up" Team member, and let loose for a bit. You can also watch bubbly and humorous movies, TV shows, and comedy shows to add a bit of lightness to your day.

- **Create a positive environment.** A positive, nurturing environment is just as therapeutic for your body as it is for your mind. Use the exercises in Chapter Eight to create a positive environment for yourself as a buffer against stress and tension.

- **Tidy up.** Even if you have little money for redecorating, a clean, uncluttered space will give you an enormous mental and physical boost. (I'll share more about how to do this effectively in Chapter Eleven.)
- **Accept help.** A great deal of pain and suffering (mental and physical) can be prevented by calling for and accepting effective help. Don't fall into the trap of waiting until the very last moment to ask for help. When you feel supported, you will be more relaxed, which positively impacts both body and mind. Your Winning Team is the ideal tool in this regard.
- **Give help.** When your life starts to feel more stable, it can be really rewarding to offer help to others who need it. You could work with a charity, do random acts of kindness in your city, or make a pot of soup for a sick friend. The key to offering help in a positive way is to make sure it doesn't drain your energy or bring you into a negative or victim space. Don't over-commit, and never offer help at the expense of your own well-being!

THINGS THAT ROB YOU OF STRENGTH AND ENERGY

Just as there are habits and actions which will bolster your energy and stamina, there are those which will drain your energy and make you more vulnerable to stress, tension, and physical illness. To keep your body strong and healthy, avoid these things whenever possible—or at least try to limit your exposure.

Don't be tempted to skip over this list, or lie to yourself if you are engaging in unhealthy behaviors. The longer you ignore energy-robbing habits, the bigger the resulting consequences will be. If you need help, rely on your Winning Team members (both personal and professional) for support.

- **Alcohol and drugs.** In periods of stress, you are more likely to overindulge in drinking, smoking, or using recreational drugs. But although these may at first seem to help relieve your stress and forget your worries, they will soon start to damage your body and your health by impacting your sleep, concentration, and emotional stability. If unchecked, these habits can create new and bigger issues for you, like addiction, financial problems, and issues in previously supportive relationships.

- **Addictions.** There are the addictions we all recognize—like addictions to alcohol, drugs, medications, and gambling—but you can also become addicted to food, social media, work, shopping, and even sports. How do you know when an otherwise positive activity—like playing a sport or working out—has become an addiction? When it robs you of so much energy that you don't have enough left over to deal with your daily activities, or when it becomes a way to escape your reality. If you feel that you're on the wrong path in this regard—or if addictive behavior was a factor in your breakup—don't hesitate to call for professional help. You deserve it! There are many wonderful resources out there that can help you get your feet under you again so you can start wholeheartedly walking the path to your happy future.

- **Mental and physical abuse.** If you have suffered abuse in your relationship or it's still happening, you should take it very seriously. This is also the case if the abuse happened in the past and you are afraid of a repetition. Abuse, or the fear of it, can cause enormous amounts of stress and panic, to the point where the fear can completely paralyze you, and cost so much energy that you can't deal with your separation. Don't be afraid to share your fears with your family doctor or other professional, and ask for the help and protection you need to feel safe, confident, and empowered not just in a single moment, but every day of your life. By standing up for yourself (and any children concerned), you will gain a great boost of energy and self-confidence, and set the stage to unravel your separation in a positive way that doesn't leave you feeling victimized.

- **Sickness and medication use.** If you are currently dealing with a health condition, or have suffered from a serious illness in the past, you need to be extra vigilant with your daily health, even if you are no longer sick. Discuss your situation with your doctor and psychologist as soon as possible, and decide if you need to update your medication regimen and/or take extra preventative measures to counteract the stress of your separation.

- **Excessive weight loss or gain.** As a result of the uncertainty, strong emotions, and related stress and tension, a great many people in separation start eating much less or much more. However, your body has more than enough to cope with right now. A sudden change in weight and eating habits forces your body to use its reserve to continue functioning normally, when those reserves have already been drastically depleted. So, even if you're tempted to treat your stress-related weight loss as a good thing for your self-esteem, make sure you don't let your health become secondary to how you look in that new miniskirt. Instead, pay extra attention to your nutritional balance by eating three healthy meals a day and drinking enough water. If weight loss is part of your happy future, consult a professional or pair up with a knowledgeable Winning Team member to be sure you're doing it in a healthy, sustainable way.

- **Negative people, situations, and thoughts.** Unnecessary mental stress creates unnecessary physical stress, which in turn drains you of valuable energy. Don't go there! (Re-read Chapter Eight if you need a refresher on how to avoid negative situations, people, and thoughts.)

- **Worrying and brooding.** Worrying is a logical consequence of a separation. When it motivates you to take action and make progress, it's not a bad thing—but when it gives you tunnel vision or creates additional stress, it can sap your energy and prevent you from seeing solutions that would otherwise be obvious. If you're struggling with worry for more than two days straight, that's a red flag. Call on your Winning Team for help so you don't take an unintended detour from your new path. If you're already predisposed to depression, anxiety, or other mental/emotional challenges, it's doubly important to be preemptive in your care for yourself.

- **Excessive TV, phone, and computer use.** For your physical as well as mental health, keep your "screen time" to a minimum. Sitting alone in front of your computer or TV can be isolating, encourages passivity, and makes it easier for you to avoid doing other things that are more important (such as taking care of your body, seeing to important tasks for your separation, or creating a positive environment for yourself). So, be disciplined. For example, after 8:00 p.m., turn off your computer and television, and take a short walk instead. Turn your phone to "vibrate" or "do not disturb" mode. If you must sit behind a computer for hours on end for your work, take regular breaks to rest and relax, and give yourself extra screen-free time in the morning and evening.

If you're not sure which of the above energy drains are actually present in your life, or how to counteract the ones you recognize, ask a member of your Winning Team for advice. Take a serious look at what's happening; together, you will come up with creative solutions that work perfectly in your life.

Note: The above tips are effective and useful, but they are not a substitute for professional medical help or advice. If you feel weak, depressed, shaky, anxious, or are thinking about suicide, call your therapist or a doctor right away. Don't wait to get professional help, and don't hide how you're feeling; doing so could be dangerous. Your well-being is in your own hands, so act wisely!

Empowered Actions

▶ Do a Body Scan

Sit on a chair in a quiet place with your feet on the ground. Turn off the television, music, and your phone so you won't be interrupted.

Close your eyes. Focus your thoughts and feelings on your body, moving slowly from the top of your head, to your forehead, eyes, nose, mouth, and chin. Continue scanning each part of your body all the way down to your feet.

Where do you feel strong, and where do you feel weak? Where do you feel inward pressure, and where is there tension? Listen and feel carefully. If at first you don't feel anything, start again. Go slowly over your body from top to bottom. If you need help concentrating, touch each body part with your hands, or Google "body scan videos" to find instructions that suit you.

Feel every pain or discomfort, regardless of how small it may seem. Are you ignoring any signals from your body? Do you feel physically and mentally fit and capable of dealing with any and all disruptions in your life—or is there some extra support your body needs to operate at its highest capacity? What can you do to take better care of your body, right now? What excuses do you make to avoid paying sufficient attention to your body?

Write down everything that comes into your mind as you ask these questions. Then, make a plan of action to give your body the support and attention it needs. If necessary, consult a physician, health coach, personal trainer, or physical therapist.

▶ Deal with Worry When It Happens

If you're worried about something, don't let stress sap your energy. Put your worry down on paper in your notebook or planner. Temporarily parking the issue on paper creates space in your mind and helps you to focus.

If you've written down your worry and are still thinking about it half an hour later, stop what you're doing and take a walk outside, or dive into an activity that requires you to use your hands, such as: gardening; clearing up your house and/or office; painting, knitting, or another creative pursuit.

▶ Track Your Actions

For a period of four weeks, write down in your notebook all the activities that empowered and energized you, as well as the activities that drained you of power and energy, keeping in mind the suggestions from this chapter. Go over your notes each week during your Power Hour, and schedule more of the activities that support you.

What Comes Next

Taking care of your body gives you a strong foundation of energy and balance in your separation. However, there are other keys to creating a positive environment and empowering yourself. In the coming chapters, we'll learn how chilling out completely and getting rid of extra "baggage" in the form of possessions and clutter can create even more empowerment, space, and positive energy for you as you work toward your happy future.

CHAPTER TEN

Chill Out Completely

S ometimes, the hardest thing to do is nothing at all. But it's in the quiet times that we learn the most about where we are, who we are, and where we want to be in our happy future.

JAMES'S STORY

To many, it would seem that James has a relaxed, even an ideal, life. He owns a guest ranch in California, and people flock to his property to escape the pressures of city life and find adventure in the great outdoors. Every day, he leads guests on trail rides, plays with visitors' kids, and sits by campfires under the stars with people from around the world.

But running a guest ranch, even a small one, is also hard work, and it never eases up—especially when you live on the property. The long hours and increasing demands of the business led to the downfall of James's marriage.

"We just didn't have time for each other. She had a job teaching at the local elementary school, and I was running the ranch. She would get home in the afternoon and I would still be running around, putting out fires (sometimes literally). Sometimes we didn't even get to eat dinner together. I would fall into bed and she would try to talk to me about her day, but I was just too tired to process it. She started to feel like I cared more about my work than about her.

"When she moved out, I was shocked. I couldn't believe it. I mean, we loved each other, and I was trying my best to make my business successful so we could enjoy our retirement in comfort. But she said she couldn't play second fiddle to the ranch anymore—that she'd never really wanted this life in the first place. Soon, she'd taken up with someone else, a guy from San Francisco with a regular nine-to-five job.

"I was angry, hurt, frustrated, and shocked all at the same time. But I still had guests booked at the ranch, and I couldn't just let things fall apart. So I threw myself into the business and worked even harder than I had before. I gave myself no time to think, or wonder what had happened, or miss my wife. I just concentrated on the tasks in front of me and kept pushing forward. At night, alone in the bed I used to share with my wife, I couldn't sleep, so I kept my mind busy making lists and planning for the next day. When that didn't work, I watched TV. A few times, I drank too much, just to knock myself out—but that only made things worse, since I still had to start my day at 5:00 a.m.

"Then, the recession hit. Hard. Suddenly, there weren't enough guests to keep me busy for fourteen hours a day. My staff were irritated with me because I kept trying to do their jobs for them. I felt like I had been sidelined in my own life.

"At first, whenever I had an hour with nothing to do, I panicked. I would make work for myself grooming the horses, or cleaning out the kitchen storage closets (I'm not kidding). You name it, I made busy work out of it. But then, something shifted. I started wondering, 'What if I spent this time doing something *I* want to do?'

"I had been so busy for so long that I didn't actually *know* what I liked doing. By default, I just did the things that were right in front me.

"I started taking trail rides alone, something my wife and I had done often when we first bought the ranch. I told myself I was inspecting the trails for when the guests came back—but in the quiet, with the mountains all around me, I felt like I was finally able to take a deep breath. I did a lot of soul-searching during those moments, and I realized that my wife had been right: I had let her become second-best to my business. All along, I'd told myself that I was doing the right thing for us by working so hard—but at the same time, I had just assumed that she would always be there, and that she would stick by me no matter what. I had taken her, and us, for granted. It was a huge mistake.

"It sounds corny, but I think I found a piece of myself out there on those trails. And when business started picking up again a year or so later, I didn't go back to working like crazy. I hired a manager I trusted, and let my awesome staff do their jobs without me looking over their shoulders. I just felt more relaxed.

"Now, I make sure that I have 'alone time' every day. It's not always trail time; sometimes, I just sit in my kitchen and do nothing, or I go into town to browse in the bookstore (instead of ordering all of my books online). This down time helps me stay more balanced. I have more fun with my staff and my guests, and I'm making plans for the future that go beyond a successful business. I want to travel to China and Nepal. I want to write a book about ranching. Mostly, I want to make sure I'm the best man I can be, so that when my new partner comes into my life, I won't make the same mistakes again."

What It Means to Relax

Rest and relaxation is the best medicine. It's as important as a healthy diet, good sleep, and proper exercise.

In the quiet pauses between activity, we can slow down our racing minds, reconnect with ourselves, and get a clear picture of where we are and how we are feeling.

It used to be that life had these "natural pauses" built in—periods of enforced boredom. A long train ride with nothing to do, a quiet winter evening with no one around, businesses closed on Sundays.

Nowadays, though, everything happens at the speed of light. Your phone, computer, and television are always on, ready to distract you and keep you busy. Agendas are too full; appointments need to be planned weeks or months in advance. It feels like you need to keep running just to stay in place and not fall behind the rest of the world.

In our 24/7 world, relaxing isn't something that happens automatically. You have to take action to make sure you have space to *not act*, and create specialized conditions to allow yourself to relax and release completely.

When you add the stress of separation to the mix, taking time to relax and unwind is no longer optional. It's absolutely necessary if you want to understand and cope with the major emotions and changes that are happening in your life. By regularly giving your body, mind, and spirit the chance to release and recharge, you equip yourself to take on your tasks in a more positive and empowered way.

REST VS. ESCAPISM

Rest is a powerful remedy against excessive stress, and can be used at any time of your choosing. It's also a great way to connect with yourself, and to assess where you are and what support you need to keep moving forward in an empowered way.

Resting your heart and mind can require some practice, especially if you are used to "living in the fast lane" or are always busy with one thing or another. If you tend to get twitchy and seek distraction when you're still, you need rest right now even more than most!

Again, rest is not optional for you right now! It is a must for recharging your batteries and dealing with the reality of your life at this moment. The more you integrate specific moments of rest into your daily and weekly routine, the more benefits you will reap.

In this chapter, you will learn how to create two kinds of rest periods in your schedule: daily rest moments, and longer rest hours. Your daily moments are times specifically devoted to breathing, meditation, and calm reflection. Your longer rest hours should not be "pre-programmed" in any way, but should be left empty on your calendar to allow you to feel what your mind, body, and spirit need. (So, while getting a massage is a wonderful way to care for your body, it's not technically "rest time.")

All of your rest times should be taken completely alone, away from your friends, family, children, and colleagues. As difficult as this may sound, it is necessary. The more you learn to just be quiet and still, without distractions, the more you will get in touch with yourself, and the more connected and empowered you will feel.

You may be thinking, "But I don't have *time* to rest right now!" I understand. With all the extra tasks that separation requires, it can be challenging to take even fifteen minutes out of your day to relax. But there could be a deeper reason you're avoiding rest: if you take time to be still, with no distractions, you will have to confront yourself as you are. You will be forced to deal with your pain, your emotions, your frustrations, and your fears. You will be forced to see the reality of your life as it is. For many people, it's easier to stay busy and distracted than face what's really going on and be confronted with so many uncomfortable feelings.

But, here's the thing: running away from your feelings doesn't make them disappear. We talked about this in depth in other chapters, so I won't rehash it all here—but I will say that refusing to rest now will mean that you are forced to rest later, when your mind or body (or both) reach overload capacity and start to break down. (Which is exactly what happened to me about two years after my breakup!)

Busyness is just another form of escapism, like drugs, alcohol, overworking, shopping, gambling, excessive computer use, or any other distraction. In some ways, it's easier to fall into the busyness trap than into other addictions, because it's so easy to justify. After all, you have *so* much to do, and not enough hours in the day to do it all.

Do any of the following sound familiar?

- Your calendar is overflowing with appointments.
- You drink large quantities of coffee (or other caffeinated beverages) to get through the day.
- You need to take pills to sleep at night.
- You are in chronic pain from headaches, digestive issues, or other stress-related illnesses.
- You often work longer hours than necessary.
- You spend all of your free time in front of the TV, computer, or tablet.
- You can't sit still without playing with your phone.
- You need to see every new TV series, and binge-watch whenever you need to unwind.

- You go out more nights than you stay home.
- You have no idea what you're feeling at any given moment. It's all a blur.
- You dive into new relationship(s) without much consideration.

If so, chances are you are falling into escapist behavior, and are sorely in need of rest and relaxation.

THE FLIP SIDE OF REST

It's true that many of us don't make time to rest, and use our busyness as a distraction. But for some, rest itself can become the distraction.

If you find yourself unable to get out of bed for days at a time, spend every free minute sleeping, or avoid all unnecessary social contact, you may be using rest as a tool for avoidance. It's okay to go undercover for a few days, but hiding from the reality of your separation won't make it go away.

If you "rest" during every hour that's not taken up with work and necessary chores, and still can't seem to process and release your emotions, you may be struggling with depression. If this is the case, contact your general practitioner or a professional therapist as soon as possible, especially if you are having thoughts of suicide or self-harm.

Chilling Out: The Magic Bullet

Rest takes a load off your mind, your muscles, and your heart so that you can function better afterward. It's a powerful antidote against overloading yourself, and you can use it anytime you wish. But, as I've said, intentionally allowing yourself to come to a complete stop requires practice (in my case, *lots* of practice)!

In order to hold yourself accountable to your daily and weekly rest periods, schedule them into your calendar. Two to three short periods of rest per day, each lasting ten to twenty minutes, is a great place to start.

Treat these daily "chill times" as mandatory. During these periods, stop whatever you were doing. Save your work, power down your computer, and turn off your phone. Come to a complete stop.

Breathe deeply for two to three minutes, in through your nose, out through your mouth. This gives your body an extra dose of oxygen and helps loosen tight muscles.

Then, relax and let go of everything. Do absolutely nothing for the remainder of your rest period. If it helps, you can listen to a guided meditation or music. You can even close your eyes if you like, but don't fall asleep. Just do nothing.

You can take your chill times at any point in your day—before breakfast, on your lunch break, in your office (with the door closed), while sitting on a park bench, in your parked car before you pick the kids up from school. It doesn't matter where you are, as long as you're in a place where you can stop and do nothing for ten to twenty minutes.

In addition to your two or three daily "chill times," also schedule two longer periods of rest per week lasting a minimum of one hour each. These are your "chill hours." Put them in your planner, and make a commitment to yourself to respect them regardless of how busy you are or how much you want to avoid them. These periods are not a replacement for your Power Hour, a workout, or any other self-care. They are simply hours in which you will allow yourself to do nothing except live in the moment and be exactly where you are.

It's important not to plan out what you are going to do during these chill hours, even in your thoughts. Remember, this is all about living in the moment! Start by simply sitting in the quiet, preferably at home, with your phone, computer, TV, and other devices turned off. Do your deep breathing, pause for a few moments—and only then start thinking about what you might want to do with your resting time. Some days, you might simply want to sit on the couch. Other days, you may feel like listening to music, cooking your favorite treat for yourself, or sitting in the garden. You might wander off to a sidewalk café, and quietly sip your cappuccino while watching pedestrians stroll by. You might head to the park, or to the beach, or to your favorite hiking trail. You might sit with your head in your hands and cry until you have no more tears. You might write an angry letter to your ex, and then burn it on the stove. You might write in your journal, then turn up the radio and dance to your favorite song. You might fidget in boredom until your hour is up. Everything and anything is possible.

There are only four rules for your Chill Hours:

1. **No TV, electronics, social media, books, or other diversions.** Music and guided meditations are the two exceptions.
2. **No other people.** This is your special time with yourself. Stay off the phone, and don't text.
3. **No substitutions or cutting your time short.** Don't use this time to go to the gym, take a power nap, do your chores, or catch up on trashy magazines. Honor your commitment to yourself.
4. **No pre-programming.** Don't decide what you will do beforehand. Instead, use this time to listen to yourself and give yourself what you really need.

The more you prioritize your chill times, the more important they will become to you. They may be hard to deal with at first, but soon, you won't want to live without them!

Empowered Actions

▶ Schedule Your Chill Times

Now or during your Power Hour, take out your planner and schedule two to three short "chill times" each day to chill out and relax, as well as two longer "chill hours" each week. Do this for at least four consecutive weeks.

▶ Keep a "Rest Journal"

If resting is a huge struggle for you, try to look at it as an exercise in observation. After each chill time, write in your notebook about how you felt during this quiet space. Were you anxious? Did you feel like the walls were closing in? Did you keep reaching for your phone? Chronicling your experiences will help you deal with the emotions that come up around resting and engage with them in a healthy, non-judgmental way. Plus, you'll get to see how your experiences change over time!

What Comes Next

So far in this Step, we've learned how you can create a positive environment, how to take care of your body, and why rest is vital to keeping you connected to yourself so you can stay strong in your separation. Next, we'll look at how getting rid of extra "baggage" in the form of possessions and clutter can free up even more energy for you to put toward your happy future!

CHAPTER ELEVEN

Get Rid of Excess Baggage

We all have stuff. Sometimes, this stuff is helpful—but sometimes it weighs us down. Sometimes, we even wonder who we are without it. Stuff really comes to the forefront of our lives in a separation. Who does our stuff actually belong to? How do we divide mutually-owned possessions? And what do we keep from our old life when we are striking out to build a new one?

AIMEE'S STORY

My creative and lovely friend Aimee discovered how freeing it could be to let go of physical baggage when she left her marriage eight years ago.

"I left my marriage, and my home, in a hurry. I'd told my ex the night before that I was leaving, but he was drunk—his addiction was a major factor in our separation—and I had no idea what, if anything, he remembered of the conversation. When I woke up in the morning, he had already left for work, but the liquor stores opened in an hour, and I was terrified that he would come storming back in a rage once he remembered my promise to leave him.

"I threw my clothes into suitcases, and my shoes into paper grocery bags. I took my essential toiletries, the good pots and pans (he didn't cook), my computer, and my guitar. Everything I took from that house fit in the back of my Mini Cooper.

"The blowup I expected never happened; if anything, my ex was conciliatory and remorseful. He let me go without a fight. But, given our history and his unpredictability when under the influence, I decided that negotiating the disposal of our mutual stuff wasn't worth the chance of a confrontation. On a day when he was working, I went back for my books, my office desk and chair, some old personal photographs, and a couple of pieces of art that my sister had created for me. Everything else, I left for him. The house barely looked different with me gone.

"For the first time since I'd moved out of my dad's house at seventeen years old, I had no possessions to speak of. It was totally freeing—and more than a little scary. I literally had nothing holding me down. No space to call my own, no retreat, no anchor. I felt as though I might float away if someone breathed too hard in my direction.

"I stayed with my dad and stepmother while I searched for an apartment. They made me feel right at home. My stepmom cooked for me, and made an effort to give me the space I needed to sort through my crazy emotions. Luckily, my job as a freelance designer allowed me to work from anywhere, so I set up shop at the kitchen table.

"It took about a month for me to find my apartment, a cozy third-floor walk-up in an old Victorian house. My amazing landlady helped me choose fresh paint colors for the walls, and even paid the painters' fees.

"Standing in the middle of my brand new, sparkling clean, very empty apartment, I felt … lost. I had nothing. No bed, no couch, no table at which to eat my meals—only my desk, my books, and my clothes in the closet. This place was mine, yes, but not really. It was a blank canvas.

"Thankfully, my family and friends rallied around me. My dad gave me the mattress and chests of drawers from his spare bedroom. My friend Joe gave me a kitchen table and matching chairs. Another friend gave me a couch and a coffee table. Suddenly, my empty space was full of objects infused with love and care. I still had to buy a lot of essentials, which stretched my budget to the limit, but the big stuff was all donated—and all of it felt like a fresh start. This wasn't 'our' stuff; it was *mine*.

"That apartment was my sanctuary. I loved living there. I loved coming home at the end of the day to a space that was wholly mine, where I didn't have to pretend, or please anyone, or work around anyone. I could laugh, dance, play music, or cry my eyes out—whatever I needed at the moment.

"I stayed in that home until I met my current husband and the love of my life. When it was time to move on, I said goodbye with an immense amount of gratitude in my heart, and with the hope that the space would become a sanctuary for someone else like me.

"Leaving behind almost everything I owned was a choice. I could have fought for the bistro table I'd loved, the dishes I'd picked out after our wedding, the crystal wine glasses, the wedding photos ... but honestly, the stuff we'd accumulated just didn't matter that much to me. I didn't want to hang on to the past. I wanted a clean break, and to leave that part of my life behind. Starting from scratch allowed me to reinvent myself, start fresh, and launch into my new life as a new and better version of me!"

What Baggage Are You Carrying?

When starting on a new journey, it's best to travel light.

Not everyone is in a situation to leave it all behind like Aimee did, but a certain amount of letting go is vital in a separation. Getting rid of excess baggage—in the form of material possessions—is a great way to energize your separation process both physically and emotionally.

For our purposes in this chapter, your "baggage" does not include the objects that still need to be divided in your separation (like furnishings, artwork, or other shared assets). Instead, we will focus on the objects that are yours and yours alone, and whose fate you can decide without input from your ex-partner. These include clothing, books, hobby items, administrative records, and computer files, as well as stuff stored with your parents, at your work, or in a storage facility.

The objects you own have a major effect on how you deal with and get through your separation and how you structure your new future. Possessions can give you a sense of security, but they can also create unnecessary stress and drain your time and energy. When the latter happens, it's better to just let go and get rid of them. The fewer sources of stress and clutter you have in your life right now, the better!

SEPARATION IS A GOOD TIME FOR "SPRING CLEANING"

A separation is a good time for separating yourself from excess baggage. You have drawn a line in the sand and disconnected from your old life; now, you get to decide what is coming with you on your new journey. This is an appropriate time to let go of objects that no longer "fit" you, and lighten your load both physically and emotionally.

By tidying up and cleaning out your surroundings, you will create new space in your head, in your heart, and in your future. More, it will create a connection between your busy mind and your true feelings.

When my father and mother separated, we were living in Reeuwijk at the lakes and in the Dutch polders. Our family home was an older property filled with nice antiques and a few 1960s modern pieces. When my dad moved out and started living on his own, he found a really sleek, modern apartment, and filled it with even more modern furniture, paintings, sculptures, and accessories. When my siblings and I first saw it, our eyes nearly popped out of our heads! We had had no idea that our father had such a love for modern style and architecture; in fact, he confessed later that he had hidden that love since he was a child. His mother, my grandmother, was very *avant la lettre*, and had built a modern house with an architect on the Zeeland Islands before the start of World War II; she died when he was only thirteen, but her love of modern art and design was planted in his heart.

When you no longer have to compromise with a partner about your home environment, you may discover new and exciting things about yourself and what makes a space "feel like home" to you.

Of course, rearranging and getting rid of things can also be a challenge, and not everyone enjoys it. But instead of thinking of this process as a chore, treat it as a golden opportunity to take an inventory of your life—and to choose, consciously, what belongs in your new, happy future, and what needs to stay in the past.

Here are just a few reasons why clearing up clutter and getting rid of baggage is a great idea right now:

- **It gives you a sense of structure, calm, and space.** When you reorganize your stuff and get rid of what you no longer need, you create structure and space in your living environment. Work in a focused and targeted manner. Decide what you want to keep, make sure it's clean, and assign it a place in your home. Pack up everything else to donate, sell, or throw away. When you're done, you will feel a sense of spaciousness, calm, and peace.

- **It helps you get rid of emotional baggage.** It's hard to fully disconnect from your old life if you are still hanging on to all of your old stuff! The objects around you are probably associated with emotions and feelings. In dealing with these objects, you are also dealing with past emotions and events in your life. You can analyze, sort, rearrange, and let go of your emotions at the same time as you clear up your possessions. Keep the objects that make you feel good, and get rid of the ones that are associated with negative images and memories. The end result is a feeling of emotional calm and space—a perfect gift to yourself during a separation! (Hint: Even if you miss your ex, put anything directly associated with him/her in boxes for the time being, and store those boxes out of sight. Keeping photos, mementos, or your ex's stuff around will only create emotional confusion and make disconnection harder!)

- **Cleaning up encourages change.** Life is a continual process of change. Every day, every hour, and every minute, change is going on around you. Change is what allows you to grow and continue on your journey. However, when change is painful—as during a separation—you may have a strong desire to resist it, and even physically protect yourself from it. This is self-defeating. You can't go back to the way things used to be, and if you try, you will waste an enormous amount of energy. Choosing to clean up and get rid of excess baggage signals to your mind and heart that you have decided to accept the changes that are now taking place, regardless of how much grief and pain they are causing you. This acceptance can be truly liberating. If it helps, visualize yourself as a tree shedding its leaves in the autumn. You need this period of winter clearing to be able to bloom in the spring!

- **Cleaning up gives your home a new look.** Once you have cleared out old baggage and rearranged things to your liking, you will have a new and cozier home that reflects your personal taste and energy. Regardless of how long you plan to stay there, creating a home space that feels uniquely yours can help keep you in a positive emotional state.

- **Cleaning up is an excellent basis for a new start.** Creating extra space and transparency (physically and emotionally) gives you the courage, clarity, and self-confidence to greet the new life ahead of you with open arms.

Empowered Action

▶ Take an "Inspection Tour"

Pick a room in your home for your inspection tour. For a maximum of thirty minutes, walk around this room, and look at everything in it with a discerning and critical eye. Pretend that you need to get rid of 50 percent of your stuff. With notebook in hand, make a list of what you would keep, and why. What associations do you have with specific objects? Which items have you been meaning to get rid of for some time now, but haven't? What are you uncertain about? Would you feel guilty if you got rid of certain objects? How would you feel if half your stuff was really gone? Would you feel lost, panicked, or relieved?

Write your answers down. Then, using your notes as a basis, get rid of anything you no longer need (or at least make a plan to do so).

Get Cleaning!

When you're ready to start cleaning and clearing, follow this formula to engage with the process in an efficient and directed way that will leave you feeling great!

Step 1: Prepare

Give back whatever belongs to your ex-partner within two weeks.

This step alone will help you avoid a great deal of negativity. Remember to consider books, clothing, music, photographs, furniture, paintings, equipment, memorabilia, and administrative records, as well as objects obtained from your ex-partner's parents, family, friends, or work.

Be decisive: what is not yours *must* be returned. Returning those objects as quickly as possible will help you deal with your separation as quickly and positively as possible. Do not try to manipulate or blackmail your ex with objects that belong to him/her. Doing so is an exercise in negativity, and will result in bad vibes not only between you and your partner, but also in your home space. Objects that you refuse to let go of, whether out of sentimentality, revenge, or as a bargaining chip in the legal negotiations—always carry negative energy.

Identify and evaluate every object that reminds you of your past relationship.

Carefully inspect all the objects in your home that belong to you but are associated in your mind and heart with your broken relationship—in particular, those objects that immediately make you feel angry, sad, weak, or lonely. Before simply discarding them, store them out of sight for a few months, or ask friends and family to hold on to them for a while. You might feel differently about them in a few months' time.

In particular, don't keep items that remind you of your ex-partner in your bedroom, living room, hallway, or study. These rooms should contain only objects that reflect your own energy, past and future.

If you have children, don't put away family photographs and reminders of family memories. If you do, you will be denying their past and memories that are precious to them. Instead, move these items to your children's rooms, or other spaces in the house where they won't affect your energy but where your kids can still engage with them.

Step 2: Sort

Keep objects that have positive emotional energy.

If you feel happy, satisfied, or comforted when you see or hold an object, it's a good idea to keep it. The object can be anything at all: a chair, a watch, cufflinks, an old teddy bear, a stone, a music recording, a lamp, a plant, a piece of equipment, a cooking pan, your bicycle, a memento, or a note on a piece of paper. If it means something to you, and serves as a source of calm, joy, or energy, keep it, regardless of whether it matches your new space.

Discard objects with negative emotional energy.

Often, you don't even realize that certain objects, including simple things that you feel attached to, can have a negative effect on you. If you see or hold an object and it brings back bad memories, elicits a sigh, places a claim on you, makes you feel guilty for any reason, or brings up a sense of unwanted obligation, you've found an object with a negative emotional charge. Such objects will drain you of strength and energy for no purpose, so your only option is to get rid of them, even if they are perfectly serviceable or attractive. What has to go, has to go. If it's a truly beautiful or useful object, the person to whom you give it will be thrilled to receive it!

Discard objects that you haven't used in more than two years.

If you haven't used something in more than two years, it's just taking up space—so why keep it? As they say, out with the old, and in with the new!

Step 3: The Cleanup

Now that you've prepared and sorted in Steps 1 and 2, it's time to do your cleanup!

Cleaning up is something you should do in a well-planned fashion. Don't be too ambitious. You don't need to collect everything in one evening and put it out with the garbage; in fact, that's a terrible idea. You don't even need to finish the process in a week, or two, or three. Take small, well-considered steps according to a plan that is appropriate to your current schedule and energy level.

If you approach this methodically, you will avoid rash decisions and disappointments, and keep yourself from feeling drained or overwhelmed. At the same time, be strict and honest with yourself. Once you start a cleaning activity, finish it! Otherwise you'll be living with more chaos and mess, which feels self-defeating and is not at all helpful to your stress level.

Before starting any cleaning project, make sure you have enough boxes, garbage bags, cleaning products, and storage space. That way, you can make fast and efficient progress. If possible, keep the windows open during the cleanup to allow fresh air and energy to circulate.

Next, divide your stuff into six different piles:

- Keep
- Discard
- Donate to charity
- Give to friends and family
- Sell
- Question marks

Keep

Make sure all the objects in this pile are clean and in good repair. Store them again in a tidy fashion, or set them out to be used as you like.

Discard

Cracked pots and vases, worn-out shoes, old magazines, clothing with holes or tears, dead plants, non-functioning appliances, and anything else that is broken, worn out, or no longer functional should be on this list. Don't promise yourself that you will darn those old socks or read those old magazines someday, when you have the time—because chances are, you won't, and they will just become extra, unnecessary items on your already-long to-do list. Put these objects immediately into garbage bags and/or bring them to a recycling center. Keep garbage pickup days in mind: the day before the pickup, you can work harder and with fewer doubts in your mind, and the stuff you're discarding will be out of your space more quickly. You can also choose a Sunday for this work, and bring your trash to a Monday morning pickup site.

Donate to charity

Within a week, donate these objects to the charity of your choice. Great options for common household goods include local resale/antique shops, Goodwill, the Salvation Army, Savers, or other charity resale organizations.

Give away to friends and family

Choose these items carefully, and assign them to a recipient immediately. If you're not sure if someone will want a particular item, ask; if they don't need it, put it in the charity bin. Avoid causing extra work for friends and family by offloading piles of unsorted goods onto them! If you have lots of unassigned stuff, hold a rummage sale for friends and family so everyone can pick out the items they want and will use.

Sell

Consign these objects at secondhand stores, or list them on internet resale sites like eBay, Amazon, etc. If you have the time and energy, you could also hold a garage sale. Try to get this done as soon as possible, preferably within two weeks. If you need assistance, ask someone from your Winning Team. If you can't sell it, don't hold onto it: give it away within three days instead.

Question marks

Some things you won't be sure about. Make a separate pile of these. On the next Sunday (or the evening before garbage pickup), hold these objects, one by one, in your hands and decide whether to keep or discard them. Remember, the first thought that comes to mind counts. Don't make excuses, and don't put things back in the pile to deal with later. Doubts only drain your energy and willpower—so make a decision, and stick with it!

Step 4: Relax

After a hard day of cleaning and sorting, open some windows, light a candle or incense, take a long, hot shower, and eat a lovely dinner at home or with friends. Pick some wildflowers or buy a plant to brighten up your space. This will help you release any clinging energy and feel refreshed and light.

TIPS AND TRICKS

- **Use cleaning as an energy booster.** If you're in a dip, cleaning up will help you feel accomplished and lighter. No task is too small. Just cleaning out your wallet, a single computer folder, a shelf, or your toolbox can help you feel better.
- **Always clean alone.** This might be challenging for you, but this process is an important part of working through your emotions and preparing to embrace your new future. Ask your Winning Team for help thinking up a system or action plan, or moving heavy furniture, but don't let your friends and family do your sorting, make choices for you, or guilt you into keeping something you don't want or need. Only you can decide what belongs in your new life. (Hint: If you need help or just want a jumpstart, you can always add a personal organizer to your Winning Team to help you create a plan to get rid of excess baggage!)
- **Keep your home neat and tidy at all times.** Although it may feel like more work on a daily basis, in the end, this will save you time and energy.

- **Make your home cozy and comfortable.** After you've cleaned, sorted, and discarded/donated, rearrange your space so it feels cozy and supportive. This creates a positive atmosphere of renewal, calm, and warmth.

- **Don't worry about how your ex-partner might respond** when entering your "new" home. This place now belongs to you (even if it's still partly owned by your ex)!

- **Ask your ex-partner, family, and friends to return things that belong to you.** A separation is a very appropriate time to ask others to return things (including money), even if they don't want to hear about it. If you find this difficult, ask someone from your Winning Team for help.

- **Set aside a box for small objects from your past** that you do not (yet) want to part with but that are emotionally difficult to deal with. Such items might include jewelry, photos, mementos, notes, and other trinkets. Open the box a year later, and decide whether to keep or discard the contents.

- **Find a new configuration.** Rearrange items in your house in new ways. Move furniture around. Change out the artwork. Paint the walls. Make your spare bedroom into your master bedroom. Reconfigure your living space so that it no longer feels like the space you shared with your ex.

- **Make your bedroom sacred.** Clean up your sleeping space. Vacuum under the bed. Clean the curtains. Get rid of any clutter. Your bedroom is your oasis, so make it feel more like a spa!

- **Create a memory book or a folder on your computer using photos of objects you are discarding, donating, or returning to your ex.** If you're having trouble letting go of attachment, this may be a way to bridge the gap—but only do it if it really helps you.

- **Don't store unwanted stuff in your house for more than a couple of weeks.** You may be tempted to wait for next year's neighborhood yard sale to get rid of your old stuff, but keeping your house full of excess clutter is not a good idea. You are in a phase of growth, inviting your new life to come in. Make sure you have room for it to fit through the door!

- **Consider your kids.** Your home should remain a familiar and comforting place for your kids. Change and rearrange things in a more subtle fashion, and don't involve them in your cleaning up or clearing out activities.

Getting rid of excess baggage is good therapy for everyone! Even if it seems trivial or silly at first, I promise that this work will help you to connect more deeply to yourself and your feelings, and put you in more positive space in your separation process!

Empowered Actions

▶ Schedule Your Cleaning Times

Now or during your next Power Hour, schedule time in the upcoming week to clean and clear one room, or one portion of your space. Discard, donate, or sell the items you no longer want as soon as possible.

▶ Do a Quick Sweep

Look around your space for a few minutes. Chances are you will immediately identify those objects which have positive, uplifting energy, and those which have negative energy. Move the positive objects to more prominent places, and get rid of the negative ones as soon as possible.

What Comes Next

By following the directions in Step 4 of the Positive Separation Method, you've established a solid baseline for your healthy, positive environment on multiple levels: mind, body, and spirit. Now, your task is to keep up the good work of disconnecting from any lingering elements of your old life, connecting to your core self and Positive IDs, getting clear on your vision and what you can influence, empowering yourself, processing your emotions, and creating a positive environment every day, from now until your separation is resolved.

Chapter Twelve, the final chapter in Step 4, is dedicated to "Special Wisdom"— tools for parents in separation, or people who are balancing a separation with a new partnership. Even if neither of these apply to you at this time, I would suggest reading this chapter anyway. There are lots of pearls of wisdom in there which can be applied to many other areas of your life. After exploring this Special Wisdom, we will move on to Step 5 of the Positive Separation Method: Move Forward with Confidence!

CHAPTER TWELVE

Special Wisdom for
Parents and New Partners

T he Positive Separation Method is unique because it is focused on *you*, not on your ex-partner, your situation, or any other outside factors. When you make yourself your highest priority, you will feel more grounded, make more positive choices, and feel more empowered to walk your path toward your bright, happy future.

However, there are special situations which add new layers to the separation process. If these are present in your world, they should be considered and navigated with care so that you can continue to honor your commitments to yourself and stay out of negative emotional spirals.

This "Special Wisdom" chapter is dedicated to helping you make empowered decisions around a few very important elements: your children and new partners. The wisdom in this chapter can be put into play from your Point of Disconnection, or the day you consciously choose to disconnect from your old life.

Supporting Your Children in Separation and Beyond

Throughout this book, I've given small tips for navigating separation when there are children involved. Now, we'll go a little deeper to create a plan and lay down some Golden Rules for supporting your children during your separation.

If you have children, creating a positive and nourishing situation for them is probably one of your biggest concerns right now. But although you may be tempted to sacrifice your own needs for those of your children, this is not a good idea at all!

So many people get this wrong. Often, the first question I hear from clients in separation is, "How can I protect my kids from this? How can I make sure that they are happy and taken care of?" My reply is always the same: "You can *only* do that by taking care of yourself."

In order to create a happy future—for everyone—you must become, and remain, happy, stable, and secure within yourself. Your children (even if they are grown) will always follow your energetic and emotional lead, and they will flourish when they have a thriving parent as a role model. After all, you are the one who creates the environment and structure in which they live every day.

The basic rule is very simple: If you're doing well, your children will also do well. If you deal with your separation positively, so will they. The opposite is also true: If you're not okay, they're not okay. If you're negative, they will feel it. Even if you bend over backward to ensure that nothing about their daily lives changes, they will suffer if you are suffering.

Where you need to go the extra mile in your separation isn't in putting on a cozy show for your kids. They will see right through it, no matter how young they are. Your effort needs to go into being a calm, responsible adult, even in stressful situations; focusing only on what you can control; processing your emotions in a positive and productive way; and taking action to create a happy, light-filled future.

Since both you and your ex-partner continue to remain parents and will need to cooperate for the sake of your children, you will never become completely separated. It's a hard truth to swallow, I know. So, to navigate these waters in a positive way, you will need to apply an extra-large dose of discipline and self-control. (If you make good use of your Power Hour, your Winning Team, and the exercises in this book, this will be a lot easier!)

Even if your children are grown and have kids of their own, they are still your children, and they still love both of their parents. If you are unsure of how to handle your particular situation, consult a professional therapist or family coach and ask for practical advice you can work with.

GOLDEN RULES FOR PARENTS IN SEPARATION

Aside from caring for yourself and keeping up your energy and positive outlook, there are numerous ways to support your kids through the separation process. Here are my Golden Rules for navigating a separation when kids are involved.

As you read through this list, put a smiley face or a check mark next to each of the rules you agree with, and an X next to those that feel challenging for you.

Consider how best to support each of your children. Every child, depending on age and temperament, requires a different kind of support. Consider consulting a professional (like a child psychologist, social worker, school counselor, or family coach) about how you can best equip your children to deal with their new situation.

Explain to your children as clearly as possible why you want to separate. If possible, decide with your ex ahead of time what you will share with the children, and how. The story you present should be a clear one, in which both parents refrain from being negative about the past and are as positive as possible about the future. This will give your children the best possible basis for coming to terms with your separation.

Do not talk negatively about the other parent. Spare your children the negative details, accusations, and finger-pointing. The reason for your separation is simply that you were no longer happy together. It may feel good in the moment to bash your ex, but in the long term, this will make things more difficult for your children.

Do not allow your new partner to speak negatively about your ex or your former family life in front of your children. New partners are outside of the situation and this creates tension for everyone.

Children have a right to both of their parents. Unless there is abuse, neglect, or other unsafe conditions happening on your ex's part, keeping your kids from their other parent will do more harm than good. Even if you would rather avoid contact with your ex, it's a 50-50 deal, so make sure the other parent has a clear parenting role to play, even if the children are still living with you.

Make clearly-defined arrangements about parenting roles, timelines, and schedules, and always uphold your end of the bargain. This creates a sense of clarity for everyone concerned.

Have fun! Joining your kids in enjoyable activities isn't just good for them, it's also good for you. Take time to enjoy your kids, laugh, and play. Your time and attention is the best gift you can give them right now.

Allow your children to continue seeing both sets of grandparents (as long as the situation is safe for them). A sense of continuity in family contact on both sides is very important for your child. Loving grandparents can provide comfort, support, and perspective during challenging times.

Don't use your children as a messenger service. If you need to exchange information or change an appointment, or if you have questions about school, clothing, birthday presents, or anything else, it's your responsibility to get that information from your ex. Period.

Never argue in the presence of your children. It makes them feel powerless and uncertain. Strive for friendly or neutral contact during pickup and drop-off times, and during all other interactions. If you need to vent, do so in private. A good stomping-around walk outside can do wonders for your mental state.

Do not ask your children to put pressure on the other parent to get what you want—even if it's something as fundamental as child support or alimony. Fight your own battles.

Never use your children to manipulate your ex-partner.

Make sure your children do not have to take sides. Don't ask them which parent they love more. Don't ask them to pass judgment on your ex-partner, even if (in your eyes) your ex has done something unforgivable. Don't compete with your partner about who is the "best parent."

Inform your children's school of your separation. Make sure that the school sends both parents information about parent evenings, school performances, etc., and that you are both on the mailing list.

Never let time with your new partner take priority over time with your children. Don't cancel plans with your kids to spend time with your new partner, and don't shuffle the kids around to babysitters so you can have a "date night." You will have plenty of time to enjoy your new partner once your separation is settled.

If you have negative emotions, deal with them yourself. Even adult children should not have to play a support role for a parent in separation. Your children are not there to comfort you or make you happy. If you struggle with this, or feel like your children are your only support system right now, seek out professional help, and revisit Chapters Six and Seven on managing your mindset and creating your Winning Team.

Remember that you are continually setting the example for your children about how to move through a crisis situation—so practicing balanced behavior can have positive long-term consequences. Be conscious of what your own behavior is modeling for them. If you take an open and positive approach, your child will copy that. If you are jealous and shortsighted, or adopt a victim mindset, your child will also learn that from you.

Teach your children to deal positively with their own emotions. Encourage them to read, write, talk, and otherwise express their feelings. Drawing, painting, making music, and other creative activities can serve as an outlet for challenging emotions. Outdoor sports and recreation are likewise helpful. If you children are having a hard time processing the emotions of the separation, don't be afraid to seek out professional help on neutral ground. Your children can benefit from therapy as much as you do!

Encourage your children to form their own Winning Team of playmates, coaches, teachers, professionals, and even teddy bears! Grandparents can also be part of a child's Winning Team, but only if they can remain positive and neutral.

Make sure you are sticking to your Five Commitments and honoring your goals. If your kids are old enough, share these goals with them so they know what you are working toward. If they see you working to create a positive future (for yourself and for them) they will feel supported.

Count your smiley faces or check marks. How many of these rules felt good to you? How many felt challenging? During your next Power Hour, give these challenging rules a second thought. What would happen if you were to stick to these rules for a week? Two? It might not be as hard as you think!

Empowered Action

▶ Make Arrangements for Your Children

The arrangements you need to make around your children in your separation will depend on your unique situation, how easily you communicate with your ex-partner, and what you have already established in terms of co-parenting arrangements.

During your Power Hour or a quiet moment, go over the following list. Place a check mark next to each item that applies to you, strike through any item that you have already dealt with, and add any items that are missing. Immediately write down any thoughts or action points that come to mind. Add necessary items to your to-do list or planner.

The basics

- The co-parenting plan (together)
- Where the children will be living/relocation arrangements
- Financial arrangements
  - Child support
  - Health care
  - Insurances
  - School and study costs
  - Bank accounts
  - Gifts and incidentals
- How to deal with contact moments like pick-up and drop-off
- Contact with schools, sports teams, and hobby clubs
- Choice of future schools/study
- Special events
  - Birthdays
  - Father's Day
  - Mother's Day
  - Holidays
  - School vacations
- Visits to doctors and dentists (who accompanies them, informing each other etc.)
- Basic house rules
  - Bedtime
  - Nutrition
  - Homework
  - Exercise
  - Mobile devices and internet use
  - Chores and duties

- Norms and values, setting limits
- Traditions that you wish to have respected (family, religious, or cultural)
- Formal and legal matters (passports, wills, guardianship)
- Contacts with grandparents and other family members
- Relationship and contact with new partners

New partners

- How and when to introduce (potential) new partners
- Rules for new partner visits, sleepovers, outings, etc.
- How new partners and relationships are discussed with the children

Yourself

- The relationship you wish to maintain with your children (changed role as parent)
- The optimum relationship between your children and your ex-partner
- The relationship between your children and family and friends on both sides
- The relationship between your children and a potential new partner (and children)
- That relationship you wish to have with the children of your new partner
- The relationship between your children and (any potential) new brothers and sisters

Take the time to carefully go over the above list of action points. Add any items that are missing. Review this list often to see which items require extra attention or action. If you need help, ask a member of your Winning Team to go over the list with you. You can also ask for help from a professional, such as your school psychologist, child therapist, or family coach. Katherine Woodward Thomas's *Conscious Uncoupling* is also a great resource for parents who want to create a positive separation and set a great example for their kids.

New Partners

When a new partner—whether yours or your ex's—enters the picture during the separation process, it can create a lot of strong emotion and drama. It's best to be prepared for this and approach the process of integrating new partners in a proactive and positive manner, even if it's painful.

If your ex finds a new partner, even if it happens months after the separation, you may feel a strong and even irrational surge of jealousy, anger, fear, or judgment. If you find a new partner during the separation (or even after it's over), the same may happen for your ex. This can make interactions regarding your separation difficult, and create blocks in the Emotional and Physical Sub-Processes of everyone involved.

If you or your ex found a new partner before the decision to separate was made, the emotions can be even more difficult to handle. Feelings of victimhood, rage, and disbelief can come up strongly. You or your ex might feel betrayed, humiliated, or struggle with feelings of worthlessness.

Whatever the situation, your separation has happened, and that old part of your life is over. Carrying old hurts isn't going to change things or help you create a new, happy future. Whenever you are struggling with new partner issues, it's best to come back to the lessons and exercises from Steps 1, 2, and 3 of the Positive Separation Method to regain your balance. Set your sights on your own happy future, focus only on what you can control, stay true to your commitments to yourself, and use the tools you've learned to manage your emotions and connect to your core. Don't try to take responsibly for your ex-partner's feelings, and don't expect your ex to take responsibility for your feelings. You are only responsible for yourself and your own conduct.

This may be easier said than done, however, because when a new partner enters the picture, lines of responsibility and involvement tend to get blurred. Your new partner, desiring to support you, may want to become involved in your separation, even to the point of coming with you to mediation sessions or court hearings. Your ex's new partner, desiring the same thing, may do likewise.

In my practice, I've seen over and over again that this shifting of boundaries is never a good idea, except in very specific situations involving medical care for you or a child, or other unforeseen circumstances.

The first and most important Golden Rule regarding new partners in a separation is: *Your separation is between you and your ex-partner, no one else!* Your separation is part of your past (even if it is taking up time and energy in your present), and your new partner is part of your future. Your new partner wasn't part of your past relationship, and s/he does not need to become part of it now.

Even if you want your new partner by your side for support, resist the temptation to bridge these two worlds. To make the best choices in your separation, you need to be free of any outside influences, even loving and well-meaning ones. Also, if your new partner is pushing through his or her own personal agenda, and something goes wrong, it could sabotage your new relationship.

Of course, how your ex involves his or her new partner is something that is beyond your ability to influence. However, if you can, ask your ex-partner (calmly and respectfully) to allow this to be decided by only the two of you, for the reasons stated above. Your request may or may not be honored, so don't get attached to the results. Just keep your commitments to yourself, process your strong emotions, and act with integrity.

GOLDEN RULES FOR HANDLING NEW PARTNERSHIPS IN SEPARATION

Here are a few more suggestions for dealing with new partners during the separation process. My suggestion is that you read and work with these Golden Rules daily. I have seen a lot of unhappiness and damage occur in situations where clear boundaries are not set for new partners. Ask for professional help if you are having emotional challenges around this, or are finding these boundaries difficult to maintain. You don't want these common pitfalls to jeopardize your happy future!

When your ex has a new partner ...

Don't take out your frustrations on your ex's new partner. Remember, your ex's actions, and those of his or her new partner, are outside of your sphere of influence. Put your energy into the things you can control, use the tools in Steps 2 and 3 of the Positive Separation Method, and hold yourself accountable to your personal commitments. If your feelings of bitterness or jealousy are clouding your judgment, it's best to seek professional help.

Renew your commitment to disconnecting from your old life. Your ex is not sharing the road to your future; s/he is on his or her own road. You can visualize this by drawing one road that diverges into two (like you did in Chapter Two). On the left branch, write your name. On the right, write the names of your ex and his or her new partner. No matter how hard it may be, imagine them following their road away from where you are standing. Wish them well. You are no longer part of their future, as they are no longer part of yours. If you need help working through this, call on one or more of your professional Winning Team members.

When you have a new partner ...

Sometimes, a wonderful new partner shows up out of the blue, as if by magic. If that happens, it's great—but don't lose touch with the work you've been doing to empower yourself, connect to your core, and manage your emotions. This is a time to rediscover yourself from the inside out, and get clear on what you really want from your future—including your future relationships. You don't want to shortchange that by striving to meet the needs of a new partner and relationship too soon. More, you don't want to exhaust yourself handling two relationships—the old and the new—at the same time!

Don't include your new partner as a member of your Winning Team during your separation. Again, your new partner is a part of your future, so keep him/her separate from your past.

Don't let your separation become the focus of your new relationship. You and your new partner may be tempted to commiserate over your past breakups. Don't. Refrain from sharing "horror stories" about your exes, or complaining about your separation process. Instead, rely on your Winning Team members, both professional and personal, to help you through tough situations.

Don't let new love create an "emotional blackout." Falling in love with a new partner is a wonderful thing. But if it causes you to toss aside all of your unprocessed or hidden emotions around your separation, it's not healthy. Sooner or later, those feelings will have to be dealt with—and if you don't do it now, they may impact your new relationship later!

Enjoy your new partner to the fullest, but be discreet. Give your ex-partner and any children involved a chance to get used to the changed situation. After all, you will have ample opportunity in future to share your new relationship with the people you love.

Don't confront your children with your new love too soon. Make sure to give your kids your undivided attention whenever possible. There will be ample time and opportunity later on for your new partner to become part of their lives.

Deal with your emotions on your own. Of course, you should talk to your new partner—but don't ask him/her to help you process your past. Take responsibility for your own healing process.

Continue working on yourself. Don't stop creating healthy habits and patterns in your life just because you found a new partner! After all, you're still creating *your* future!

Empowered Action

▶ Create a "New Partner" Strategy

If you have a new partner already, or plan to start dating again soon, take the time to map out your "new partner strategy." This is your plan for introducing and including a new partner into your life.

Even if you don't have a new partner yet, make some commitments to yourself about how you will operate in the space of new love. How will you separate your past from your future? How long do you want to wait before "going public" with your new relationship? What parameters will you set around the pace and progression of your new relationship? How long do you want to wait before introducing a new partner to your children?

Knowing the answers to questions like these beforehand will help you avoid making emotionally-charged judgments in the heat of the moment. Also, setting clear boundaries will actually help your new partner support you as you continue to finalize your separation.

What Comes Next

Your new life is waiting—and your children and any new partners in the picture are fortunate to be able to share in the vibrant new future that *you* are creating. There will be times when things will get tough, or feel complicated and sticky; when this happens, always go back to your Positive IDs, your Five Commitments, and your vision for your bright new future. Ask the members of your Winning Team for help, and seek professional assistance if you need it. Do whatever it takes to hold on to your vision of a positive, happy future. You will be happy again—and if you are happy, the ones you love will be happy as well!

POSITIVE
SEPARATION
STEP 5

Move Forward
with Confidence!

Move Forward with Confidence!

I n Steps 1 through 4 of the Positive Separation Method, you focused on creating a solid, positive foundation for yourself during your separation. You disconnected from your ex-partner and your old life, you created a framework and accountability system to keep yourself aligned with your new life, you looked within yourself to find your Positive IDs, you made supportive commitments to yourself, you learned to take better care of your body to support your energy and build up your reserves, and you cleared up your space, schedule, and relationships to create a positive environment. In short, you've put all the pieces in place to support a new, happy, fulfilling life, and become a new, empowered version of yourself who you can really fall in love with.

Step 5 of my Method is the "Happy Step," and your energy should feel like it's rising to match your vision for a new future. It's time to congratulate yourself! You have made it through the hardest part of your separation process. Even if the legal part of your separation is still in the works, or you still have a bit of climbing to do to get where you really want to be, you can see the summit of your "uphill journey" ahead, and you know you will make it. Your reward for all of your hard work, of course, is a brighter, more effervescent you!

Before you engage with this Step, it's important to ask yourself if you truly feel ready to move into this new energy. The art of positive separation is no different than any other art form; it takes time and repetition to master. I have seen my clients, friends, parents, and grandparents master this art. It doesn't always happen straight away, but with time and patience they shed their old layers to become the fullest versions of themselves. This new radiance shines through in their relationships with children, family, friends, and new partners.

When you are a parent, this Step will be extra-valuable for you. Your role has shifted from a romantic partner/co-parent to co-parent only, but you will always maintain a certain connection to your ex-partner. In Step 5, you will clearly map out your new parenting relationship with your ex, and step into your new role from a loving, empowered place within yourself that takes into account your desire for everyone's happy future.

If you're not quite ready to move into Step 5 yet, don't worry. Some people reach this point in six months, while others need a year or more. There is no good or bad, right or wrong. It takes time to integrate all of actions, emotions, and processes from Steps 1 through 4 into your life in a full way. Sometimes, your heart needs extra time to heal, and your emotions need extra time to catch up with your vision. That's why it's imperative that you keep up with your Power Hour, honor your Five Commitments, focus on only the things you can influence, manage your emotions in a healthy way, take care of your body and your environment, schedule daily and weekly chill times, and follow all of the other instructions in Steps 1 through 4, even after the bulk of your separation tasks have been resolved. Don't stop doing your work just because you're feeling better—it's *because* you're doing the work that you feel so connected to yourself!

You are ready to launch into Step 5 when things have settled down in your life quite a lot, and you feel a strong connection to your inner core. You might still have a tough day here and there, but in general you are feeling pretty relaxed and at home in your life. More, you are ready to close the door on your old life for good, and welcome in the next phase of your life and all of the opportunities that come with it.

Remember, mastering the art of positive separation isn't about just going through the motions. It's about being the healthiest, happiest, most connected, and most empowered version of yourself—because that is the *best* way you can contribute to yourself and others. As your new life continues to evolve and expand, always return to your core: your vision, your dreams, your Positive IDs, and your commitments to yourself. The more you take care of your body, mind, heart, and soul, the more amazing your future will be!

CHAPTER THIRTEEN

Embrace Your New Life!

I t's time to congratulate yourself. You've done a lot of work, and now you're ready to leap with both feet into your new, happy future. You are 100 percent ready to love, value, and care for yourself through thick and thin—and with a foundation like that, the future can't help but be radiant!

Debra Poneman, keynote speaker, popular seminar leader, and best-selling author, discovered this after she separated from her husband, Fred.

DEBRA'S STORY

"I was married to the most wonderful man on the planet. He was kind, loving, giving, funny, brilliant, a generous lover … but it was over. He wasn't cheating on me, and I wasn't cheating on him. I just didn't want to be married anymore.

"I once heard someone describe a similar situation in this way: 'The marriage part of our friendship was over.' Looking back, I can see that this is essentially what happened, although at the time I didn't exactly see it that way.

"We had talked about divorce for years, but we just kept trying because it wasn't like there was anything really 'wrong.' We went to individual and marriage counseling, and several different couples seminars, but for me, it was all an exercise in futility. It was just not where I wanted to be.

"I would say things to him like, 'I don't deserve you. You should be with someone who loves and adores you and wants to be married,' and he would say, 'No, I want to be with you.'

"'But you deserve so much more! You think you want to be with me, but you really don't!'

"If you had asked me back then why I finally left, I might have said things like, 'He was too nice to me,' or 'He didn't take charge in a macho kind of way,' in order to justify leaving; but really it was just over for me. So at this point, I don't want to look back and try and make it more than it was or make him wrong. Instead, I want to look back and see where I could have shifted and where I didn't take responsibility.

"For example, I've always been a perfectionist. I like to do things my way. When Fred didn't get things 'right,' I would get really tense. The truth is that if he did things his way, 99 percent of the time they would end up turning out fine—but I had no patience. It's not that I enjoyed making him wrong, but I was gripped by my impatience and my certainty that I knew the best way to do things. Eventually I got into this place of expecting him to not do things right and I guess my commitment to the marriage wasn't strong enough for me to do the emotional work to pull myself out of that place. I realize now it was more about commitment to myself; he was just there for me to see my reflection.

"Would it have saved my marriage if I had been fully conscious of all of this back then? I don't know—and, really, it doesn't matter. I love my life now, and I love my space. I'm wired to be independent.

"Fred and I had both been doing inner work for decades. We were both meditation teachers, and had done lots of personal growth workshops. We both had many tools in our toolkits to use when we split up. We are still really, really close.

"Our divorce was completely amicable. When we needed to divide up our possessions, we would have arguments, only they were like, 'No, you like that more, you should keep it.'"

"But as smoothly as it went, I felt like the bad guy. I was the one who left. I was 'Bad Debra.' This wasn't feedback I was getting from most people (when I told our twenty-four-year-old daughter, Deanna, that I was going to leave, she said, 'Well, it's about time, Mom. You haven't wanted to be married for years!'); but there were some people who would say things that made me feel very guilty—and it was how I felt inside.

"I didn't need tools to deal with the practical stuff about our separation. I found myself a cozy little apartment that I loved, and Fred stayed in the big five-bedroom, five-bathroom house. I wasn't worried about the kids—I mean, it wasn't a cakewalk for either of them, but they were young adults and out of the house, so it wasn't a major trauma in their lives—and they both knew it was coming. What I really needed were tools to deal with the nagging guilt I was feeling. Fred was such a nice guy. I couldn't stand seeing him hurting. Was I really a horrible person?

"About five months after I moved out, we decided to sell the house. As we planned for the estate sale, I was in and out of the house daily. One day, when I came over, I guess he didn't hear me come in; I overheard him talking on the phone saying. 'I miss you too, sweetheart.'

"*Oh, he must be talking to our daughter*, I thought. *He's such a loving dad.*

"Then he went on: 'Yes, I'll see you tonight. Do you want to meet at the restaurant, or at your place?'

"'What the heck?' I was floored. Here I was, beating myself up every day and feeling like the worst person for hurting this precious man, and he had already found a new woman! I felt like I had been totally duped. There was more to his conversation, something about going dancing, but I didn't really want to hear it and quickly went upstairs.

"*You jerk! You should have told me!* I raged at him in my head. *You knew I was suffering. You knew I was taking the blame.*

"At that moment, I had to make a choice. I could blow up at him, and unleash all the rage I was feeling, or I could use my tools.

"I went in the bathroom, closed the door and started working with the Ho'oponopono technique. '*I'm sorry. Please forgive me. Thank you. I love you.*' The Ho'oponopono is a technique not simply for forgiving the other person, but for forgiving yourself for that part of you that contributed to the situation. After repeating these four phrases many times, and then 'destroying and un-creating' my rage using my Access Consciousness clearing statement, I was able to calm down and allow truth to come in.

"This wasn't about Fred or what he had done. It was about feeling and acknowledging my own feelings. Fred's choices had nothing to do with me. He hadn't done anything wrong. He was just living his life and didn't need to be accountable to me.

"I felt free, and so much lighter. I was able to walk back downstairs and look Fred in the eye. 'I don't know if you heard me coming downstairs earlier,' I said. 'But I overheard you on the phone, and I know that you have a new girlfriend. I'm happy for you.' And I really was.

"It's not that the emotional charge didn't come back again during the process of separating, but each time, I was able to diffuse it using my tools, and at the same time, learn something about myself. It was no longer about seeing how Fred needed to be different. That wasn't my business. What was my business was seeing where *I* needed to grow.

"Today, Fred and I are still really close. We talk a lot and are always there for our children. He dated a couple of different women after our separation, and has now found a wonderful partner who is perfect for him. She's really a doll and loves him the way he deserves to be loved. Because we had done our work together before the divorce, and kept doing it during and after, we've been able to keep the good parts of our relationship intact.

"Now, I can see clearly that when you're not full inside, you might think you're loving someone, but really you're not. You're trying to get something from them: approval, a sense of completion, love, security. You think you're giving love, but if you don't have great self-love first, you're really just twisting yourself into a pretzel trying to get your needs met from the other person. Only when you're full inside and have done your inner work can you really have an authentic relationship. You have to be full of love to really give love.

"Relationships and even divorces are great opportunities to take your attention off the other person; to stop trying to make them into who you think you need them to be, and start looking at who *you're* being. Have gratitude for the gift of what they reflect back to you, what they allow you to see about yourself. The only person you can ever change is *you*."

What It Means to Move Forward with Confidence

At this point in your life, you are setting out on a journey of exploration. Now that you have reached Step 5 of the Positive Separation Method and reconnected to the core of who you are, you're doing the "happy dance." Your past is behind you; your radiant future is ahead.

You're probably still discovering what empowers and motivates you on a daily basis, and which of your old habits and patterns no longer serve you. This work is ongoing, and hopefully you will continue to explore it for the rest of this year and beyond. More than a decade after I committed to mastering the art of separation, I am still discovering new things about myself and deepening my connection to my core. It's a fun and rewarding process!

You may, like Debra, also be discovering things about yourself that you didn't think were true, or uncovering feelings you didn't know you were holding on to. This uncovering is healthy and necessary. The more you can get in touch with who you truly are, what you want, and why you do the things you do, the more easily you will be able to create a happy, stable future full of love, joy, and promise.

Moving forward is about doing the work to reconnect with and empower yourself so that you can feel full of love—for yourself, your dear ones, and your new life. The first four Steps of the Positive Separation Method were centered around rebuilding your foundation and doing what was necessary to create stability, certainty, and inner connection after the shock of your separation. This sets the stage for whatever level of continual inner work, self-discovery, and healing will help you create the new life you desire.

ARE YOU READY FOR STEP 5?

As you move forward into your new future, the foundation you built in Steps 1 through 4 will continue to serve you well—but there comes a point where you need to close the door on your separation process and leap with both feet into your new life. In this chapter, we will do just that!

But how do you know when you are ready to make that leap?

When you are ready to move from your separation phase into your brand new life, you will feel it in your gut. There is no right or wrong. However, it has been my experience that most people need to work with the first four Steps of the Positive Separation Method for at least six months before they are truly ready to move on to Step 5. Some (like Isabelle from Chapter One, and Aimee from Chapter Eleven) were ready after just a few months. Others, like Jane from Chapter Two and Sophia from Chapter Eight, needed more than a year before they were fully ready to step into their new lives. Heather from Chapter Nine was ready when she saw her new self in the mirror in her apartment. Robert from Chapter Three was ready once he was certain that he would retain shared custody of his children. I personally needed a little over a year to feel fully connected to myself and what I wanted from my new life.

So, if you're not absolutely certain that you are fully connected to yourself and ready to move on, be patient. You are in a healing process, and healing cannot be rushed. Think of it as coming back to your favorite sport after ankle surgery. First, you have to deal with the trauma of injury, and the frustration of being in a cast. Once the cast comes off, you have to put weight on your foot again little by little, and deal with the pain and twinges as you heal your bones and tendons. Day by day, week by week, it gets better—until, one day, you decide you're ready to run headlong onto the field again.

You cannot rush this process; if you do, you will ultimately set yourself back. So be kind to yourself. Pamper yourself a bit. And let things unfold in their own good time.

Your "Big Leap" Day

The actions in Step 5 are all about launching you into your new life—and what better way to do that than with an all-day "launch party"?

When you decide that you are ready to make the break from your old life for good, plan a "Big Leap" Day (or, if you prefer, a "Big Leap" Weekend) where you can spend several few hours on your own to celebrate your journey and look back on what you've accomplished. This is a powerful way to wrap up the energy of your separation process and close the door on that phase of your life once and for all. You have done a lot of hard work to move yourself into a loving, empowered place, and it's time to acknowledge your efforts!

You can celebrate your Big Leap Day in any way you like, but I suggest making it a sacred time just for you. Prepare your space by cleaning up and opening windows (if the weather permits). Set up a table or altar with candles, flowers, scented oils, books, artwork, or anything else that makes you feel connected or inspired. Make yourself some fresh food, brew a pot of tea, and put on clothes that make you feel comfortable and happy. Turn off your phone, tablet, television, and computer, and minimize any other distractions as much as possible. This time—like the Power Hour you've been working with since Step 1, or the Chill Times you implemented in Step 4—is all about you!

YOUR BIG LEAP DAY: THE PLAN

When everything is ready, spend some time in quiet reflection. Then, work with the following six Empowered Actions (all of which are detailed in the sections to follow):

1. **Looking Back, Finding Purpose: Your Retrospective**
2. **Your New Road**
3. **Your Personal Pyramid, Revisited**
4. **Your Future Pyramid**
5. **Your Future Winning Team**
6. **Your Future Goals and Commitments**

All of these will help you look back on your journey in a tangible way, and prepare you to step fully into your new future.

Allow yourself at least several hours to do this work. At the end of your Big Leap Day, you may want to indulge in some private relaxation time, or you might invite some or all of your Winning Team members to celebrate with you over dinner or champagne. Either way, this day is all about you!

Empowered Action: Your Big Leap Plan

▶ 1. Finding Purpose, Looking Back: Your Retrospective

Before we begin the exercises for your Big Leap Day, I'd like to share a short story from world-renowned motivational speaker, thought leader, and best-selling author Lisa Nichols. I discovered Lisa's work in 2011, when I read her inspiring book, *No Matter What!* I fell in love with her "bounce-back muscles" and her determination. Later, when I learned more about her experiences in past relationships, I knew I would love to get her insights and share them as part of this book.

Finding Purpose: Lisa's Story

Lisa grew up on rough turf in Los Angeles. Twenty-plus years ago, she was a single mother dependent on public assistance and jumping from one job to the next. She had a young son, Jelani, whose father was in jail. One day, with just $11 in her bank account and needing to buy diapers for her son, she decided that something big had to change in her life. No one was going to rescue her. She had to become her own rescuer in order to provide a better life for herself and her son.

Later, already on the track to success, she became engaged to a new love. However, she discovered that he wasn't the man she thought he was. He began abusing her emotionally and physically. Now, she had to rescue herself in a different way by separating from her toxic relationship.

What I truly admire about Lisa's story is how she disconnected from a negative relationship and dire circumstances by connecting to her deeper self again and again, trusting her inner wisdom, being honest with herself, and taking care of her own needs. Today, she has created the wildly successful life of her dreams, and inspires people the world over with her radiance and wisdom.

"I decided I deserved a better life," Lisa said. "I had a dream to help and inspire others, but before I could do that I needed to rescue myself. I had to be my own biggest cheerleader; only then could I break out of the defeatist mindset, negative behaviors, and habits that were holding me back from success."

That's the attitude in a positive separation, too—the attitude you have been cultivating through your work with the Positive Separation Method. No one is going to do the work of your breakup on your behalf. No one is going to pave the way to your bright future for you. You need to take yourself by the hand and come into action day by day, step by step, with trust and faith in yourself and your own potential.

But that's not all Lisa had to share with me. When I asked her what helped her move past her old relationships in a healthy way that left her feeling whole and empowered, this is what she shared:

"The key piece of awareness that got me through not just one breakup, but several, was learning that there are three types of relationships. There are *lifetime relationships*—the kind you are in forever. There are *life-giving relationships* that let you know that you are still in the game, but which only last a couple of years. And then, there are *purposeful relationships*.

"Most people are in purposeful relationships, which are exactly what they sound like: relationships full of purpose, purpose-full. And once that purpose is fulfilled, the relationship either shifts or completes itself.

"At first, I would look at my relationship after a breakup and ask, 'What happened? What went wrong?'

"Then, when I learned about the three types of relationships, I shifted my perspective. I started asking, 'What was the gift here? What was the awareness, the opportunity?'

"When I started seeing that each relationship served a purpose, I could pull something from that relationship. It was no longer a loss or a waste of time. Every relationship I had ever been in, even the really challenging ones, served a purpose. They taught me things I needed to know about myself, and about love."

Looking Back: Your Retrospective

Set aside at least thirty minutes to do this exercise.

Now that you have been working with Steps 1 through 4 for a while, I am convinced you have the strength, clarity, and love for yourself to look back and see the purpose of your broken relationship, and identify the important lessons you learned from it.

Drawing on the wisdom of Lisa's story, think back on all the ways you have learned and grown since your Disconnection. What positive things have your old relationship—and your separation process—taught you? What did you need to face in order to grow as a person? Be open to whatever comes up when you ask these questions, and don't dwell in the negative. There is a reason why this relationship was part of your life. As Lisa described, it was "purpose-full."

For example, my own separation helped me to learn how to deal with my emotions in a positive way, and not be scared of my "big" feelings. Instead of running from what I felt, I learned to take the time I needed to explore my emotions and handle them with grace.

There is no right or wrong in this exercise. It's all about acknowledging what is true for you in your current reality, and seeing with the clear vision of hindsight. So write down all of the positive lessons you have learned from your past relationship and your breakup on a piece of paper. Feel as much gratitude as you can that you were able to live through and learn from this experience. Then, take a deep breath and let it all go.

▶ 2. Your New Road

Set aside about five minutes for this exercise.

Take a moment to sit quietly and take a few deep breaths. Then, on four separate pieces of notebook paper, newsprint, or even paper towel, draw the four parts of your path, one after the other: the path before your separation, the Point of Disconnection, your path from the Disconnection until this moment, and your future path. Place a special mark or symbol on your Point of Disconnection, and another symbol (like a star or a smiley face) on your future path.

Put all the papers in a line. Think of all the things that have changed, and all of the good things you are taking with you on your new road. Feel gratitude for where you have been, and where you are going. Congratulate yourself for everything you have achieved, and marvel at how far you have come. Then, when you are ready, put away the papers symbolizing your past, your Disconnection, and your separation process up until this moment. Keep the paper with your future path with you, or hang it where you can see it easily. You have stepped fully out of your old life and into the new!

> *Note: Some people like to lay down the drawing of their new path on the floor, and actually take a leap onto it to symbolize leaping into their new life! Others dance across the line, or do a frog-jump with both feet. Do what feels joyful to you—just don't slide across the paper, dragging the past into the present!*

▶ 3. Your Personal Pyramid, Revisited

Set aside about thirty minutes for this exercise.

Back in Chapter One, you created your Personal Separation Pyramid and assessed how your needs were being addressed on all five Levels. Now that you are ready to move out of the initial phases of your separation, we are going to revisit the Pyramid so you can see how far you've come since you started this journey.

For example, you might have been struggling with basic physical needs (Level 1) when you first separated. Now, you've got a cozy apartment and your finances are mostly sorted out, so you are feeling much more secure in this area. You may notice that your self-confidence and self-respect grew on Level 4, and that your self-fulfillment on Level 5 is glowing like a happy sun. Celebrate the amazing personal growth you have achieved!

So, get a big sheet of paper, and draw your new Personal Pyramid and its five Levels. Look back on all of the positive things you've achieved in the past year. Write down your achievements on each Level, and how you feel in each area of your life. Consider how you have reconnected to yourself and learned to value yourself more deeply. You have practiced patience, compassion, and love for yourself and others. You have received strength from your Winning Team and others around you. You have built new structures in your life. Look how you have thrived! Compliments to you!

Once your Pyramid is complete, write down the five things you have achieved since your Point of Disconnection of which you are most proud. If you feel inspired to do so, compare your progress to the vision for your new life you created in Chapter Two, and the goal list you completed in Chapter Three (especially your Focus Goal). Enjoy the feeling of accomplishment!

▶ 4. Your Future Pyramid

Set aside about thirty minutes for this exercise.

Now that you have tracked your progress and seen how far you've come, your next step is to create your Future Pyramid—a plan for creating happiness and stability in every area of your life over the next few years. (I still do this exercise at the beginning of every year!)

Get out the vision you created in Chapter Two, back at the beginning of your separation. Does this vision still hold true for you, or do adjustments need to be made? If necessary, rewrite your vision statement so it feels authentic and exciting to you.

Now, draw a big, empty Pyramid with five levels. Where are you now, and where do you ideally want to be? What is your ideal for stability on each Level? Fill in each Level with your wishes and aims. If you like, place a radiant, happy picture of yourself at the top layer of the Pyramid. Surround your picture with magical light arrows, or stars, or whatever gives you the feeling of expansion and possibility.

Next, start a list of goals and actions (see Chapter Four) that will help you get to where you want to be on each Level of the Pyramid. For example, if you want to move to a new neighborhood or a bigger home, your actions might be around saving extra money each month, researching real estate prices, etc. When you have goals and actions complete for all five Levels, set your Future Pyramid and list aside; we will work with them in Exercise 6.

▶ 5. Your Future Winning Team

Be sure to set aside enough time to fully engage with this exercise.

Although you initially asked your Winning Team to come on board for three months, it's beneficial to keep working with your Winning Team until your separation process is resolved. Certain Team members might become less involved as you get back on your feet, but keeping your supportive connections is vital to getting through the first year of your separation (and beyond).

Now that you are ready to leave your separation process behind and move forward into your new, empowered life, you can create an updated Winning Team as well. This is the Winning Team for your happy future—the people you will depend on to help you create the new life you envisioned.

I like to call my own Winning Team my "Brady Bunch Team," because it's comprised of a blend of trusted friends, family, and professionals. You might call yours a "Happy Future Team," your "Live-Along Team," your "Joy Team," or something else entirely. Choose a fun title that reminds you why the people on this Team are so important in your life.

This new Team will be a much broader circle of people than your initial Winning Team, will be more flexible, and will grow over time. It can be small or large, structured or free. Some of the people on your original Winning Team will naturally become part of your new Team; others will take on different roles as you learn and grow. All that matters is that your Team is full of people you love, trust, and have fun with, and who you really want in your life.

There's no need to formally ask people to join this new Team (although you can if you want to!); just know who each Team member is to you in your life, and how they make your present and future richer and brighter!

Some good additions to your new Team could include:

- A new partner (see my guidelines in Chapter Twelve for new partners)
- Your children
- New friends
- New professionals who support your growth
- People who inspire you
- Anyone else who helps you be the best version of you!

Your new Winning Team will have new members and new roles. Now that you are so much more deeply connected to who you are and what is good for you, you will automatically attract people who support you and your vision for your happy future. With a stellar new Team by your side, you will be able to handle anything your new future brings!

▶ 6. Your Future Goals and Commitments

Set aside at least thirty minutes for this exercise.

In Steps 1 and 2 of the Positive Separation Method, you created a vision for your future, set practical goals, made commitments to yourself, and learned to focus on what you can control (instead of on things you cannot influence). The good news is, these things don't expire once your separation process is complete! You can take all of those actions and techniques and bring them into your bright future alongside you.

Your Focus Goal and the Personal Goals you established in Step 2 of the Positive Separation Method have done their jobs and run their course. Now that you are leaving that part of your life behind with gratitude, it's time to update them to reflect your new, exciting future.

Look again at the updated vision for your future you prepared in the Future Pyramid exercise. (Or, if your vision hasn't changed, use your original one.) What has shifted for you? What new Focus Goal can you set that will help you reach what you envisioned?

Now, look at the goals and actions you identified in the Future Pyramid exercise. These are your Personal Goals for the year. Ask yourself how you can work these new goals and actions into your weekly schedule so that you keep moving steadily forward on your path.

I do this exercise at the start of every year as a kick-off, too. It is a wonderful way for me to create structure and energy for the upcoming year, and get excited about what I'm creating in my life. Sometimes, if I'm striving toward something big, I create a new Focus Goal. Other years, I create a Happy Goal, or a Loving Goal—an overall standard for happiness and love that I want to meet in my life. You can call your big goal anything you like, as long as it feels inspiring to you!

Write your small and bigger goals on a clean sheet of paper and post them where you can read them often.

Keep Up with Your Power Hour

Even when you've moved beyond the immediate crisis phase of your separation, keep up with your weekly Power Hour. This has become a lifelong practice for me, and it can for you as well! Instead of my Power Hour, though, I now call it my Love in Action Hour, because I fill it with loving support for myself.

Check in with yourself. How do you feel? What emotions have been triggered in the past week? If any of them were challenging, how can you find gratitude for what has happened and look differently at the situation? How can you connect more deeply to yourself and your Positive IDs? Where can you offer yourself more love and support? Where do you need to take action? Where do you need extra support from others? What events, milestones, or challenges are on the horizon for you, and how do you plan to deal with them?

Also, use your Power/Love in Action Hour to plan your weeks and months, including chill times, time to take care of your physical body, and time with family and friends, as well as time to manage and implement your self-loving activities and create positive circumstances every day.

Invite a Wonderful New Partner Into Your Life

If you have done all of the exercises in this chapter to tap into the energy of gratitude and celebration, you probably feel pretty amazing. You have closed the door on your old life, and are stepping out into the sunshine of your new life.

If you feel in your core that you are ready to invite a new partner into your life, this exercise is a great way to get clear about how a new partner will compliment you and fit into your happy future. (Even if you do have a new partner, you can do this exercise. You can even work on it together—it's a great way to get to know one another even more deeply!)

On a clean sheet of paper, write down everything you are looking for in a new partner. What are this person's dreams and goals? What does s/he value? What are his or her hobbies? What about this person inspires you? Be specific, and don't hold back. Write down your ideals for everything from great, loving sex, to financial situations, to growing old together. What kind of life do you want with this person? How does he or she complement your vision for your future?

Note: Now that you are connected to your core and feeling empowered in yourself, these traits might be completely different than those you have looked for in past partners! Trust what comes up as you write.

This exercise is powerful. Besides getting clear on what you actually want from your new partnership, it can help you actually attract your new partner! Remember Aimee from Chapter Eleven? This exercise worked like a miracle for her. Here's what she had to say.

AIMEE'S STORY

"I had been separated for about six months when I decided I was ready to explore the idea of a new relationship, if not the reality. I figured I could reasonably expect to stay single for about two years—but hey, why not get a jumpstart on creating the life I wanted?

"About two weeks before my birthday, I made a list of everything I wanted in a new partner—and I mean *everything*. I got super-specific about every detail of my ideal man, from personality, travel preferences, and career (someone in engineering or the sciences—no more 'rock stars' who needed my money to pay their bills!), to music choices, movies, and favorite books (must love sci-fi fantasy), to hair color and body type. I even made a note about the amount of chest hair he should have!

"My list took up four notebook pages. I looked it over after I was done, and wondered if this guy actually existed outside of my dreams. Then, I promptly closed my notebook and forgot about it. After all, I was going to be single for a while yet—or so I thought.

"Two weeks later, on my birthday, I received a Facebook message from Matt, a guy I had gone to high school with. We hadn't talked in fifteen years, but my birthday notification had popped up in his news feed and he sent me a note to say hello. We started messaging back and forth, and I ended up inviting him to my house for tea that afternoon. Tea led to lunch the next day, which turned into dinner, and … suddenly, we were dating. A few weeks later, I was head over heels in love.

"I knew Matt was pretty close to my ideal guy, but I didn't realize how perfect he really was for me until I opened my notebook a few months later and found my list. He matched *every single one* of my qualifications—all four pages of them. Sometimes my 'requests' had been fulfilled in unexpected ways, but they were all there. It was pretty miraculous, actually.

"I don't know if I would have fully appreciated all that Matt had to offer if I hadn't taken the time to get clear about what I really wanted from a new relationship. He was, in many ways, the polar opposite of every man I'd been with before. But my list was concrete proof: he was a perfect match for what I wanted in my core. Six years later, we are happily married with two magical daughters—and I still call him my 'birthday present!'"

What Comes Next

What comes next is the rest of your amazing, happy, empowered life—so get out there and live it!

You have done the work of connecting with yourself, created the beginnings of a bright new future, and mastered the art of positive separation; now, it's time to practice your art of positive living. You have an amazing life ahead of you, and I know it will be full of blessings, beauty, and love. Enjoy the radiance that your new life has to share with you!

Afterword

We entered one another's lives through this book and the connection of our hearts. Now, it's time for our paths to diverge. I leave you to step into your new future with great trust, pride, and love. I know that you will share the beautiful lessons of your loving actions over the course of your work with this book with everyone you meet on your path. Your positive stories, tools, and lessons might be the key to unlocking the secrets of positive separation for someone in your world. The more connected to your inner core you become, the more you will shine as an example to others of not only the art of positive separation, but also the art of positive living.

So go off and live your *joie de vivre*, your effervescence, and your abundance. The heartbeat of your life is in the now. Remember, always, to fully love yourself so you can be a loving and enlightened lover, parent, child, sibling, friend, mentor, and teacher. When you love yourself, you become the change the world needs.

In Love, Happiness, and Hope,

Eveline Jurry

APPENDIX A

Star Actions

I always say to my clients, "A Star a day keeps trouble away."

I developed my Star Actions for a dear friend who was in a separation crisis more than fifteen years ago. I advised her to pick three shining stars from the heavens every day when she had done three things she knew she needed to do, but feared or didn't feel like doing. (For example, going to the neighborhood supermarket, where she might run into her ex, was a huge fear for her.) From that day on, she updated me regularly to share her little "Star achievements." Soon, she had walked over her own fears, and done things she had never thought of or wanted to do before, and was feeling much more empowered.

And so, the Star Actions were born.

If you are at the beginning of your separation and don't have the energy to do all of the Empowered Actions in Steps 1 through 4 of the Positive Separation Method, you can tap into these Star Actions to give your day a little boost. These are practical actions that you can take quickly to boost your mood, create a more positive environment, rebuild your energy, motivate you to meet your goals, or just bring a smile to your face on a hard day. Some of them are completely fun, and some are like little "jobs," but all of them will leave you with a sense of accomplishment.

Even once you are past the immediate crisis phase of your separation—meaning, the legal battles have died down, you have a stable place to live, and you aren't facing minute-to-minute emotional turmoil—it's incredibly important to take good care of yourself and create a positive environment every day.

The Star Actions in this section are connected, directly or indirectly, to your Five Commitments and the first four Steps of the Positive Separation Method. (If you have already been working with the Steps, you will recognize some of them as pieces of the Empowered Actions!) They are broken into groups based on level of difficulty. Each action will earn you between 1 and 5 stars. If you want to make a game of it, aim for 10-15 stars a week (or 40-60 in a month), and give yourself a little reward when you reach your star goals.

Your Star Actions

1 STAR

These actions are easy, fun, don't take much time, and will give you an energy boost.

General

- ★ Get your jacket, go out, and **buy the most beautiful and cheerful bunch of flowers** that you can find. Place them in a vase in your home or on your desk at work. Smell them often throughout the day.
- ★ When it's raining hard, **bicycle or walk in the rain without a hat,** rain jacket, or umbrella and allow yourself to become completely soaked. Jump in puddles like a little kid. Do a rain dance. Whatever brings a smile to your face.

★ If daily exercise isn't a habit, **take a walk of at least one hour each day for three days in a row.** Take note of how you feel after three days.

★ **Take a long, hot shower** and let your tears, sorrow, frustration, and anger mingle with the water and disappear down the drain. This can be an effective daily ritual to rid yourself of built-up anger or sorry, or a quick fix after a hard day or a fight with your ex-partner. Give yourself a star every time you consciously let go of a negative emotion and let it swirl down the drain.

★ **If you managed to stay in control of your emotions** and avoid a nasty scene during a confrontation, reward yourself with one star for each incident.

★ **Make a list of things that immediately make you feel better** after going through a difficult moment (for example, lying down for 10 minutes, meditating, listening to a particular song, or taking a walk). All the items on the list must be possible without the need for another person. Save this list in your daily planner or wallet. When you have a tough moment, do one of the activities.

★ **Find or buy an object from your past that brings back the feelings of happiness** that you experienced at the time. This could be a photo, a certain aftershave or perfume, a toy, or something else.

★ **Make a list of your heroes/role models from your childhood** until the present. This list could include friends, family members, neighbors, colleagues, teachers, celebrities, writers, musicians, or anyone else who has inspired you. How did each of them have a positive influence in your life?

★ **Try a new type of coffee or tea,** a new food, or another new product. New things and activities hold no echoes of the past, and belong only to the present. Trying something new means you are consciously taking a step forward in your new life. Once you try it, you can decide if this new thing belongs in your future, or not.

★ **Put on your favorite music.** Download the lyrics (if you don't know them) and sing along as loudly as you wish.

★ For a change, **take a different route to your work,** to school, or to do your errands. What caught your eye on your new route?

At Home

★ **Hang a radiant photograph of yourself** taken before you were in the broken-up relationship, or when you were still a child, in a very visible location in your home.

★ **Stand in front of an open window in the evening.** Spread your arms wide, breathing deeply in and out. Blow away all your negative feelings into the air and watch as they are carried away by the wind.

★ **Give people who are important to you and who you rely on a copy of your house key.** Ask relatives or friends with who you no longer feel comfortable to give back their keys. If necessary, ask someone from your Winning Team to help you.

★ **Get rid of keys that you no longer use,** including keys to your old storage unit, lost bike locks, your former car, etc. If you're not sure what door or lock a key belongs to, create a container marked "Unknown Keys" and put it in a safe place.

★ **Give back any keys that belong to your ex**—including keys to your old house. If you don't want to see your ex, leave the keys in the mailbox or ask a friend to deliver them.

★ **Bring all empty bottles, cans, old newspapers, magazines, and other recyclables to the nearest recycling center** (or put them out for curb collection).

★ **Cook your favorite recipe from when you were a child** for yourself, friends, or family.

Social

★ **Invite a friend** whom you haven't seen recently to join you for dinner, a film, or a hobby or sports activity.

★ **Send a card to someone you like** but have not had any contact with for some time.

★ **Send a letter of support or a book** to someone who is ill or has gone through a trying time.

★ **Reconnect with friends outside the country.** Talk about what's going on in the world outside your hometown.

- ★ **Help a stranger.** Open doors for a mother who has her arms full. Help an elderly person to cross the street safely. Give directions to someone who looks lost. Unexpected gestures on your part cost very little time or energy, but they make you feel great!
- ★ **Give someone a sincere compliment** that really makes them glow.

Coping/Emotional

- ★ **Every time you sit down for your Power Hour, give yourself a star.** Getting there is half the battle!
- ★ **Go carefully over the "Uphill Model" in Chapter Six.** How is your climb going? Where do you think you are now? Where were you one month ago?

2-3 STARS

These actions take a bit more time or are more challenging, but they help keep your energy elevated and flowing.

General

- ★★ **Go outside with a plastic shopping bag** and fill it with street litter. Bring the bag to the nearest recycling center.
- ★★ **Make a playlist** of three hours of your favorite songs.
- ★★ **Write a letter to yourself** describing how you feel and about your vision for your future (a minimum of two pages).
- ★★ **Write down all your most fun experiences from your life so far.** Think of your best birthday parties, vacations, days with special people, adventures, achievements, etc.
- ★★ **Watch the sunrise or sunset from a quiet place outdoors.** Spend a minimum of one hour sitting quietly to witness this transition between day and night.
- ★★ **Write down what you think are your best characteristics.** Why do you value these things about yourself?

★★ **Go outside on a radiant day** and take photos of everything that cheers you up.

★★ **Ask two or three of your best friends what they think are your best characteristics.** Write down what they share, and post the information someplace where you will read it often (like on the bathroom mirror, next to a photo of yourself, or as a screensaver on your smartphone).

★★ **Write and send five postcards to family or friends.** Add notes about anything fun. (E-mail doesn't count—they must be handwritten!)

★★ **Read a book on any topic that interests you**—preferably a topic that you've never had time to dive into before.

★★★ **Take a day or weekend course** on personal development.

★★★ **Take your chill times and chill hours** (see Chapter Ten) for a week without missing a single one.

★★★ **Keep a gratitude diary.** Record three happy things per day for 30 days (see Chapter Six: Marci's Story on page 121, and Chapter Eight: Daily Gratitude Practice on page 174.).

At Home

★★ **Purchase several new pieces of kitchenware** that you will use every day (i.e., ladles, whisks, frying pans, etc.). This makes it clear that you are about to start on a new chapter of your (culinary) life.

★★ **Clean up the stuff lying beneath or next to your bed or sofa.** Immediately get rid of everything you no longer need.

★★ **Cook a family recipe** or a new recipe from a cookbook you have never tried out before.

★★ **Remove your old nameplate from your door** (or, if you've moved, replace the nameplate from the previous residents). Claim your home as your own.

★★ **Buy some plants and herbs** for your balcony, garden, or a pot in your house. Plant them the same day.

★★ **Organize and clean up your writing desk** or the area where you deal with your paperwork. (Find some great tips in Chapter Eleven.)

★★ **Remove all pictures and photos which make you unhappy right now** from your living and work spaces. Replace them with new, up-to-date photos.

★★ **Remove all art and decorations from your walls that make you feel depressed,** or which you don't actually like. Don't be afraid of empty walls!

★★★ **Paint an old chair or table in your favorite color.**

★★★ **Go through all of your books.** Do you still need those travel and old study books, or those depressing titles? Return books which are not yours, and give away any that you will not read again. Then, pick up a few new books that interest you!

★★★ **Enjoy a "Light Night" during the winter.** Buy a bag of tea lights. Place them through your whole house (away from anything flammable, of course). Light them, then turn out all the other lights. Keep them lit until they all burn out.

★★★ **Change an eating or drinking pattern.** (Changing a pattern or habit can work wonders to help you disconnect from your past!) This can be simple, like changing your brand of coffee or taking your tea in a different mug, or more far-reaching, like switching to non-dairy milk, giving up fried foods, or cutting back on alcohol consumption. You need to keep up with your new pattern for at least two weeks before you can claim the stars!

★★★ **Sort out your clothing.** Take at least two hours to go through everything you own. If you haven't worn something in two years, give it a new home. Throw away all clothes which are torn, broken, or faded (and which can't be mended to look new again). You are in a new phase of your life now, so it's important to feel good!

★★★ **Sort your shoes.** Donate or throw away those which are old, broken, or no longer fit. If a favorite pair needs some TLC, make a trip to the shoe repair shop. Clean, polish, and properly store the pairs you are keeping.

★★★ **Make a space in your clothes cupboard for your "Happy Clothes"**—clothes that are soft, comforting, or make you feel good. When you are upset or need an energy boost, put on an item from this space. A soft shawl, sweater, or coat can do wonders for your mood!

Social

★★ **Bake a cake, buy a good bottle of wine, or prepare a home-cooked meal** for someone who is really helping you out, and deliver it spontaneously. Making a pot of soup for someone who needs it is also an excellent gesture.

★★ If you have historically avoided going out on your own and it's uncomfortable for you, **take yourself to a solo dinner and a movie.** Get your favorite food and treats at the theater. (Hint: You also get stars if you go on your own to a concert, show, auction or exhibition.)

★★ **Bake a tart, cheesecake, or any other dessert from scratch.** (Don't cheat and use a boxed mix!) If you're not comfortable with baking, ask a friend to help. Then, take your dessert to work, your children's school, or the local retirement home to share.

★★ **Look in your local paper and/or online forum for free activities** you can participate in over the next couple of weeks. Sign up for or plan to do at least one activity.

★★ **Go to a (free) lunch concert** or open mic night.

★★★ **Visit an older friend or relative whom you haven't seen in two years or more.** Take along a snack or a game. Ask them to share their wisdom around how they coped with life's challenges. Be interested in their past and what they have to offer. You may be surprised at what you learn!

Practical

★★ **Read Chapter One and Two of this book again.** Ask yourself if you have fully disconnected in all areas. If not, do the exercises again, and feel how wonderful it is to let go!

★★★ **Get all your insurances (home, car, liability, etc.) switched into your name.** You will get your stars after all policies have been adjusted.

★★★ **Take a financial inventory for yourself.** Write down all of your daily, weekly, monthly, and yearly costs. Then, compare your costs to your income. What needs to be adjusted? (Hint: You can ask your "numbers whiz" Team member to help you with this! Reference Chapter Seven.)

★★★ **Cancel all subscriptions you no longer need,** including e-mail subscriptions. More often than not they cost you either money or time, and they might keep you in old patterns or habits.

★★★ **Clean out your filing cabinet.** Throw out or shred all paperwork you no longer need. (Chances are you don't need your credit card bills from ten years ago!)

★★★ **Write down every penny you spend for an entire month**—from daily shopping to monthly bills and expenses. At the end of the month, tally everything. Were you spending what you thought you were spending? Where did you surprise yourself? Where do you need or want to make adjustments?

★★★ **If you have children, reread the Golden Rules for Parents in Chapter Twelve** and write down all rules which are still a challenge for you. Then, write about how you might approach them with fresh eyes and a positive attitude. (Hint: Ask a member of your Winning Team for help if you need a different perspective!)

4-5 STARS

These are some of my favorites that will really make you feel like you've hit the ground running. However, you need to feel good about starting them, otherwise they won't give you the same energy boost. If necessary, build up your energy and momentum with a few 1 or 2-Star Actions first.

General

★★★★ **For one week, turn off your phone, computer, and television after 8:00 p.m.** Don't turn them back on again until 8:00 a.m. the next day (or whenever you are finished with your shower and breakfast).

★★★★ **Make a "body health plan" that you will stick with for two weeks.** Set three rules that you absolutely will not break—such as eating three meals a day, walking for an hour every day, sleeping for eight hours a night, etc. (Hint: Revisit Chapter Nine for more ideas.)

★★★★ **Sort and clean out your hobby gear** (e.g., your toolbox; sports gear, painting supplies, knitting basket, music gear, books, or scrapbooking supplies). Clean, organize, and store anything that is in good shape and which you still use. If your items are broken, or if you won't use them anymore, throw them away or donate them.

★★★★ **Plant a fruit or nut tree in your garden** (such as a chestnut, avocado, lemon, or apple tree). Tend to it diligently for at least six months, or until you start to see it grow and blossom. As the tree grows, remind yourself that you are growing as well through your own caring, positivity, hard work, and inner power.

★★★★ **Schedule a "Magic Day" for yourself.** Take the day out of work (or cancel your other activities), and go out and enjoy yourself. Let your intuition rule the day. Your only job is to let beauty and magic show up.

★★★★ **Start a new collection and keep it up for three months.** It doesn't matter what you collect; the goal is to focus. For example, one of my clients collected different clothes hangers. Another collected special teas. Yet another collected small glass jars, which she then filled with wildflowers. During my own separation, I collected little stones on my walks and built miniature towers with them.

★★★★ **Pick up an old hobby that you used to love,** such as making music, singing in a choir, collecting antiques, playing a sport, riding horses, walking shelter dogs, or anything else. The point is to do something that connects you to yourself and makes you feel good.

★★★★ Using pictures from the internet or out of magazines, **make a dream board of all the vacations destinations you would like to visit** in the next ten years.

★★★★★ **Plan your first birthday celebration after your separation** (even if your birthday is months away). Include about an hour of time on that day to reflect on the positive changes you want the next year to bring.

★★★★★ **After living on your own for a month, give yourself five stars.**

At Home

★★★★ **Empty your refrigerator, including the freezer, and give it a thorough cleaning.** Throw out everything that reminds you of your ex-partner—like that certain brand of mustard or chili sauce—or is past its expiry date.

★★★★ **Clean out your coat closet, mudroom, and entryway areas.** Get rid of old jackets, worn-out boots, broken umbrellas, and other stuff that you no longer need. Wash and repair anything that needs it.

★★★★ **Clean the windows of your bedroom and living room,** as well as all the mirrors in your house.

★★★★ **Thoroughly wash and clean the inside and outside of your car.** Afterwards, take a ride to a place you've never been before.

★★★★ **Change the bed you slept in with your ex.** Paint it and get new linens, or sell the bed or give it away. If possible, change the bed's position in your bedroom, or choose a different bedroom in your house to call your own.

★★★★ **Dispose of any chair, table, or other piece of furniture that holds too many bad memories.**

★★★★ **Approach people to whom you have lent certain items (such as hobby gear, household goods, or money), and ask for them back** within a week. If you find this hard to do, ask a member of your Winning Team for help.

★★★★ **Return any items in your possession that aren't yours.** If you can, repay any money you owe to friends and family.

★★★★★ **Give yourself five stars for every room you set up after you move,** or every room you clean and reorganize if you're staying in your old house.

★★★★★ **Paint one room in your house, on your own or with help.** Enjoy the happy atmosphere that room's new look brings. My living room got painted raspberry red after my separation. I loved it!

Coping/Emotional

★★★★ **Form your Winning Team.**

★★★★ **Make a list with twenty Star Actions you make up yourself**—ten easy ones, and ten hard ones. Then, do one of each within a day, and give yourself bonus stars for each one you complete!

★★★★ **If you are looking for a new place to live, approach a real estate agent.** Give yourself five stars for every property you physically visit.

★★★★★ **Give yourself five stars on the first day your children sleep at your ex-partner's house.**

★★★★★ **Give yourself five stars the first time you take a vacation as a single person** (whether or not you are traveling alone).

★★★★★ **Give yourself five stars the first time you get through a holiday, birthday, or special event as a single person.**

***

Have fun with your Star Actions. Play with them. Make them your own. Let them become part of your daily life, even after you've moved on from your separation. Treat your new, happy future like the adventure it is!

APPENDIX B

Resources

Now that you have created your new life and your positive separation, you may want to take a break for a while and just enjoy your life! However, if you are relishing the personal growth and development you've experienced through the Positive Separation Method, you may want to delve into these resources to gain additional insight and information about yourself and your journey toward your happy future.

Books

INSPIRATION

- Drew Barrymore. *Wildflower.* (Penguin Random House UK/Virgin Books, 2015)
- Ingeborg Bosch. *Rediscovering the True Self: Past Reality Integration.* (Atlas Contact, 2000-2009)
- Bill Burnett and Dave Evans. *Designing your Life. How to Build a Well-Lived, Joyful Life.* (Alfred A. Knopf, 2016)

- Doc Childre, Howard Martin, Deborah Rozman and Rollin McCraty. *Heart Intelligence: Connecting with the Intuitive Guidance of the Heart.* (Waterfront Press, 2016)

- Louise Hay. *You Can Heal Your Life.* (Hay House, 2004)

- Bryna René Haynes. *The Art of Inspiration. An Editor's Guide to Writing Powerful, Effective Inspirational & Personal Development Books.* (Inspired Living Publishing, 2016)

- Titia Hennemann-Heering. *Pluk de Appel.* (Uitgeverij Elikser, 2016)

- Arianna Huffington. *Thrive: The Third Metric to Redefining Success and Creating a Life of Well-Being, Wisdom, and Wonder.* (Harmony Books, 2014)

- Dalai Lama and Desmond Tutu with Douglas Carlton Abrams. *The Book of Joy: Lasting Happiness in a Changing World.* (Avery, September 20, 2016)

- Sage Lavine. *Women Rocking Business.* (Hay House, 2017)

- Frédéric Lenoir. *L'Âme du Monde.* French and European Publications Inc. (August 21, 2014)

- Lisa Nichols and Janet Switzer. *Abundance Now: Amplify Your Life and Achieve Prosperity Today.* (HarperCollins Publishers/Dey Street Books Paperback, 2016)

- Barack Obama. *Dreams From My Father: A Story Of Race and Inheritance.* (Canongate Books, 2016)

- Judith Orloff, MD. *The Empath's Survival Guide.* (Sounds True, 2017)

- Margaret Paul. Ph.D. *Inner Bonding: Becoming a Loving Adult to Your Inner Child.* (HarperCollins, 1992)

- Michael Puett and Christine Gross-Loh. *The Path: What Chinese Philosophers Can Teach Us About the Good Life.* (Published in the Netherlands by Uitgeverij Ten Have, 2016)

- Eric Ripert with Veronica Chambers. *32 Yolks: From My Mother's Table to Working The Line.* (Random House Books, 2016)

- Don Miguel Ruiz, Jr. *The Five Levels of Attachment: Toltec Wisdom for the Modern World.* (Hierophant Publishing, 2015)

- Sheryl Sandberg & Adam Grant. *Option B: Facing Adversity, Building Resilience, and Finding Joy.* (Knopf, 2017)

- Marci Shimoff with Carol Kline. *Happy for No Reason. 7 Steps to Being Happy from The Inside Out.* (Atria Paperback, 2008)

- Marci Shimoff with Carol Kline. *Love for No Reason. 7 Steps to Creating a Life of Unconditional Love.* (Free Press, 2010)

- Susan Smit. *De Eerste Vrouw.* (Lebowski Publishers, 2016)

- Susan Smit and Marion Pauw. *Hotel Hartzeer: Eerste Hulp Bij Liefdesperikelen.* (Lebowski Publishers, 2017)

- Michael A. Singer. *The Untethered Soul: The Journey Beyond Yourself.* (New Harbinger Publications, Inc., 2007)

DIVORCE/ SEPARATION/ BREAKUP

- Keith Anderson, M.D. with Roy MacSkimming. *On Your Own Again: A Down-To Earth Guide To Getting Through a Divorce Or Separation and Getting On with Your Life.* (McClelland & Stewart, 2007)

- Debbie Ford. *Spiritual Divorce. Divorce as a Catalyst for an Extraordinary Life.* (HarperOne, 2006)

- Kathryn Lankston. *Help for Healing from Divorce (Elf Self-Help).* (Abbey Press, January 1, 2002)

- John Gray. *Mars and Venus Starting Over, A Practical Guide for finding Love Again after a Painful Breakup, Divorce, or Loss of a Loved one.* (Perennial Currents, 2005)

- Katherine Woodward Thomas. *Conscious Uncoupling: 5 Steps to Living Happily Even After.* (Harmony Books/ Yellow Kite, 2015)

- Katherine Woodward Thomas. *Calling in "The One": 7 Weeks to Attract the Love of Your Life.* (Three Rivers Press, 2004)

- Tonja Evetts Weimer. *Thriving After Divorce. Transforming Your Life When a Relationship Ends.* (Atria Paperback/Beyond Words, 2010)

HEALTH

- Heather Mills McCartney. *Life Balance: The Essential Keys to A Lifetime Of Wellbeing.* (Michael Joseph Ltd., 2006)

- Dr.Stephen S. Ilardi. *The Depression Cure: The 6-Step Program to Beat Depression without Drugs.* (Da Capo Lifelong Books; Reprint edition, June 1, 2010)

- Dr. David Servan-Schreiber. *The Instinct to Heal: Curing Stress, Anxiety, and Depression Without Drugs and Without Talk Therapy.* (Rodale Books, 2004)

- Dr. David Servan-Schreiber. *Anticancer: A New Way of Life.* (Viking; New edition, December 31, 2009)

EMOTIONS, GRIEF, AND MINDSET

- Jack Canfield. *How to Get from where You Are to Where You Want to Be. The 25 Principles of Success.* (Harper Element/HarperCollins Publishers, 2007)

- Pema Chödrön. *When Things Fall Apart: Heart Advice for Difficult Times.* (Shambhala; 20th Anniversary ed. Edition, June 7, 2016)

- Tian Dayton, PhD. *Emotional Sobriety: From Relationship Trauma to Resilience and Balance.* (HCI, December 10, 2007)

- Dr. Anne Dickson. *Trusting the Tides. Self-empowerment through our emotions.* (Rider & Co, January 1, 2000)

- Mira Kirshenbaum. *Everything Happens for a Reason: Finding the True Meaning of the Events in Our Lives.* (Harmony; reprint edition, April 26, 2004)

- Paul McKenna. *I Can Make You Happy.* (Transworld Publishers, 2011)

- Brooks Palmer. *Clutter Busting: Letting Go of What's Holding You Back.* (New World Library, March 1, 2009)

- Susan Piver. *The Wisdom of a Broken Heart: How to Turn the Pain of a Breakup into Healing, Insight, and New Love.* (Atria Books, December 28, 2010)

- Dr. Sonja Lyubomirsky. *The How of Happiness: A New Approach to Getting the Life You Want.* (Penguin Books; reprint edition, December 30, 2008)

- Dr. Phil McGraw. *Real Life; Preparing for the 7 Most Challenging Days of Your Life.* (Free Press; reprint edition, September 15, 2009)

- Caroline Myss. *Why People Don't Heal and How They Can.* (Bantam Books,1997)

- Lisa Nichols. *No Matter What! 9 Steps to Living the Life You Love.* (Grand Central Life & Style; reprint edition, March 22, 2011)

- Dr. Christiane Northrup. *Mother-Daughter Wisdom. Understanding the Crucial Link Between Mothers, Daughters, and Health.* (Bantam, March 28, 2006)

- Karen Salmansohn. *The Bounce Back Book: How To Thrive In The Face of Adversity, Setbacks, and Losses.* (Workman Publishing Company; 1st edition, May 14, 2008)

- Jamie Sams. *The 13 Original Clan Mothers. Your Sacred Path to Discovering the Gifts, Talents, and Abilities of the Feminine Through the Ancient Teachings of the Sisterhood.* (HarperCollins; 1st edition, April 22, 1994)

- Gary Zukav and Linda Francis. *The Mind of the Soul: Responsible Choice.* (Free Press; reprint edition, October 4, 2004)

CHILDREN AND SEPARATION

- Alec Baldwin with Mark Tabb. *A Promise to Ourselves. A Journey through Fatherhood and Divorce.* (St. Martin's Press, New York, 2008)

- M. Gary Neuman and Patricia Romanowski. *Helping Your Kids Cope with Divorce The Sandcastles Way.* (Random House; 1st edition, August 1, 1999)

- Edward Teyber. *Helping Children Cope with Divorce.* (Jossey-Bass; 1st edition, April 5, 2001)

Programs, Methods, and Websites

CONTRIBUTORS TO THIS BOOK

- Workshops, programs, and coaching with Katherine Woodward Thomas (KatherineWoodwardThomas.com)

- Marci Shimoff's *Miracle Mentor Program* (MarciShimoffMentoring.com)

- *The Miracle Zone* with Marci Shimoff & Debra Poneman: Get ready for a breakthrough in happiness, success, and abundance! (YourYearofMiracles.com)

- *Yes to Success!* With Debra Poneman (YesToSuccess.com)

- Workshops and programs with Janet Bray Attwood and Chris Attwood (ThePassionTest.com)

- Chris Attwood: Pilgrimage to Wholeness (DiscoveringDharma.com)

- Inspiration for speakers and leaders from Lisa Nichols (MotivatingTheMasses.com) and creative Visualization Training (CreativeVisualization.com)

- The Heart of Writing: Education, resources, and services for inspired writers with Bryna Haynes (TheHeartofWriting.com)

- Jack Canfield: *Maximize Your Potential* (JackCanfield.com)

- John Gray: Relationship expert for men and women (MarsVenus.com)

- Marcia Wieder: Global visionary leader, founder of Dream University (MarciaWieder.com)

- Nikki Green: sexual/marital therapist and founder of "The Art of Lasting Love." (NikkiGreenOnline.com)

GENERAL INSPIRATION

- Sheryl Sandberg's Option B: Build resilience and find meaning in the face of adversity. (OptionB.org)

- Ingeborg Berghuijs, Independent Art Director based in the Netherlands (magazines, books). (IngeborgBerghuijs.com)

- Jim Halfens' Divorce Hotel: An innovative divorce concept where couples get divorced in a weekend in a positive way. Jim and I meet regularly to promote positive separation in the world. (DivorceHotel.com)

- Workshops on nature, crystals, and energy with Judy Hall. (JudyHall.co.uk)

- Kim Forcina: A coach for dreamers and creatives, offering support, strategy, and guidance for your creative projects and expressive spirit. (KaleidoscopeSpirit.com)

- Past Reality Integration (PRI) from Dutch psychologist Ingeborg Bosch shows you how to remove blockages and live more fully in the now. (PastRealityIntegration.com/en)

- Dr. Elaine Aron: Information on Highly-Sensitive People and how they function in love and relationships. (HSPerson.com)

- Collaborative Practice: A resource to discover professionals who are in favor of amicable divorces and separations. (CollaborativePractice.com)

- The HeartMath Institute: Find out more about the coherence of your heart, and learn how simple meditations can help you become more balanced in stressful situations. (HeartMath.com)

Acknowledgments

With Love and Gratitude ...

Happy Again! The Art of Positive Separation is a work of great love, generosity, inspiration and collaboration.

My personal journey to mastering the art of positive separation started when I watched my grandparents, Omoes and Grootvader Baardje, as well as my parents, separate in my youth. They gave me a blueprint for positive separation— and, even better, a vision (and eventually the reality) of a happy future after their breakups. Their mutual efforts ensured that I and my siblings could enjoy an abundant family life, and taught me that joy, ease, and deep bonding between family members is always possible, even after the "official" family relationship has changed. And, as both my parents found new partners (Oom Hans and Brigitte) with families of their own, we got "bonus family" who have added enormous richness, love, and inspiration to my life.

The family blueprint inspired me in my own search for a positive separation after my own breakup. I created my Positive Separation Method in the Netherlands in 2008, and followed that with my first book, *Je Wordt Weer Gelukkig* (You Will Be Happy Again) in 2013, published by the respected Dutch publisher Bruna/Lev. This was followed by a "pocket version" in 2016.

I am grateful to have met many people on my path who helped me to develop my talents and passions. I feel that, from the moment I opened my eyes on this planet, I had "believers" around me to inspire me and push me in the right directions in life. My family and Winning Teams have helped me greatly over the years, not only by meeting my wildest plans with openness and honesty, but also with their *doe maar normal* attitude—the Dutch expression for "stay cool, act normal, and keep your feet on the ground." This balance saved me from lots of trouble and turbulence in times of big change and exploration.

What I've learned over the years is that, if I want to change something, reach a goal, or conquer events which are hard or sad, there is only one road. With a positive approach and a big dose of discipline, I had to get up and keep going—even at times when my self-confidence felt like it was at absolute zero. Taking small actions in trust and confidence, keeping a smile on my face, and asking for help when necessary was the best way for me to move forward. When you can do this, everything in Heaven and on Earth is possible!

My "Brady Bunch"

I want to thank my "Brady Bunch" of friends, family, mentors, teachers, and colleagues who have inspired, guided, and loved me through the years. There are a lot of them, so here we go!

First and foremost, I want to thank my wonderful children, Boudy, Fréderique and Charlotte: you are my greatest gifts of love and joy, and so much more. From the days you were born, being your mother has given me a shine, a glow, a strength, and a love beyond description. Thank you for loving me as I am—with all my good and bad, adventures and oddities, pinks, books, and flowers all over! I love you from my head to my toes, forever!

John Fiszbajn, my soulmate, my biggest love, you have supported me since the day we met. You have taught me so much, and have inspired me tremendously. Deep in wisdom, full of love and the greatest compassion, you let me shine even more, and grow into who I am today. I feel so lucky for our relationship, as well as our blended family.

Avital, Gidon, Lyvana, and Davita, my fabulous bonus children: since the day I met you, you have embraced me with your love and smiles. I love our blended family of nine, which is so full of love, respect, joy, happiness, traditions, and possibilities. I feel we are on a great adventure!

Mammie, my creative, loving, elegant, feminine, super-eye-for-detail, talented, traveling, out-of-the-box-thinker mum; Pappie, my joy-for-any-daughter, go-getter, keep-me-on-track, ever-listening, great-advice-giving, naughty dad; Arjan, my strong, true-to-your-nature, always-bring-a-smile-to-my-face brother; and Flo, my best ally, most-fun-to-play-with-since-I-opened-my-eyes-under-the-chestnut-trees sister: all of you have been the wisdom and light on my path.

Ingeborg Berghuijs, my talented, fun, and inseparable friend since our advertising days: you are a great gift, joy, and inspiration. The pink cover you designed for this book is a symbol of our friendship spreading her wings over America and the world.

Also, for fun, laughs, love, tears, teaching, and wisdom: Wendela van Swol, Jannie de Graaf-Kruithof, Katy Rage-Ewing, Marielle Gielink, Titia Henneman, Frederike Hollander, Madelon van Lookeren Campagne, Florens van den Bosch, Claudia Jurry, Cathleen Beerkens, Willemijn Beerkens, Leontine Beerkens, Marit Stofberg, Akelei Hertzberger, Klaske van der Mandele, Jane Diemont, and Madelene van den Berg; my teachers, Mijnheer Keuken, Loekie van Wingerden, and Mijnheer van Harte at my elementary school in Gouda; the friends and teachers at Ancaster House, Bexhill-on Sea, England (UK); my boarding school buddies at Eerde, Ommen, the Netherlands; Geraldine Coughlan, my great Geography teacher who taught me how to learn anything I wanted with joy and discipline; Ankie Looman, who taught me that any learning goal is achievable; my student club 'Track of the Cat' from Leiden; Professor Eric Japikse, whose passion for teaching Maritime Law showed me that living and sharing your passion is the greatest gift you can give yourself and the world, and still brings a huge smile to my heart; my advertising gangs from the 1980s; my sunny and always-supportive Bermuda family (Oom George, Marijke, Flora, Bregitta, and the Kitchen); the Florence 2014 group (Marianne Bezem, Gila and Nadav Belfair, Ingrid Gerrits, Sandy Colombo, Tommaso Mario Scutti, Jesse Ianniello, Patty Aubery and Jack Canfield); and my Grane Tribe from France, Spring 2017: Barbara Wilkes, Elfin Moningka, Ineke Bannink, Eduard Saris, Annemarie Woestijne, Lidewij Leijten, Robert Erdbrink, and Ingeborg Bosch.

You all make my heart sing with joy!

Two Writers, One Big Ocean in Between!

We made it, Bryna—and I love it more than I can express in words!

Bryna Haynes, thank you from my deepest of hearts for sharing all your talents, love, and magic with me. You are not only a "word alchemist," but a "love alchemist," too. Your caring for the people who read this book, the creativity which goes beyond words, but enters your heart with a joy and comfort I cannot describe.

Let me backtrack a bit.

When I was seven, I moved temporarily with my parents to Geneva. I was a young kid, and I loved to talk. Talking was my *thing*. Moving to Switzerland made a huge impact on me. I did not speak French, and I suddenly felt like my mouth was pasted shut. I wanted to express myself, but couldn't at first. If you do not know a language well or at all, you are so limited in your ways to share your feelings and thoughts; it feels crippling.

Rewriting my Dutch book, *Je Wordt Weer Gelukkig,* in English took me by surprise in nearly the same way. My spoken English is pretty much perfect, but the writing process knocked me off my feet in the beginning. For the English-speaking market, a different approach was needed, one with more personal stories and a new explanation of my Method. It wasn't just a translation; we had to create a whole new book.

I'll be honest: I felt like that seven-year-old girl again, not knowing which words to use on my first days in Geneva. How could I share my Method, and the art of positive separation, with thousands of people going through what might be one of the most difficult times of their lives, in a language not my own?

Bryna, you took me by the hand, opened your energy to my heart, and opened your voice to my voice. Together, we brought the wisdom of my Positive Separation Method to the English-speaking world. Thank you from the bottom of my heart.

(And thanks as well to Bryna's husband Matthew and daughters Áine and Aelyn for adding a little sparkle to our Skype conversations!)

My Mentor: Marci Shimoff

This book would not be here at all if Marci Shimoff—my mentor, my happiness guru in color and light—had not been sent to me by the Universe.

In 2014, I had the honor to participate in a week-long program with Jack Canfield (creator of the *Chicken Soup for the Soul* books) and a wonderful group of people in Florence, Italy. It was there that I first heard about Marci and her work. Jack was her mentor, and when I heard her name I could already sense her shine. She is my biggest fan when I need encouragement, but also adds a layer of deep strength, wisdom, and joy, and pushes me beyond the lines of "doe maar normal" and into her Miracle Zone. She introduced me to Bryna and her work, as well as to her lifelong family of friends—including Katherine Woodward Thomas, Debra Poneman, Janet Bray Attwood, Chris Attwood, and Lisa Nichols—who in turn shared their powerful and inspiring stories in this book.

Marci, thank you for everything! You have been a great gift to me, and to this work. Big hugs and kisses for all of your wonderful guidance and deep teaching.

The Contributors

Katherine Woodward Thomas, I am so immensely grateful how you opened your heart to my work, and to me. The moment I finished my English manuscript, I knew I wanted to share my work with you. I've followed your work with excitement since *Conscious Uncoupling* became a hit in 2014. You set the tone and inspired a new, loving, wise approach—not only for individuals, parents, and families, but for professionals like me as well. I never expected our friendship to emerge as it has (in fact, I'm still a little starstruck by you!) but I'm eternally grateful that you have come into my life. By joining forces across oceans, languages, and cultures, we can plant love and healing in the hearts of people who need it most. Thank you for your honest, beautiful, and sparkling Foreword. My book is more complete for having your grace within its pages.

Thanks to David Hancock, Jim Howard, Margo Toulouse, and the rest of the publishing family at Morgan James for helping me get my book out into the world. You opened your arms straight away when my manuscript arrived, and I knew my book had found a home.

Deep gratitude as well to all who contributed their personal separation stories to this work. Your generosity in sharing your vulnerability, wisdom, and lessons is a great act of love. Without your contributions, this book would not have the same depth.

A huge thank you to my "guests of honor" Chris Attwood, Janet Bray Attwood, Debra Poneman, Nikki Green, Lisa Nichols—and of course Marci Shimoff—for sharing your stories of separation and healing. Your wisdom, as always, leaps off the pages and into readers' hearts.

And, of course, grateful hugs and love to my friends and clients, Isabelle, Jane, Robert, Sophia, James, Heather, and Aimee: you are angels in my world, and the reason I created my Positive Separation Method.

My Miracle Sisters

Thanks to my dear Nanci Donohue, Nikki Green, Heather Bennett, Gina Robichaux, Sara Laalamen, Beth Larsen, and Kirsten Ward, for sharing your light and happiness over the course of the past year. We have formed our lifelong bond forever in abundance and miracles. Kim Forcina, your warmhearted kindness, wisdom, and great love made a deep impact on me. Gina Lombardo, thank you for being "Angel Gina." AlexSandra Leslie and Suzanne Lawlor, you made me understand 'being present' while writing this book, and your knowledge was an energizing gift.

In the Netherlands ...

Thank you to Joost van den Ossenblok from Bruna/Lev Publishers: you were my first and strongest believer in spreading the word for positive separation in the world. Your talent is unique and I am honored that you shared it with me.

Eliezer Birnbaum, my translator from Dutch to English: you have a pen like a rockstar and an angel. Nelleke van Lindonk, my Dutch mentor: I love your clarity and strength. Nils Kroese, thank you for your creativity, patience, and fun days of working. Benjamin van Kessel, thanks for always being happy to help with positivity and expertise regarding any law-related questions. Mirjam Bleeker, famous travel photographer and friend, thanks for capturing me in a relaxed way. Janneke Paalman, thanks for your lovely illustrations. Chris Mulder, thank you for sharing your design talent in the moments when I need it most. Annelies Dollekamp and Elise de Bres, you know how to do things perfectly! Great thanks as well to Mark van der Voort and Fred Leeman, my computer gurus: you all made my work shine even more.

Annelies Hendriks, internationally-renowned professional in the field of separation and children: I love your heart, your smile, and the ease and expertise you bring to everything, and feel deeply honored to work with you.

Susan Smit, please keep sharing your beautiful words with the world. I am proud of you in many different ways.

My professional Winning Team members from my separation in 2004, Emma van Hilten, Ruud Kroese, Edwin Lankester, Willem de Jong, Hans van Baaren, and Annemieke Rodenburg: you guided me in a professional, loving way, and helped me to build a new foundation from which my family and I still blossom today.

And, Last but Not Least ...

Thanks to you, Reader. I believe in you!

About the Author

Hello! I'm Eveline Jurry, creator of the Positive Separation Method™ and an expert in applying practical action to create greater happiness and positivity in all areas of life.

Born in the Netherlands and educated in the Netherlands and England, I hold a Master's degree in corporate law from the University of Leiden (the oldest university in the Netherlands, established in 1575). Prior to launching my coaching practice in 2008, I worked in the advertising sector and contributed to various magazine publications. My first book, *Je Wordt Weer Gelukkig* (You Will Be Happy Again), was published in 2013 by the prestigious Dutch publisher, Bruna/Lev; the successful first edition was followed in 2016 by a more compact new edition, *Je Wordt Weer Gelukkig! Positief en Daadkrachtig door je Scheiding in Drie Stappen* (Empower Yourself & Be Happy Again! Getting Through Your Separation in Three Steps).

How the Positive Separation Method™ Was Born

The Positive Separation Method™ was born in the years following my own divorce. I knew I wanted to unravel myself from my old life in a positive way, but there was no handbook for the process, and no one to teach me what I needed to know to do this in a way that conserved energy and propelled me toward a new, happy life.

Four years later, happily engaged to my new partner, John, I decided to make it my mission to help and empower people in one of the most vulnerable times of their lives. Millions of people go through divorces, breakups, and separations every year. I knew there were many positive stories and tools available that could help others avoid the traps and pitfalls I experienced in my own quest for a positive separation, and I was determined to find the best and most direct path for those who wanted the same happy outcomes that I had created for myself.

I studied the topic of separation and divorce for three years. I spoke to the most experienced and successful professionals, not only in the Netherlands, but also in the rest of Europe and America. I met with success and happiness gurus. I looked for the right combination of tools, stories, and examples, and from these, I developed my Positive Separation Method: a clear path and empowering approach for navigating daily life during and after separation, with a happy future as a goal.

My Method can benefit everyone in separation, regardless of age, gender, economic status, religion, location, family structure, or other factors. It focuses solely on the individual using the Method, so it doesn't require the participation of a partner. It is particularly beneficial to individuals with children, as I've discovered the best way to encourage healthy parenting is to get oneself back on track physically and psychologically as soon as possible.

What I'm Creating

Today, I advise individuals, companies, and governments on positive separations using my trademarked Method, and train lawyers, psychologists, therapists, mediators, and other coaches on how to guide their clients through positive separation processes. I inspire my clients and colleagues in the art of positive living through the creation of new and practical actions and concepts.

In addition to my work with positive separation, I am an active board member of several nonprofit organizations in the Netherlands which encourage professionals to team up in a more positive and constructive way, and to share knowledge on the vulnerability of adults in separation situations. I am also engaged in creating The Love Fountain, an art project aiming to create more love between people, cultures, and nations so that every heart can shine in its own beauty.

Connect with Eveline

Learn more about my work, programs, and coaching services at

PositiveSeparation.com

MethodePositiefScheiden.com

Connect with Me on Social Media

Facebook.com/PositiveSeparation

Twitter.com /PosSeparation

Instagram.com/PositiveSeparation

Morgan James
Speakers Group

www.TheMorganJamesSpeakersGroup.com

We connect Morgan James published
authors with live and online events
and audiences who will benefit
from their expertise.

Morgan James makes all of our titles available
through the Library for All Charity Organization.

www.LibraryForAll.org